IN THE HEART
OF CAIRO

Mahi Wasfy

First Printing, 2016

ISBN-13: 978-1512031744
ISBN-10: 1512031747

Typeset and edited by www.nownovel.com

For permissions please contact the author: mahitabw@gmail.com

For my boys, Omar and Karim:
No matter how far you go in life, may you always remember
where you came from. Love always.

CHAPTER ONE

"We are all alive now. We are all going to die some day. No one can escape this cycle, no matter how hard they try. What lies beyond is unknown to everyone. So why does everyone forget that?" Mrs. Magda asked her students, all of whom looked like they couldn't care less about what she was saying. A vibe of nonchalance dominated the air. Nobody answered the question, because in fact nobody heard what it was in the first place. Maha was busy doodling in her notebook. Laila was contemplating the party she was planning on Thursday. Mahmoud was thinking about his soccer game on Friday and all Ossama wanted to do was listen to his music.

With fierce eyes, Mrs. Magda looked at each one of them and said, "You know what? If you all continue like this, you will all fail."

At that moment, all the students stopped what they were doing and paid attention to what Mrs. Magda said.

"What do you mean, we will fail?" Laila asked in a sarcastic, 'do-you-even-know-who-you-are-talking-to?' kind of tone.

"Well, Laila, I'm surprised that as seniors attending the best school in the region, you don't know what 'fail' means. Too bad…

I thought I had set appropriate expectations for this class. It looks like I'm going to have to re-evaluate that now."

"I still don't get it," Mahmoud protested. "It is only the first week of school and you just decided that you're going to fail us for no reason."

"Just because you don't know the reason, does not mean that there isn't one! Now please, I'll make this clear to you all. In this class, you speak to me with respect, the way you do when you speak to Mr. West, your Math teacher, or Mrs. Hamilton, your English teacher. I know you all wouldn't dare talk back to any of your other teachers the way you just did with me," she said. "As for your grades," she continued, "I will fail anyone who does not take part in class. Your participation in class counts for much more than tests and quizzes. This is a Theory of Knowledge course! So it is necessary to speak, question and debate issues in our class discussions! And you must meet this requisite to get your International Baccalaureate Diplomas."

"Fine. So the only way to get an A in this class is to take part in it? Does that include attendance and tardies as well?" Ossama asked.

"Yes," Mrs. Magda replied.

Then Mrs. Magda realized that class time was up. The students were fidgeting and eager to go to their lunch break. "Hold on! Before any of you leave! Your homework for next week is to write a one thousand five hundred word essay on what you think your life's purpose is. Explain whether you are living it or not, and if not, think about what it is you need to do in order to live it," she said.

Mahmoud responded with his infamous eye-roll. Laila pouted. Ossama yawned. And Maha couldn't have cared less.

"This homework is important for your participation. So good luck with it! Class dismissed!" Mrs. Magda said.

And as soon as she said that, the students were gone in less than 60 seconds.

As soon as Mahmoud, Ossama, Laila and Maha made it past the hallway, they looked around and then at each other with the assurance that it was safe to speak.

"Looks like it's going to be a so-not-good year with Mrs. Magda!" Mahmoud exclaimed.

"Why is she so on fire? It's so strange that she's so not easy-going, funny or relaxed! She is not like the rest of the Egyptian teachers who teach French or Arabic!" Laila said. "Do you think it has something to do with her veil? I mean, this is the first time I've spoken to one who is a core subject teacher!" she continued.

"I don't know. But whatever it is, I think she needs to go fly a kite!" Ossama joked.

"I think you all need to go fly a kite!" Maha said in disbelief. "This is ludicrous, Laila. I can't believe my ears! The nerve you have to speak like that about Mrs. Magda, just because of the way she's dressed. I'm sure that if she wasn't veiled, you wouldn't be judging her the same way you are doing now!"

Maha wondered what had happened to her friend, who had now become alien to her. Ever since transferring to this school four years ago, she had slowly morphed into some different form of being. An unrecognizable kind of being. The kind you would never want your best friend of 11 years to change into. One would have thought that she was immune to the changes that this school inflicted on anyone who got accepted to it. *How could Laila forget the years before, when she made fun of all the people in the school?* The arrogance. The pettiness. The fakeness. The opportunism. Now all these qualities had gotten to Laila. And they had rotted her. This put pressure on the expiry date of their friendship. Maha was sad that this was so. But deep down, she knew that it was only a matter of time before they would walk their own separate ways. She knew that she could not sell her soul to a life of glitz and glam in exchange for her self-respect and integrity. "It's so sad that you consider yourself to be among the most educated in the country.

How is it that you advocate for social justice and equity, when you can't even practice what you preach?" she continued.

"What are you talking about Maha? Do you not know that these people are ignorant?" Laila asked.

"What do you mean by *these people?*" Maha asked in shock. She was getting angrier and angrier by just listening to her speak. Had Laila forgotten about her roots? Her previous schooling in her old ordinary Egyptian school? The women in her extended family who were mostly veiled? Her old friends who came from simple middle-class families?

"Duh! The religious ones, of course. The ones who are blind and follow religion only. Do you not remember Karl Marx when he said that 'religion is the opiate of the masses'?" she asked, trying to act all intelligent by name-dropping an intellectual.

"Karl Marx? You're quoting a philosopher and economist to prove a point of view you have on Islam? Does he even know it?" Maha asked incredulously, thinking of Laila's ludicrous reasoning. Rather than mention any of Islam's greatest thinkers and scholars – like Ibn Sina, Al Ghazali or Ibn Khaldun – she's supporting her argument with Karl Marx? *Yup… Yeah… Uh-huh, makes perfect sense, right!*

"Karl Marx is an excellent philosopher! So that must mean something!" Laila retorted.

"Fine. So on that basis, Laila," Maha said, knowing that she had to take baby steps to get her point through, "if you had to choose between two rockets to go up to space, one designed by NASA and the other by Ralph Lauren, would you choose Ralph Lauren because he is an excellent designer?" Maha asked.

"No! I would choose the one designed by NASA, of course! Even though I know the one by Ralph Lauren would be more stylish," Laila said with a smirk.

"Excellent! So you would choose NASA because you know for sure that they are leaders in the field and you trust them! Right?" Maha said with relief.

"Yes. But what does this have to do with Karl Marx, religion and Islam?" she asked.

"It's not rocket science, Laila! Karl Marx's authority on the subject of Islam is as flimsy as Ralph Lauren's if he were to design a rocket!" Maha exclaimed. "It's more credible to support your point with the appropriate scholars – the ones who dedicated their lives to studying and understanding the Quran! Like Ibn Sina, Al Ghazali and Ibn Khaldun," Maha explained. "Who are these people?" Laila asked.

"Exactly my point!" Maha cried. "You made a judgement about something. You supported it with someone who knows nothing about it. And you aren't even familiar with the people who know anything about it," Maha said. Now she wondered whether this discussion was even worth it. The truth was that Laila, hypnotized by the belief that they were inferior, wanted to have nothing to do with her roots.

"Whatever! As if I care-like! Come on... We all know that you cannot value what Mrs. Magda teaches the same way you would Mrs. Hamilton. Also, I don't get it, why do we have to call her by her first name and not her last name, like the rest of our teachers?" Laila wondered.

"Oh, please stop," Maha said in disbelief that her friend was being outright biased. *So much for the respect and diversity that the school preaches it instills in its students.* "Just stop!" Maha said, wanting to walk away. At that point, she was sure that she could not do anything but walk away.

"Yo, chill... you're taking this too personal! You're gettin' too emotional 'bout this," Laila said.

"Yeah, I guess you're right! I get emotional when it comes to issues of bias. I have no tolerance for it," Maha said, wondering how in the world Laila forgot about respect. Conversations like this always made Maha angry – she could not believe that there were people in the 20th century who could judge others like that!

Be it for the color of their skin, religion or even social class. This made Maha sad.

"Stay cool, M. No need for all this," Laila said. "Let's change the subject to somethin' lighter, like my PAARRTTAAYY!" she exclaimed. "How excited are you?"

"Well, about that… I wanted to let you know…" Maha started to say, and then was cut off.

"Noo… Don't tell me, M! You are coming?" Laila exclaimed.

"Well see, that's the thing, I have to go with my mom to my aunt's. You know what family obligations are like," Maha said, hoping that she would get away with this excuse. Everybody in Egypt suffered from that pressure of family visits. Those who said no to such obligations were categorized as rebels.

"Oh no! Then pass by after," Laila insisted.

"I will do my best," Maha said, knowing that she wasn't going to. She was finding any excuse to distance herself from Laila. Besides the fact that she had changed, Maha had also recently found out from Leena that Laila was the cause of the fallout between her and Sultan. She realized that she could not trust her anymore. Also, she couldn't let on that she knew, because she swore to Leena that she wouldn't tell. But anyway, Maha had found out from Leena that Laila told Sultan that Maha was the cause of the problems between him and Noha, his girlfriend. And both Laila and Sultan were Maha's best friends. Laila's motives behind this were unclear, but whatever they were, Maha did not want to be a part of this drama. For there was nothing she hated more in the world than melodramas.

"You'd better, M," Laila screamed.

Maha then turned her back to Laila and walked towards the Art building. She got her Discman out, put on her earphones and played "I Used to Love Him" from her all-time favorite album, *The Miseducation of Lauryn Hill*. She softly sang along to the words, "Now I don't… I used to love him… but now I don't."

Ossama, Mahmoud and Laila stood in silence.

"I don't know why, but I have a feeling that Maha is distancing herself from me," Laila told the boys.

"Don't think that!" Mahmoud said. "You know how respect is important to Maha."

"What do you mean, Mahmoud? That I'm disrespectful? Statin' my opinion is me exercisin' my freedom of expression," she said.

"Sure. Feel free to express yourself! Just be respectful. And make sure your info is legit and causes no harm to anyone," Ossama said.

"Whatever, guys! Forget about it! I'm so hungry. Please, let's go get some food," Laila pleaded.

As they walked across the field to Carlitto's Restaurant, they saw Mrs. Magda hurry into the gym. They looked the other way and scurried off to get their food.

CHAPTER TWO

Mrs. Magda was new to the campus, and had so many places to explore. She hurried to the gym area in hopes of finding a changing room. She wanted to complete her ablution and prayers before the end of break. It was a shock for her to discover that there were no prayer rooms on her first day at school. She struggled to find a peaceful place to pray in. She had just moved from Dubai, where it was common that all public places had prayer rooms for Muslims to pray in. She was shocked that a huge school in a Muslim country did not have prayer rooms on their campus.

After negotiating a maze of hallways and stairs, she found the changing room. It was in a separate building connected to the gym. When she finished her prayers, she realized that she had some time left before her next class, so she decided to go see Mrs. White, the high school principal, to discuss the prayer room issue at school. After all, she knew that the school had been pressured into hiring her to meet the International Knowledge Authority's new requirements. Her objective was to help the school become more culturally appropriate. According to the new standards, it was not enough for international schools to have diversity among students. Teachers, administration and staff were expected to show diversity as well, among many other things. This was a problem for ACS, because 98% of their teaching and administrative staff members were white and American. Actually, ACS was not the only international school that had this problem. Many suffered from a similar lack of diversity. In fact, prior to moving back to her homeland Egypt, Mrs. Magda had worked at a British School in Dubai for five years, and had helped the school become more bicultural. Even though Mrs. Magda started her professional career as an educator, it was not until eight years ago that she became an anti-bias one. She had earned her Master's Degree in anti-bias education in the US, after which she'd joined a consulting firm that helped schools enhance the quality of their programs. The research indicated that the positive impacts of biculturalism at schools outweighed those that weren't bicultural. It significantly maximized the cognitive, emotional, social and physical development of students. And because of that, the International Knowledge Authority decided to set culturally appropriate standards as new requirements for this year's inspections. Mrs. Magda was aware of that. She knew that ACS wanted to maintain the best ratings. The school had built its reputation on consistently having the highest rankings. This is what motivated her to take the job – and to make some serious changes at the school.

She adjusted her veil in a rush and hurried across two soccer fields to get to the high school building. When she arrived inside the main entrance, she found the two elevators occupied. To save time, she decided to take the stairs instead. By the time Mrs. Magda reached the fifth floor, where Mrs. White's office was, she had run out of breath. She stood for a minute to catch it, gasping for some air. Even though she was not the muscular and fit type, she had a healthy and strong physique. She had the figure of an ex-ballerina. And it was obvious from her body type that she preferred to walk and do yoga to keep fit. Once she had recovered, she composed herself and walked towards Hala, Mrs. White's secretary, and asked to speak to Mrs. White.

"Do you have an appointment?" Hala asked, staring at her computer screen and adjusting her glasses.

"No. I just need to talk to Mrs. White for a few minutes," she said.

"Hold on a minute. I will have to check with her first if she can meet you now," she said, picking up the phone to call Mrs. White.

After a brief exchange of questions and answers, Hala told Mrs. Magda that she had only 10 minutes to speak to Mrs. White.

Mrs. Magda walked into Mrs. White's office and found her finishing up her lunch, which looked like what remained of a once-upon-a-time homemade tuna corn salad. Mrs. White took the last mouthful of salad and stood up to shake Mrs. Magda's hand.

"Hello, Magda. How are you doing?" she asked, still chewing her food.

"I'm fine, thank you, Mrs. White. Still adjusting. I'm aware that I have so much adjusting to do," she said.

"Sure. Transitions take time. Please let me know if you need help with anything," she said.

"Thank you. I appreciate it. In fact, it's funny you've just mentioned it, because I'm actually here to ask for your help," Mrs. Magda said.

"Sure. How can I help?"

"Well… I was quite shocked to learn that there are no prayer rooms at school. It is so strange for many reasons. First, we are in a Muslim country and there are many staff members and students who need a place to pray. Second, the standards for high quality programs are changing. Schools must be inclusive, culturally appropriate and ensure the healthy wellbeing of the whole child. Isn't this why you hired me in the first place?" she asked.

"I'm sorry that you feel this way, Magda, but this is a secular school. We do not promote religious practices here. If we were to introduce prayer rooms on campus, it would complicate things. Then we would have to establish equality for all, and create small chapels, synagogues and temples, so that all religions are similarly catered for," she said.

"Sorry, but I don't understand your point. I think you might be misunderstanding something here," Mrs. Magda interrupted.

"No, I don't think I am. And let me tell you, we hired you because we respect the new standards. We understand that being inclusive and culturally appropriate must go for students as well as teachers. That's why we hired you."

"You think hiring one veiled Egyptian teacher for core subjects amongst a pool of two hundred teachers makes you culturally appropriate? And *inclusive*?" Mrs. Magda asked, wondering where the logic was in what Mrs. White was saying. It was not going to be enough for the school to hire her. There needed to be more changes in this culturally schizophrenic school.

"It's the first step, Magda. The administration has a five-step plan that I must follow and adhere to. It's not in my hands to change things as I want."

"Well, say that to the inspectors from the International Knowledge Authority when they come later in the year to rate the school. Seriously, if you want me to help you maintain your outstanding rating, you are going to have to do a lot more than just hire me," Mrs. Magda said, remembering the first interview she had with Mrs. White. She had promised Mrs. Magda that she would support her in making the changes needed to ensure that the school was genuinely inclusive and culturally appropriate.

"My hands are tied for now. I'll have to get back to the administration before I make any changes around here."

"Well, you should've told me that before you hired me. And I don't see why you need to go back to the administration to create prayer rooms. FYI, in Islam, it is an obligation that all Muslims pray five times a day. Muslims at this school must fulfill three of those prayers during their working day. So this, Mrs. White, is not about equality. It is about equity. Respect for the needs of every religion is non-negotiable."

"Fine. I get it."

"Good. I am confident you can find a place for Muslims to carry out their prayers. Do it for the staff members that work at least twelve-hour days at this school to clean out *your* garbage, classrooms and even toilets. The least *you* can do is find a place for them to pray in," she continued.

"Ok... Ok... Let me think about where and get back to you," Mrs. White said as she looked at her watch.

"Sorry. I cannot accept this. I moved my whole life from Dubai to Cairo to help your school become bicultural. I will have to report this to the inspectors when they come," Mrs. Magda raged.

Fearing the implications of the report that Mrs. Magda could give to the inspectors, Mrs. White agreed to her request. "Fine," she agreed. "I can create two prayer rooms. One for men and the other for women. Unfortunately though, due to limited space, it will be next to the side gate and behind the janitors' service area. I'm sorry! But this is the only empty space that I have available now," she said.

"Ok... That will do for now, because this is just temporary. Anyway, I have to go now! I don't want to be late for class," Mrs. Magda said as she hurried out of the office.

"Good riddance!" Mrs. White whispered to herself as Mrs. Magda walk out of sight.

Mrs. Magda was glad that the third day of school had come to an end. She was so exhausted from the day's tension and negativity. When she walked out of the main gate, she found Sayed, the driver, waiting in her Jeep Cherokee. As she walked towards him, she doubted whether this was a job she could handle for the rest of the year. And it wasn't because she didn't like it and wasn't up for the challenge – it was much more than that. She worried about the dominant culture at school, especially its impact on Egyptian students. They were so disconnected from themselves, their roots, their culture and their country. They made the Egyptian identity look more useless than a stale commodity collecting dust. It was of zero value to them.

Being cool trumped any core value in that school. It dictated the way students dressed, talked, behaved and even ate. The Egyptian identity had no chance of survival next to the towering giant American one. The longer Egyptians were in that school, the deeper they buried their identities underground. With no funeral processions to remind them of what they had lost, they led soulless lives – and they didn't even know it. Instead they filled their minds with American culture and covered themselves with labels. They defined, excluded and judged others to justify their 'coolness'. They adopted the infantile ideologies of the West, without questioning their credibility. 'Isms' crowded their minds. They borrowed styles of clothing without understanding their sustainability. People on horses playing polo covered their clothes. It was obvious that they surrendered to what they could see rather than what they couldn't, when in essence it was the guidance of the unseen that true believers sought.

Mrs. Magda's train of thought came to an end as she got into the car. She noticed the AC was blasting, and she found relief in the cool atmosphere. She snuggled into the backseat and hoped to enjoy a quiet ride home. She asked Sayed to turn on the sound system and was happy to hear one of Julio Iglesias' songs play in the background. She just loved how the sound of his voice had the power to ease all her troubles away.

After an hour of flowing through the most organized chaotic traffic, they finally arrived at their destination.

"Madam! We've finally arrived back home," Sayed said.

"Oh! We're home! I must have slept through the whole ride. I must be so tired! Ok, Sayed," she said as she woke up from the most lucid power nap. "Thank you. I'll go in now and you go get Maher," she continued as she jerked her neck back from her seat and got out of the car.

She was so happy to have arrived home. It was where her heart belonged. She walked into her ground floor apartment and felt a sense of comfort overcome her. Her home was in a building that was unique in style and rich in historic culture. And that's why she was happy to live in this Heliopolis-style building. She had always been fond of beautiful architecture. And this building was representative of that. It unified and fused the aesthetic and functional benefits of different exotic styles. It juxtaposed Moorish and Persian facades with Arabic spatial volumes, while European, Neoclassical and Moorish influences dominated its interiors. What made this place particularly special was the big, beautiful, green and lush garden at the back entrance. It provided a great opportunity for her to connect with her love for nature. She loved growing different kinds of vegetables and fruits in it.

When Mrs. Magda passed the main entrance of her home, the smell of cooked food greeted her senses and reminded her of how hungry she was. She rushed into her room and changed her clothes. She then took off her veil and let her thick, medium length black hair down. She freshened up and then hurried to the kitchen to greet Saneya.

"Hi, Madam! How are you today? How was your day at school?" Saneya asked while chopping up the vegetables for the salad.

"I'm ok, Saneya. School was fine. It could have been better, though," Mrs. Magda replied.

"Why? Did anything happen? Are you ok?" she asked.

"A few things happened. I had to talk to the principal today about making prayer rooms for the Muslims at school. And it was stressful. You know, I sometimes feel that the only thing the principal wants is to secure that 'Outstanding' rating and that's it. I just wish she was more sincere in her intentions to create a bicultural school," Mrs. Magda sighed.

"Don't worry about it. You know with every difficulty comes ease. It's in the Quran. Something good will come out of this. This is the way life is, Madam Magda. Conflicts always give birth to change. It will be fine. Trust yourself," Saneya claimed.

It was strange how Saneya's words enlightened Mrs. Magda. It always perplexed her how it was the uneducated people she met in her life that were the wise and happy ones. And it wasn't ignorance, like Adam Pascal had once said, that brought about this bliss. Rather, it was their ability to accept and surrender to anything. This ability empowered them. It set them apart from the educated, who lived in their minds and struggled with their thoughts constantly.

Maher walked into the kitchen with that 'feed-me-now' look on his face, interrupting their conversation.

"Hi Magda! How are you? How was your day?" he asked.

"It was fine, Maher. How was yours?" Mrs. Magda asked.

"It was good. I want to tell you all about it, but I'm so hungry I can't speak now," he said.

Mrs. Magda looked at her husband of 20 years and smiled at him, knowing what he implied by that.

"Sure, love. I'll have lunch ready in five minutes! And I can't wait to hear all about your day," she said.

"Great!" he said as he walked out of the kitchen.

Saneya and Mrs. Magda served the food on the dining table. Maher arrived just in time. He grabbed the oven-baked potato crisps off the serving dish.

"Delicious!" he said as he crunched it all up.

"I'm glad you like it. So, tell me about your day. How was it?" Mrs. Magda asked.

"Well, today was a fluctuating day for the currencies. No stability whatsoever. I'm going to have to look into what is impacting this, but it's almost impossible in a place like Egypt. I've been facing so much difficulty understanding this market. I know we've only been here for a month and there is so much I still have to learn. But to be honest, the market in Dubai was so much easier to understand. I guess I got used to working in the National Bank of Abu Dhabi. After being there for ten years, it seems I've forgotten what it's like to be vulnerable to instability," he said, shaking his head. "Anyways, enough about me. How was your day?"

A look of disbelief came over his face as Mrs. Magda told him about everything that had happened at school that day. "Unfortunately, Maher, the dominant culture at school is worrying me. I don't see how it's serving these students. I believe that at school the trend is to be cooler than cool. It's a *faux pas*, even shameful, to not be the coolest. Speaking in Arabic, being Egyptian and Muslim is like a one-way ticket out of cool. Egyptian students at that school are ashamed of themselves, their families and their roots. And they don't even know it," she sighed.

"I'm sure they know. It's obvious they do. If they didn't, they wouldn't try so hard to be something they are not."

"The sad thing is that the professionals with postgraduate degrees are blind to this. They are supposed to be experts in the fields of education, psychology or child development! And it's just strange that they cannot see how the culture at school is ruining these students' lives. There is a huge contradiction between what the school preaches and what it practices. On one hand, they encourage their core values of respect, independence and diversity. But on the other hand, they can't even acknowledge, let alone respect, students for who they are!" she continued.

"You put it nicely when you say it's a contradiction. This is a mess. I mean, there is nothing wrong with being exposed to other cultures. But there *is* something wrong when you don't know where you come from."

"Exactly, Maher! The research and science show that these students will suffer – be it from cognitive dissonance, mental health issues, extremism or what have you. And that's sad. Because these students have an infallible right to be proud of and happy with who they are," Mrs. Magda declared. "Social and emotional wellbeing is what maximizes cognitive abilities in people. And if these students continue like this, they will never be able to achieve that. They will *never, ever* be able to maximize their cognitive abilities, let alone reach their full potential."

"I agree with you, Magda. This age is already a difficult time for most teenagers, no matter what part of the world they're from. But can you imagine what it's like for all these students? They have to deal with all these teenage issues while trying to survive in an environment that is hostile towards their cultural identity and roots!" Maher exclaimed.

"These students cannot continue like this."

"And you know what... You're right! People perform their best when they feel good about themselves. So this just makes me think about all the Egyptians who are already beating the odds and thriving in academics, sports or arts. Can you imagine what it would be like for them to be in an environment where fitting in was not an issue? Where it would actually be an advantage to just be who they were? It's sad that the circumstance of their nationality and religion has them at a disadvantage in their own country. It's heart-breaking that no matter how hard they try, they will always be second best because of it," he continued.

"Maher, the thing is... When you come to think about it... They're treated like second best both in and out of school. The dilemma outside of school places them at second best as well. Foreigners have more privileges in Egypt than Egyptians do. They are more respected in Egypt than Egyptians are. So it's like they're stuck in this vortex of disadvantages," Mrs. Magda added.

"Well, that's another issue," Maher said with a deep breath. "This has been the plight of the Egyptian people since ancient times. It has been a long part of our history, Magda. So many empires occupied us. And we always struggled with our identity. But the difference is, in the past it was obvious what we were struggling against. But now the struggle is so elusive and discreet. You can barely see it, let alone feel it. It is camouflaged by the backdrop of global citizenship. With the advent of technology, more people want to become 'global citizens', but nobody really understands what that means and what it requires from us. Children and adults worldwide are forgetting their roots to join this trend. The question is, how can we become global citizens without rooting ourselves somewhere?" Maher asked.

"I don't know, Maher... I guess this explains why students at school are so lost. They need to ground themselves. But it's impossible for the Egyptians to do that. I mean, the Arabic language, their mother tongue, is not allowed at school. And detention and humiliation is the fate of many students when they speak it. Over and above that, students don't learn any important life skills. They just memorize, write essays and take tests. I don't understand how they'll be able to face any of life's challenges with only these skills," she said.

"Now that would be impossible."

"It's so overwhelming, Maher... I don't know which issue to address first. I didn't think that this job would be so difficult. I thought I made the right decision to come back to our home country. I thought I would contribute to a positive change in our community. But I'm scared I was wrong," Mrs. Magda sighed.

"Don't worry about it. This is just your first week. Take it one step at a time," Maher advised. He pushed his empty plate away and took an apple from the fruit bowl placed at the end of the dining table.

"Hmm… I guess you're right. I'll have to wait and see," Mrs. Magda agreed as she grabbed a clementine from the fruit bowl. In an attempt to change the subject, she asked, "Would you like to listen to some music and have our tea outside in the garden?"

"Great idea," he said. "But first I want to get my cigar from the living room."

"Sure," she said, resisting the urge to argue with him about not smoking. "I'll make a head start outside."

"Ok," he agreed, relieved that she did not put up a fight with him by delivering one of her anti-smoking lectures.

CHAPTER THREE

Maha's Home
Tuesday, August 24, 1999, 5:15pm
Cairo, Egypt

Maha walked into her house, relieved to smell the scent of homemade food. The high ceiling of her family's apartment marked the elaborate style of a now-extinct architecture. The grandiose space helped breathe air into her life.

Just as Maha was about put her green Jansport bag at the entrance of her house, she was startled by loud screams. Maha hated nothing more in the world than loud noise. It irked her. More importantly, though, it reminded her of the pain during the time of her sister's divorce. Her sister Ayah had gotten divorced last year after a two-year marriage. Her husband was a stingy mama's boy. He had two sisters who were also controlling. Ayah did her best to please everyone at first. But just like the fate of most people-pleasers, she became their doormat, marked with a big 'WELCOME' sign. But Ayah's 'come-step-over-me' behavior came to an end one day. It happened when her mother-in-law reviewed her son's monthly financials. She discovered that too much money was being spent on mineral water. So, to resolve the issue, she told Ayah to not buy any more water. Instead, she thought that since they lived in the same building, it would be best that Ayah and her husband go to her apartment to drink water whenever they needed to. Her mother-in-law wanted to refuse her the right to drink water in her own house! Ayah was grateful she didn't have children yet, because it made her choice to end her marriage that day easy. It was a no-brainer. She called her father and told him the story. And that was when he insisted that she come back home.

That night, Ayah had drank eight litres of mineral water. Her mother even made sure to donate mineral water to remote villages. The whole family prayed that night and thanked God for everything He had given them. They committed themselves to helping those in need. And at that point, Maha decided that she never wanted to get married. She knew that life was not worth living if one could not have the freedom to do simple things such as drink water in one's own home or even help those in need of it.

As she walked into the dining room she saw Ayah and her friend Maya in a heated debate with their mom.

"Mommy! You don't get it! Transcendental Meditation, yoga and chakra workshops are good for you," Ayah said.

"I'm not saying that they aren't. I'm just saying be careful. Some of these teachers are phonies and are in it for the money," Maha's mom countered.

"Ayah, you know, your mom is right…" Maya said.

"What? Really, Maya?" Ayah exclaimed, glaring at Maya.

"Well, remember my story about Veronica, the Sivananda yoga teacher? The one whose yoga class I was injured in?" Maya asked.

"No! How did that happen?" Maha's mom interrupted.

"Well, during one of her yoga classes, she asked us to 'seize the day' and bend all the way backwards into the camel pose. Because I'm flexible, I went all the way back. But because I was not strong enough I injured myself when I tried to get back up. I strained all my neck and back muscles," Maya explained.

"Oh yes, I remember. I was there. The worst thing is that she passed right beside you as you were trying to get back up," Ayah said.

"Yes. What's even worse, Tunt, is that she then asked me to take same private yoga therapy sessions with her to heal my injury," Maya said.

"And why was that a bad thing?" Maha interrupted the conversation.

"Well, because I started a few sessions with her and then I stopped in the middle of April last year. Then I received an email from her on April 30 saying that she's doubling the price of the private sessions starting from May 1st," Maya explained.

"What?" Maha's mom exclaimed.

"Yes. I swear she did that," Maya said.

"See, that's why I'm telling you to be careful, Ayah," Maha's mom said. "Sometimes these people are just in it for the money!"

"You know what's even worse?" Maya asked.

"There's even more?" Maha asked in disbelief, wondering what could be more contradictory than a materialistic yoga teacher.

"How about a materialistic yoga teacher and a spiritual healer-to-be?" Maya said.

"What! No way!" Maha exclaimed in disbelief. What had the world come to when someone calling themself a spiritual healer judged others? These stories made Laila look like a saint, because at least she didn't pretend to be something she wasn't!

"What happened?" Maha's mom asked, intrigued.

"I was attending a Chakra workshop with five other women. One of them was Veronica, by the way. During one of the breaks, Clara, a classist artist, talked about a recent trip she'd taken to Iran with her husband," Maya began.

"Ok, and?" Maha's mom prompted.

"She talked about how Iran was a beautiful country, with its rich history and architecture. Then she started talking about the role of women in Islam," Maya said.

"Let me guess," Maha interrupted. "She started talking about the inequality and mistreatment of women." Maha wondered how people were so careless about the information that came out of their mouths. She believed that people needed to take responsibility to share credible information. It was so simple! People didn't have to talk about subjects they knew *nothing* about. Such a statement was ludicrous, especially coming from someone who knew nothing about the religion or the Quran! It ticked her off that people felt they had the liberty to bash a religion they knew nothing about.

"Exactly! Information memorized, not understood! She just regurgitated what everyone around her said," Maya said.

"I feel sorry for people like her," Maha's mom said.

"Yes, they end up wronging so many people," Ayah agreed.

"Must make for a heavy heart and life," Maha said.

"That's an understatement. Anyway, during this conversation I found out that Veronica was half-Egyptian and Muslim. Because as soon as I started to speak about the importance of sharing credible info, Veronica blew up," Maya continued.

"What? No way! Get outta here!" Maha exclaimed.

"No, I'm not going to get out of here! I want you to listen to this. So Veronica got all worked up. She bashed Islam, the religion of thousands of years and billions of people. She was like, this religion mistreats women and does not give them rights! She said that she hated the inheritance laws most, and the fact that when her father dies her brother will get double her inheritance," Maya said.

"Wait, wait, wait. Hold on. The spiritual yogi teacher is thinking about the amount of her inheritance, and her father is still alive?" Maha asked, wondering what the world had come to. She preferred an out-in-the-open materialistic person over a closeted one anytime.

"No, wait, and she's pissed off that her brother is getting double hers," Ayah added.

"She's got it all confused. A married woman will inherit half of what her brother will because she will inherit from her husband as well. As for a non-married woman, she will inherit what she was supposed to get from her husband from her brother instead. It's all fair in the end. She cannot take things out of context," Maha's mom said.

"And then what happened?" Maha asked.

"Then the spiritual healer went on a full rage and rant attacking all Muslims. And not just about how Islam mistreats women – she said that bearded Muslims living in *her* country ticked her off. Also women wearing the hijab and burqa," Maya said.

"Oh no, stop! I'm sorry you had to endure that, Maya. But you know, it's not their fault," Maha's mom said.

"No I don't know that…" Maya countered.

"What do you mean by that?" Maha asked.

"What I mean is that you can't blame them for thinking that way. They live in societies that feed them this information," she said.

"But still, mommy, how can people make such obscene statements without taking the responsibility to understand what it is they are talking about in the first place?" Maha said. She wondered how it was not obvious for people to see. Imperialists hijacked many cultures worldwide; fundamentalism was an unintended consequence of it. Colonized people fought hard to preserve their identity and earn respect. People who earn that respect by default can never understand how and what *others* need to do to get it.

"Exactly!" Maya agreed.

"So what did you do?" Maha asked.

"I walked out," Maya said.

"Good for you," Maha's mom said. "There is no point in exposing yourself to this kind of negativity. Discussing things with respect and in a constructive manner is one thing. But this is just awful."

"Yes. Thank God it's over. It was an important learning experience for me," Maya said.

"How so?" Ayah asked.

"Well, first, there are many phony teachers in the spiritual world. The ones who aren't are a rarity, but they do exist," Maya said.

"See, I told you, Ayah," Maha's mom said.

"Second, all the labels that people get worked up about are essentially weightless. Yet hate makes them heavy in weight. Like the spiritual healer hating on men with beards and veiled women," Maya said.

"Exactly! A veil or a burqa, for example, is a piece of cloth at the end of the day. What difference does it make if someone decides to cover their hair with it? Is it necessary to wage a war on those who do?" Maha agreed. She thought that it was insane that some people felt superior enough to judge those who did. She had faith that there was no such thing as 'superiority'. And she believed that God guided all those who sought his goodness into light.

"I know. It's just a piece of cloth," Maya said.

"Hmm, true... It *is* just a piece of cloth! I pray that these people become more enlightened. May God guide them to live a peaceful and safe life," Ayah said.

"And help them become more mindful of the fact that diversity exists. Look at your own hands and remember this old Egyptian saying: Even the size of your fingers are not all the same," Maha's mom reminded them.

Maha looked at her hand and was so grateful for her family. She loved them so much. There was nothing in this world that could ever compare to the love for her family. She felt whole because of them. No one in the world had the power to ever replace that.

"Ok, so how about we take our beautiful hands and get them washed before we have lunch?" Maha's mom suggested.

"Sounds like a great idea, mommy," Ayah said as she got up and hugged her mom. Maya and Maha followed.

After lunch, Maha walked into her room to finish up her homework. As soon as she neared the door, she heard her home phone ring. It was her own private line, so she knew that it was for her. Her heart skipped a beat as she wondered whether it was Sultan calling. But then realized that it couldn't be – he hadn't called her in a long time, and there was no reason for him to call her anyway. She ran and picked up the phone

"'Allo," Maha said, hoping that it would be him.

"'Allooo…" Sultan said, trying to make fun of Maha.

"Yoooou, ugh…" Maha groaned, suddenly regretting the very thing she had hoped for. There was nothing in the world that Maha hated more than listening to Sultan make fun of her. He was so annoying.

"My one and only," he said.

"Yeah, your one-and-only, soon to be once-upon-a-time friend because of your terrible sense of humor," Maha retaliated.

"Haha," he laughed. "Take it easy. I'm just tryin' to be a funny bunny."

"Hmm," Maha hummed, trying to remember the last time he asked her to say these rhyming words. Maha had never known the secret as to why he always insisted she say these two words. It was one of those things that mystified her throughout their 10-year friendship. "I'm not stupid, Sultan. I know what you're trying to do. And guess what – I won't say the words."

"Yo, come on, please!" he begged. "I love it when you say it. You sound so funny!"

"I won't do it. So *for*get it, bro."

"Fine sis… Have it your way," he sulked.

Maha knew he was trying to make her feel guilty about upsetting him. "Oh, come on, Sultan! Grow up," she chuckled.

Sultan joined her laughing. They joked for a few minutes. And for a single second there, it felt like the good old times. Ever since third grade, this was how it had been between them. They would spend hours on the phone, talking about anything and everything. They listened to music together. They even read to each other on the phone. Sultan was very finance and sports savvy. He planned to major in Economics and earn a scholarship for track and field at NYU. Maha wanted to go to New York and major in Art and Design History and Theory at Parsons.

"Ok, whatever... Suit yourself," he conceded.

"Fine, I will. So what's up?" she asked.

"Nothin' much," he replied. "I was about to start working on my NYU application, so I wanted to call you first to see how you're doing with yours."

"Oh, how sweet of you, bro," she said. "I haven't started mine yet. But I will soon."

"You'd better. I'm not going to New York without you," he warned.

"Haha," Maha laughed. "Let's see about that."

"Ok. So let me know when you've finished it," he said.

"Sure thing," Maha replied. "First things first, though – I have to finish English homework."

"Oh really! What's your homework about?" he asked.

"I need to write a Haiku poem. I have to personify my motherland, Egypt, and give her humanlike qualities," Maha explained.

"Wow! Sounds like fun."

"Yeah, like soooo much..." Maha said sarcastically, catching herself before she made the big mistake of saying the word 'fun'.

"Oh man! I was *so* close to hearing you say fun/funny!" he groaned.

"I told you I'm not stupid," she said.

"Ok, if that's so, then go do your homework by yourself. Title it '*Masr Om El donia*'. But make sure you translate it to English first!" he said.

"If I translate it, it will be 'Egypt Mother of the World.'"

"Hahaha," he laughed. "This is fun. Can I help you out with this?"

"Sure. I'd love that," she replied. "Let me go first."

"Fine, go ahead."

Maha read the lines she'd written out loud:

> "My name is Egypt
> All my people neglect me
> This makes me very sad."

"Haha, nice. Ok, now my turn, I'll continue," Sultan said.

"Ok, but don't forget lines 1 and 3 need to be five syllables long, and line 2 needs to be seven," Maha reminded him.

"I got it, Maha. I know what a Haiku is. You need to have more faith in me and my abilities," he joked.

"Hmm, whatever, Sultan," Maha rolled her eyes.

"Ok so here goes…" Sultan took a deep breath and recited his poem:

> "My people put me down
> They dump much trash everywhere… Hmm…
> They'd rather live elsewhere."

"Wow, you did it!" Maha smiled, impressed. "My turn again:

> "Even though it is green
> My passport is an insult
> That brings to most shame."

"Wow… This is heavy, Maha…" Sultan said.

"Tell me about it."

"Ok, my turn now, and I'll wrap it up," he said.

"Cool."

Sultan took another breath.

"Why? is my question
Do you treat me like you do?
I'm mom of the world."

"Hahaha, nice twist," she laughed. "I have to add one more stanza, Sultan:

"So please be careful
What you sow is what you reap
So don't trash me then."

"Amazing ending, Maha. You so rock, girl! Like I've always told you since we were young. You're so creative and I know you will be a successful fiction writer when you grow up," he enthused.

"Oh, please stop. As if I believe anything you say," Maha laughed.

"Trust me. And when you get awarded for your first book, I will be sitting in the front row clapping for you," he promised.

"Oh, Sultan," Maha sighed, wondering whether he was joking or being serious. Sultan was the kind of guy that talked a lot. He liked to charm people. But he had his way with sarcasm as well. And this, to Maha, felt like sarcasm. She thought that there was no way that someone like Sultan could ever believe in her. Especially when she didn't even believe in herself. "We'll have to see about that…"

"Hmm, you'll see Maha. I know, and you know that I know," he declared.

"Haha, I don't know anything," she said.

"Oh, come on, just admit it: you're an open book."

"Well, stop before I close that book on you," she retorted.

"Haha, whatever. It's no use. You're so stubborn."

"Better stubborn than stupid and sorry."

"Listen, watch and learn from the best," he crowed.

"Yeah, the best… Haha… Fine, Mr. Best, have it your way," she relented. "I need to go now because my mom is calling me."

"Ok, but before you go, why did you give in so easily? It's not like you to agree that I'm the best."

"Well, Sultan," she said, wondering why she always loved to have the last word. "That's because I'm better."

"Hahaha! Oh no! What have I done to you now?" he exclaimed.

"Nothing. I listened. Watched. *And* learned," she said in hopes that she impressed him. Not that she really understood why she wanted to impress him in the first place.

"And I'm going to get you back for that. Remember: "Like dust, I rise,'" he quoted.

"Well, get ready to rise real high, bro. I'd love to see you rise up," she said. "I have to go now. Thank you for helping me finish my homework. I had so much fun!"

"I did, too. Peace out, sis. See you de-main," he said.

"Hahaha, you're polishing up your French as well! Wow, you've come a long way. Well then, *hasta luego*, bro. FYI, that's 'see you later' in Spanish," she explained.

"Duh," he said.

"Oh no… Here we go again… We're never going to hang up, are we?" Maha smiled, remembering how this was standard protocol with them. Sometimes it would take them up to an hour to hang up. Somehow, the phone call had relieved her of the worry that whatever it was that Laila had told him about her, it had not ruined their friendship. She couldn't wait to tell Leena all about it.

"No… You hang up," he said.

"Oh no, Sultan, please. I really have to go talk to my mom," she pleaded.

"Fine, fine… I'll let you go," he relented.

"Thanks, bro. See you later, *hasta luego*, *adieu*, *salaam*. By the way, that's a real special bid farewell. It's only for you in English, Spanish, French and Arabic."

"I'm honored," he said.

"I'm glad. Bye now."

"Bye, sis," he said.

CHAPTER FOUR

American School in Cairo
Sunday, August 29, 1999, 7:16am
Cairo, Egypt

Dear Salwa,

Hope all is well. Thank you for your email. Yes, I hope this week will be easier than the last one. Anyway, as per your request, my reflections about the school based on my first week are below.

I will contact you if I need your help with any issues. I appreciate your support.

Kind regards,

Magda

In the heart of Cairo, one of the world's poorest cities, is the most expensive private school in the region. Its location is in the arid desert land of New Cairo, a developing city. It's isolated from mainstream life - only a few shops, cafes and a supermarket surround the school. Its ironclad gates and tall brick walls are landmarks that set it apart from what exists beyond. Its outdoor landscape is as sophisticated as an exotic resort's. The shrub trees are formed in little pyramids. And nature's vibrant colors fill the wide range of flowers at the entrance of the school.

This school is nothing but perfect. Engraved on its main wall is the Ancient Egyptian symbol of the Key of Life. It represents the promise of a bright future for these students. Only 300 Egyptian students, out of the millions living in the country, can attend the school. They are the privileged few who have this opportunity. The school promises to provide students with the skills to become 21st century learners. It applies the latest teaching methods, and it hires exceptional professionals. It has the latest technology and facilities. It has three tennis courts and gyms, two soccer fields, a basketball court, and a swimming pool. Also, it has arts, music and choir centers, a library, and fast food restaurants and cafes. The classrooms have the latest resources. There are five computer labs that utilize Apple computers and laptops only. The science department has high-tech gadgets that allow students to carry out sophisticated scientific experiments.

The system at school follows the American curriculum model. In high school, students have the opportunity to do the International Baccalaureate (I.B.) Diploma. Many universities worldwide value the I.B. Diploma. In fact, students who score well can receive up to 30 credits at university and skip their freshman year. Test scores, grades and universities are top priorities in high school. Students who have the potential to get into Ivy League schools receive special attention. In general, students do not learn about their social or emotional development at school.

The diversity amongst teachers is limited. Most teachers are of American origin. The ones who are not, teach elective subjects such as foreign languages and P.E. classes. I am the only veiled, let alone Arab and Muslim, teacher of a core subject at school. Most of the staff are Egyptian, and seem to be underpaid and overworked. Until last week, there were no prayer rooms for anyone to pray in. I resolved that issue with Mrs. White last week.

The dominant culture at school is American. This is an issue for Egyptian students. They struggle to fit in because the values of their Egyptian culture are not in line with American ones. Unfortunately, this is not serving their social and emotional wellbeing at all. There is a disconnect between their cognitive and social, emotional and physical development. The school fails to ensure their healthy and holistic development.

On that basis, I recommend that the school needs to make serious changes. It must establish systematic changes that will resolve this issue. This is the only way that it can ever achieve a genuine bicultural environment. High quality programs must be inclusive, and this school is not. In the next few weeks, I will email you my specific suggestions to resolve this issue.

Mrs. Magda arrived at school early on Sunday morning and was glad she had time to reply to Salwa's email. Salwa was the head consultant at Ta3leem Consultancy Group (TCG). She oversaw how international schools in the Arab world integrated culturally appropriate values. Keeping in contact with Salwa was important for Mrs. Magda, as her support was beyond necessary at this point.

By 8:00am, Mrs. Magda saw Mahmoud, Ossama, Laila and Maha walk into class. They all, except for Maha, looked like they had not slept. Their hair was messy and their eyes looked narrow from the darkness that circled underneath them. At a glance, Mrs. Magda figured out that they must have pulled an all-nighter.

"Good morning, class!" Mrs. Magda said. "How was your weekend?"

"It was great!" Mahmoud enthused. "Well... It was great until last night. I had to stay up late to finish up the assignment," he complained.

"Us too," Ossama and Laila chimed in.

"Well, I didn't, because I completed mine on Thursday," Maha said.

"Yeah? Well, that's because you're a loser! Who does their homework on a Thursday?" Laila sneered, looking at Mahmoud and Ossama to back her up.

"Oh! I'm sorry that I'm not cool like you! And I wasn't busy partying Thursday night," Maha retorted. "And if I'm such a loser, Laila, why do you hijack my phone and MSN with so many messages?" Maha exclaimed. She then realized that Mahmoud and Ossama did not want to take sides.

"What? How dare you speak to me like that? And how could you not answer my calls or messages? What's the deal with you?" Laila asked in disbelief.

"Nothing much."

"What! I'm sure there is something up!"

"Hmm, strange, you think? So ask yourself then..."

"No, I won't, 'cause I know I didn't do anything."

"Sure, sure. Well anyway, it really doesn't matter what you say to my face. What matters is whether you can stay loyal behind my back."

"What are you talking about?"

"You know very well."

At that point, Laila turned away and looked down at the ground. Mrs. Magda did not know what to do and how to support both girls. Because at the end of the day, she knew the truth: their behavior had less to do with their natures and more to do with their environment and how it shaped them. This was especially true in an environment like ACS, where it was common for friends to betray each other. It wasn't like ACS was the only place where betrayals existed; what was different at ACS, though, was that it was uncool to get upset about betrayals. At ACS, one had to be cool with hurtful and heart-wrenching betrayals. It was uncool to get emotional. It was uncool to be human. In this case, Mrs. Magda understood what the issue was. It was obvious that Laila had expected Maha to react in that typical manner, to brush off betrayal and just be cool with it. But that was difficult for Maha; she just could not do it.

"Ok girls, this has to stop! Please let me help you resolve your issues after class," she suggested.

"I'm sorry about taking up class time, Mrs. Magda," Maha apologized while Laila stayed silent.

"No worries," Mrs. Magda said. "So… now let's get back to where we left off."

"Yes… As I was saying before getting interrupted, I did my assignment on Thursday. And I enjoyed it because it allowed me to put my life into perspective," Maha reported.

"I'm glad to hear that, Maha. I look forward to reading all about it!" Mrs. Magda said. "You all had more than five days to do this. This should not have been difficult, unless you decided to leave it until the last minute! And in that case, the problem is yours and not mine. So tell me, Mahmoud. Why did you find the assignment difficult?"

"Besides the fact that I did it last night, I felt overwhelmed by trying to find the answers to the questions," Mahmoud said.

"Interesting! Why did you feel that way?" Mrs. Magda asked.

"Well, I don't know if you know, but the only love I've ever felt in my life is for soccer. Nothing makes my heart pound like the game. This past summer, I was fortunate enough that scouts selected me from a thousand players, and I received a scholarship to pursue a career as a soccer player for one of the teams in England," he said.

"Wow! That's excellent, Mahmoud! Congratulations on such an achievement," Mrs. Magda exclaimed.

"No… no… There is no need for you to congratulate me, Mrs. Magda," Mahmoud said.

"Oh? Why is that so?" Mrs. Magda asked, looking confused.

"Well, when my father first heard of it, he completely shattered any hope I had of considering it as an option. He made it clear to me that my only career path is the one related to the family business," he explained.

"I'm sorry to hear that, Mahmoud. All I can say is that you never know what good can come out of this," she said.

"I guess so… Even though I don't know what kind of good can come out of living a life you don't love," he said, looking dejected.

"Interesting point, Mahmoud. I think it would be a good idea to have a class discussion on Tuesday about this. I should be finish grading the papers by then. We can talk about the life skills needed to live fulfilled and loving lives," Mrs. Magda said.

With a sudden change of heart, Laila decided to break her silence and take part in the discussion.

"Even though I did my assignment yesterday, it was a positive experience for me. I realized that despite my falling out with Maha, I'm living a fulfilled life. I have all the clothes I want. I get invited to all the best parties. I'm always on VIP lists. I get what I want all the time. I don't have anything missing," Laila said.

And it was at that point that Maha realized how different she and Laila had become. She imagined that her life would be simpler if she only cared about parties and clothes, rather than having to endure the misery and agony she put herself through in trying to find the answers to life's big questions.

"I guess if you're speaking only on the material level of things, then you are right, Laila," Mrs. Magda said.

"Well, I'm sorry, Laila. I don't think that's enough to live a fulfilled life," Ossama interrupted. "Working on my assignment made me recognize that there's more to life than just the material stuff. I realized that I would love to have my family's support to pursue a career in music. But that's almost impossible! The music industry has such a negative image in Egypt! And my parents are not supportive of it," he continued.

"This is interesting, Ossama. I cannot wait to read all of your papers tonight," Mrs. Magda said. "As for homework for our next class, I would like you to prepare three questions that you want to discuss. The questions must address your personal lives. The objective of the discussion is to help you find your life's purpose in order to help you live a fulfilled life," she continued. "Now that that's done, I want to start today's lesson. I would like to discuss the origin of knowledge, and its relationship with discoveries and inventions. Can you tell me what it is? And can you give me examples to support your point of view?" Mrs. Magda asked.

"Easy!" Maha shrieked as she raised her hand.

"Go ahead! Tell us Maha," Mrs. Magda said.

"Well, the relationship is obvious to me. Discoveries are the gateway from the unknown to the known. They expand our knowledge base. Through them, we learn more," Maha said.

"True," Laila interrupted. "Like nobody knew America existed before Christopher Columbus. After he discovered America, everybody knew about America."

"What do you mean by that, Laila?" Mrs. Magda asked, feeling a lump in her throat harden. "Do you *really* believe that Christopher Columbus discovered America?"

"Yes! Christopher Columbus discovered America. The Americans and Europeans discovered so many things. And they are responsible for the great advancements in modern history," Laila declared.

Mrs. Magda could not believe her ears. Her face turned pale. She felt nauseous. She couldn't believe that in the 21st century, educated 16-year-olds regurgitated mindless information like that. The thought of it made her feel like she was stuck in the Dark Ages.

Mahmoud was the first to sense that something was wrong with Mrs. Magda.

"What's wrong, Mrs. Magda?" he asked her.

"What's wrong is the information that Laila just mentioned. Christopher Columbus did *not* discover America! What's even more wrong is that none of you *realize* that there is something wrong with it!" Mrs. Magda exclaimed. It was at that point that she pitied the parents of these students. They paid US$20,000 in tuition per year. They had the conviction that their children received the best education possible. In reality, though, the school was as bad as the next big scam. It led many astray from the truth.

Mrs. Magda realized that it was 9:30am and that class time was up. She was so relieved that it was over. She did not know how she could have continued the class discussion after that point. "Ok, so it looks like class time is up. I will have to explain everything to you during our next class. I'll do it after the homework discussion. So in preparation for that, I would like you to write the definition of the word 'discovery' on a small notecard. Class is over for now. See you all on Tuesday," she said.

Mrs. Magda took a few deep breaths after the students left class. She needed a minute to calm down and clear her mind. She was trying to think of ways to address the catastrophe that had just happened. She decided that the best thing she could do at that moment was to call Salwa, so she grabbed her phone from her handbag and walked out to the field. The fresh air helped her relax. At least it released the tension in her throat.

Mrs. Magda did not have another class for the rest of the day, so she had ample time to speak with Salwa. She took out her phone and dialed Salwa's number, and after two rings, Salwa picked up.

"I can't believe you're calling me now," Mrs. Magda heard Salwa say on the other end. "I just finished reading your email and was about to reply to you."

"Oh, great!" Mrs. Magda said, appreciating this sign of divine intervention.

"It is unfortunate that the situation and environment is like that ACS," Salwa said.

"It just keeps getting worse, Salwa. The students are so lost. They need appropriate guidance," Mrs. Magda interrupted.

"Oh no! How so?" Salwa asked.

Mrs. Magda told her all about what had just happened in class.

"I can't believe this! This can't be happening at the turn of the twenty-first century! What a disgrace this is to the field of education! I do not doubt that you will resolve this misunderstanding with the students," Salwa exclaimed. "Yet… This school is in dire need of systematic changes that will address the real issues! It needs to be bicultural and current, Magda! I suggest that the first step to bring about this change is to introduce something in Arabic as a core class. That way, all students will learn both English and Arabic, and both languages will be set on an equal standing."

"I think that's an excellent idea!" Mrs. Magda said. And it was at that moment when a sudden epiphany hit her.

"I've got it, Salwa! I think I know how we can achieve just that!" she exclaimed.

"How?" Salwa asked.

"Arabic Calligraphy!"

"What do you mean?"

"We can propose to the school that they offer Arabic Calligraphy as a core class. It will be an all-encompassing course. That way, the students will learn the Arabic language, as well as aspects of its etymology, history, art, spirituality and culture. Also, the immersion of two languages in school will benefit students on a holistic level. This will certainly create a more bicultural environment at school," Mrs. Magda said.

"Brilliant! Excellent job, Magda! Go for it! I'll be waiting to hear updates from you!" Salwa replied.

CHAPTER FIVE

Maha got to school early. That always happened when she didn't pass by her friend Yasmine on the way. She went to the kiosk and bought an apple juice. There she saw her friend Jessica sitting in the corner reading a book. Jessica was from Brooklyn, and used to be Maha's best friend in elementary. But unfortunately, Jessica had moved back to the US right before the sixth grade. After so many years of living in the US, Jessica and her family had once again moved back to Cairo last year. Even though Maha wanted to maintain their friendship, it was very difficult, because they were so different now – or so she thought.

"Hey, Jessica," Maha greeted her.

"Hi, Maha," Jessica said with a very cold stare.

Sensing she was not welcome, Maha regretted having started a conversation with her.

"How are you?" Maha said.

"Fine. You?" Jessica said as she grabbed one of her braids and twirled it around her finger.

"I'm ok, I guess. Just very stressed about my college plans," Maha said.

"Tell me about it… What are your plans?" she asked.

"Umm… Parsons New York, if I get in," Maha replied. "You?"

"Most probably NYU," she said.

"Oh wow, so New York too, huh?" Maha said.

"Yeah. Can't wait to get outta here and go back home" she said.

"I can imagine… I feel the same way about wanting to get outta here," Maha agreed, realizing that they weren't really so different. "Anyway… Best of luck to both of us, I guess," she continued as she caught the sight of Sultan from the corner of her eye.

"Yeah, I guess so," she said.

"Ok… Enjoy your book and see you later," Maha said as she turned around and saw Sultan avoid looking at her. He walked past her as if he didn't know her.

What the… How could he? She couldn't imagine what had happened between the time of their conversation on Tuesday and today. *What was going on?* Her heart pounded, stomach flipped and legs cramped. That weird feeling crept into her gut *again*. And she did not like it. She turned her back to Sultan and tried to think of something to do to escape this feeling. She walked to the kiosk to pick her backpack up. She had left it there before talking to Jessica. She then took her long, thick black-brownish hair and tied it into a high ponytail. She looked like she was ready to box anyone who got in her way, even if it were Mohammed Ali himself.

"Hey, what's up? You have PE this morning?" Yusuf asked Maha as he came from behind her.

"Oh… Yusuf… I didn't see you coming," Maha said. Yusuf was a great guy. She had known him since she was six years old. He was grounded, brilliant, athletic, charismatic and had a passion for music. He also had this unique ability to understand people. Sometimes it scared her how well he could read her mind.

"Yeah, I was inside the building printing my homework in the computer lab. My printer got busted last night," he explained while he put his blue hard disk in his bag.

"Oh, ok…" Maha said, struggling to focus on what he was saying. She looked troubled. It was obvious. She could not hide how she felt.

"Maha, are you ok?" Yusuf asked.

"Ummm… Yeah. It's just whatever," she said vaguely.

"You know we have a few minutes before class… You can talk to me," Yusuf said.

"Yeah, I know I can… But I can't now. I'm so sorry," Maha said as she turned around and saw Sultan standing with Laila. They were laughing and joking around. He was squeezing her cheeks, then her waist. Maha could see his dimples appear even from so far away when he did that. And that for her was a shock, because Sultan's dimples never showed. Well, unless he was really over-the-moon kind of happy. And in the past, that had only happened with Maha. It didn't make sense to her, what was happening with her two best friends.

Was she naïve to think that Sultan would never believe what Laila had said about her? Losing a best friend was difficult enough, but losing the two to each other at the same time was like Brutus stabbing Caesar in the front and back. But not only that – Laila was really taking on Maha's role in the group, too. Ever since Laila had transferred to ACS, the dynamics of the group had shifted. Now all outings, trips and hang-outs revolved around her. She didn't understand why Laila tried so hard to copy and compete with her in everything. *Why was Laila doing this to her?* She felt like her identity was being hijacked, and she couldn't do anything about it. It's not like there were copyright issues for such a thing. How could she protect her individuality amongst the copycats and wannabes? Even though she did not want to face the truth, it was clear that she did not fit in, let alone belong to this place. She was like a mask without a face. Deep within, she secured herself by setting up a defence system that attacked anyone who dared to get in.

"Ok, I understand," Yusuf said as his hazel eyes followed the direction of where Maha was looking. "I see you're not as close to Laila and Sultan as before."

"Yeah, we're not... So many changes, you know. I guess it'll be ok," she said as she forced herself to make sense even though she was really not aware of what she was saying.

"I know it will. You know I never will let anything bad happen to you. I've always got your back, sis," Yusuf assured her.

"Thanks, bro," Maha said, reflecting on how Yusuf had always been such a good friend to her ever since elementary. "I'd better get going."

"Ok, lemme walk you to class," Yusuf offered.

"Ok, cool," Maha agreed as she reveled in the effect that he had on her. Yusuf was a Godsend to Maha. He certainly was not the kind of person to come in the disguise of a genuine and supportive friend when he actually had ulterior motives. He was the real-deal kind of friend. And in some weird way, she knew that things were going to be fine.

CHAPTER SIX

As soon as Mrs. Magda hung up with Salwa, she hurried to Mrs. White's office. Mrs. Magda realized that the principal was busy when she saw the door of her office closed.

"She's busy and she's in a meeting," Hala said as she rolled her eyes and puffed.

"Yes, I can see that!" Mrs. Magda told her. "Can you please book me an appointment? I need to talk to her soon."

"Hmm. Sure," she said as she looked at the calendar on her laptop for availability.

"Unfortunately, she is fully booked this week. How about next week?"

"What? She has no availability this week at *all*? Not even for fifteen minutes? I can meet her before or after school. This is urgent!" Mrs. Magda exclaimed in disbelief.

"She's busy. I'm sorry," Hala said firmly.

"Fine. Book me an appointment please for Sunday next week," Mrs. Magda said.

"Ok. It's done. I've booked you in at 7:45am, right before first class," Hala confirmed.

"Thanks," Mrs. Magda muttered, trying to think of what good could come out of waiting so long.

Mrs. Magda was a firm believer that 'every delay had its benefits'. It was life's experiences that had taught her this lesson. So she was resolved not to struggle with what she could not control. Instead, she used the time to look for the benefits that hid behind such delays. Resisting the urge to dwell on her disappointment, Mrs. Magda decided to let it go. As she walked out of the main building, she thought that she could use this time 'waiting' to write up a proposal for her meeting with Mrs. White. In it, she would show the numerous ways in which Arabic Calligraphy classes could benefit the students, through technical, historical, linguistic and spiritual knowledge. In that moment, Mrs. Magda felt confident that this proposal was the great leap forward that she needed to achieve her goals.

When she reached the soccer field next to to the main building, she saw many students walking out of the school. It occurred to her that it was an early release day and the school day must have come to an end, so she had to hurry back home. Her best friend Hana, her husband Khaled, and his brother Mohsen were coming over for a late lunch. They had all been looking forward to meeting up for about a month now. She ran to her classroom, gathered her stuff and ran to the main gate. She found Sayed parked at the end of the block.

As soon as she got into the car, she asked Sayed, "Please can we go home as fast as possible?"

"Yes! Sure, Madam. I'll have no problem beating the traffic today. You know how Cairo's streets are. There are so many ways and shortcuts to reach any destination," he assured her.

"I'm glad to hear that, Sayed," she said with a smile as she took her mobile out of her bag. It annoyed her, how difficult it was to unlock the keypad. It was the new Nokia 6150 cell phone that Maher had gotten for her during his last trip to Dubai. He'd had to go two weekends ago to complete handing over their old apartment to their ex-landlord.

Finally, on her third try, she was able to access her phone. She called her home number so that she could talk to Saneya and check on her progress with the food. After the fourth ring, Saneya picked up the phone.

"Hello, Saneya," Mrs. Magda said, relieved to hear her voice on the phone.

"Hello, Madam. How are you?" she asked.

"I'm good. I'm on my way back home now. Tell me, how is the cooking and food? Were you able to get anything done?" Mrs. Magda asked.

"Yes, Madam. I finished the rice. The moussaka is in the oven. The vine leaves are simmering on the stove. I finished preparing the vegetable sauté, *vol au vents* and roasted chicken. The only thing left is the Sharkaseya. I have the walnuts, bread and chicken stock ready for you," she reported.

"Excellent! What about the fattoush and fruit salad?" Mrs. Magda asked.

"Both are done as well! The only thing left is for Mr. Maher to get the baklawa for dessert," she said.

"Perfect! Also, what about the foil plates? Do you have some at home or should Maher get those as well on his way back?" Mrs. Magda asked.

"Of course! There are plenty of foil plates. I would love to let you know all the drivers and security guards passed by earlier this morning. I don't know how word about the invitation spread, but they are all excited about today's feast. They love our food, Madam," Saneya said.

"Wonderful news, Saneya! I'm so happy to hear that! God bless you. I will be home in twenty minutes," she said

Hearing Saneya's news lifted Mrs. Magda's spirits and put a smile on her face. Doing good made her feel good. That's why she seized the opportunity to always feed, give to and help those in need. Everybody in the neighborhood knew that about Mrs. Magda. Her house was open to everyone. It had become a custom now that whenever she was catering for a special occasion, she fed everybody else as well. She prepared a hundred foil plates and filled them with the food that she and Saneya cooked, and distributed them to everyone on the block. Mrs. Magda inherited this tradition from her mother, and she was grateful for it.

As a young girl, Mrs. Magda saw how her mother's compassion crushed cruelty. She saw how God rewarded those who did right. Her mother was one of those people, always committed to be the best that she could be. She was a tower of strength. She never let negativity get the best of her, even when it would have been so easy to do so. She had lost her husband when she was only 33 years old, becoming a widow and a single mother of three children, one of whom had Down syndrome. She could have wallowed. But she didn't. Later, after Egypt's 1952 revolution, she lost her family wealth and assets, and was left with nothing. It was at that point that she realized one of life's undeniable truths: that in the blink of an eye, life can shift anyone's course. It was that swift. Mrs. Magda had been too young to understand that, though. She was only 9 years old on the day her father did not come home. And it had hurt her that he didn't. But it was her mother's compassion that allowed her to cope with the pain, even though it would never fill the void that replaced the connection she had once shared with her father. It was enough for her to believe and get on with life.

It was perfect timing when Hana, Khaled and Mohsen arrived. Mrs. Magda had finished preparing the Sharkaseya. The smell of Arabic Oud incense filled the air. Julio Iglesias' album, *My Life: The Greatest Hits*, was playing on low volume. Mrs. Magda looked so classy and modest. She wore her new Escada green twinset that she had gotten on her last trip to Paris. She topped it with her beige pants, also Escada, purchased during another trip to Switzerland. And she wrapped her beige Dior scarf over her hair.

When she had finished dressing up, she took a moment to stare at her reflection in the mirror. She realized how she was the by-product of her parents' upbringing. Her father was the typical traditional Arab family man; he was the son of a man who had fought to preserve the Egyptian identity and culture under British Imperial rule. In fact, his father had been so influential that the pro-British government, threatened by his popularity amongst the people, exiled him for 11 years. He spent his years of exile in Tunisia, where he fell in love with a Tunisian woman whom he eventually married. Later, they returned to Egypt and had their son, Mrs. Magda's dad.

Mrs. Magda's mom, on the other hand, was the complete opposite of her dad. She came from a family that benefitted from pro-British rule. They were the Europeanized aristocrats, and their life stories were even documented in between the lines of palaces and sweet streets. The undeniable desire to be together was what prompted Magda's mom, Aida, to marry her husband Nasser. Despite their differences, Aida and Nasser always found a way to work it out. Even when Mrs. Magda was born, Aida and Nasser had argued tirelessly about choosing a name for her. Nasser chose the name Magda because it was of Arabic origin. Aida had wanted Nelly, because it was of European origin. To resolve the dispute, they agreed that on the birth certificate, her official name would be Magda, and her nickname would be Nelly. And so she became the woman with two names that clashed culturally.

It was interesting how, when she looked at herself in the mirror, she realized that she was also the woman who embraced all influences without sacrificing identity, be it from the Middle East, West or even East. She embraced all values and respected them equally. She didn't let labels define her. She could wear Western brands as well as Arab ones. She could listen to Arabic, Western and even Eastern music. The way she thought and lived her life was not divisive. In fact, it was anything but. It was very rich in depth of understanding. She knew how to embrace differences without selling her self or soul. And it was because of that, that she could turn a Dior scarf into a veil.

Mrs. Magda's train of thought came to an end when she heard the doorbell ring. Maher greeted their guests at the door before her. They brought with them a delicious cake and tart from Fauchon.

"Oh, you shouldn't have!" Mrs. Magda told Hana as soon as she saw the pink boxes.

"Oh please! I so should have!" Hana responded with a smile.

"Fine! You so should have! You know how much I love this patisseur! It's my greatest weakness!" Mrs. Magda admitted with a laugh.

"Of course I do! I wouldn't have gotten it had I not known," Hana said.

"Haha, Hana! You know how to make things difficult for me. It's so good to see you all! Especially you, Mohsen!" Mrs. Magda said. "It's been such a long time since Maher and I last saw you!"

"Yes, it has. Unfortunately, I have been experiencing dramatic, life-changing events! Divorce is not easy. I seriously don't understand how people do it," Mohsen said.

"I'm sorry to hear that, Mohsen. Yes, I can imagine! Divorce is no simple matter. And unfortunately, it has become more common now," she replied.

"Yes. I've heard about so many couples splitting up, too. It's so contagious this year. It's sad. So many broken families, homes and hearts," Hana said.

"Oh well," Mohsen sighed.

"It is what it is. But perhaps what you hate is good for you, and what you love is bad for you," Mrs. Magda said.

"Yes, true. Some good must come out of this," Mohsen said, forcing a broken smile.

"So, is the food ready?" Khaled asked, desperate to change the subject.

"Yes," Maher confirmed with a chuckle. "Why? Are you as famished as I am?"

"Without a doubt, Maher," Khaled laughed.

"Come in. Please, after you," Maher said as he gestured to his guests to walk forward into the living room.

"You know, there is a calming sense of peace that I always feel when I'm at your place. All is beautiful and well here," Hana told her hosts. She walked towards the corner of the living room and relaxed into a comfortable burgundy armchair.

"Tell me about it," Khaled agreed.

"I'm happy to hear that. *Mi casa es tu casa,*" Mrs. Magda said. "Here, please take a seat and enjoy some of the nuts and crackers. I will need about fifteen or twenty minutes to serve lunch," she continued, hoping that the snacks could ease the pain of hunger that was so visible in their eyes.

"Wait! I'll join you in the kitchen and help," Hana offered, jumping up from the armchair.

Mrs. Magda could tell that Hana was hoping to use this time to bond. And right she was, because as soon they arrived in the kitchen, Hana vented about Mohsen and his ex-wife, Lisa.

"Can you imagine that after ten years of marriage, Lisa and Mohsen have divorced? I understand that they had a difficult marriage. And that it was not easy for her to conceive. She had four miscarriages. But they loved each other, Nelly! And I know that it did not bother Mohsen that he did not have kids," Hana exclaimed. "I can't imagine what it might feel like to let go of the one you love just because of social pressure. Such a coward."

"Social pressure? What social pressure are you talking about?" Mrs. Magda exclaimed.

"Don't pretend like you don't know. My in-laws were desperate for Mohsen to have a child. They even manipulated him into making the decision to leave Lisa. They offered him a higher stake in their family business if he did," she said.

"I didn't know any of these details! I promise! What happened?" Mrs. Magda asked.

"Hmm… I thought you knew. Well, listen to this. He refused their offer and told them that he could not live without Lisa. And that it was not an option. He even told them that they were both considering adopting a child!" she said.

"Ok… I hear you… continue," Mrs. Magda prompted her.

"They panicked. They couldn't handle the social stigma that an adoption would bring to the family. So they made him another offer," Hana continued.

"Offer? You speak of this as if it were a business proposal," Mrs. Magda said.

"Well, that's what it's like nowadays. Marriages like that outnumber actual mergers and acquisitions. They've become excellent investment opportunities for all business professionals! The love in these marriages is a disguise for all things business, while the true intentions hide in between the lines of marriage contracts and settlements. I hope you know what I mean," Hana said. "Anyways, the sad truth about the next part of what happened is that it *actually* happened. This is not a story from some lame soap opera. My in-laws masterminded the whole scheme. They suggested that he marry a second wife from a lower socio-economic background, have children with her, and not let Lisa or anyone know about it."

"*What*? What are you talking about? This can't be true!" Mrs. Magda exclaimed.

"It is true! It happened, Nelly. But things did not go as planned. Lisa, God bless her, found out about the whole plan coincidentally. A friend of hers hired the second wife to work as a waitress at her restaurant! And she divulged everything to her co-workers," Hana revealed.

"Is this for real?" Mrs. Magda asked. "I feel like this is a melodrama written by a heartless screenwriter. Please tell me this ends well."

"Trust me, every bit of it is true. The good thing is that Lisa has a strong support system. She's so intelligent, smart, beautiful and creative. She knows her self-worth. And I'm glad for her that she got that divorce," Hana said.

"I know what you mean! And indeed, those who choose to do no wrong are always guided and guarded. I'm glad to hear that she has this positive support. It's disheartening though, that social pressure is the root cause of all people's misery. I mean, it's not her fault that she couldn't bear him any children. But do you think she would have asked for a divorce had this not happened?" Mrs. Magda wondered.

"What do you mean?" Hana asked.

"I mean… Do you think she was waiting for an excuse to leave the marriage? And that she didn't have the guts to do it because of social pressure as well?" Mrs. Magda asked again.

"Interesting! I didn't think of it like that before. I guess there might be some truth to it," Hana conceded. "Whatever it is, Nelly, this woman is a symbol of strength. And we must honor her for her courage."

"Of course! It's about time we have more role models like her. Women need to embrace their strength. They have the right to live their lives out of love and not fear," Mrs. Magda agreed. "And I don't know how you feel about this, but I would like to visit with her soon."

"I think that sounds like a great idea! I'll call her tomorrow and arrange for a breakfast or brunch. I think she will appreciate it!" Hana said.

"Great! Let me know the details as soon as you confirm anything with her," Mrs. Magda said.

"I'll do that!" she said. "Also, you know... On a sad note, this story has got me thinking about my in-laws. It has allowed me to gain perspective on who they really are, especially my mother-in-law. It just made me realize how much power our in-laws and parents have over our lives."

"How so?" Mrs. Magda asked.

"Well, it's especially true with many mothers-in-law. The way a mother-in-law treats her daughter-in-law is directly proportionate to how much she loves her son. The more she loves him, the more difficult she will be with his wife."

"Oh, come on. Stop exaggerating!"

"No! I'm serious, Nelly. The influence that in-laws have could make or break a marriage. What is even worse is the role that many men play in the middle of all these relationships. It's difficult for men to stand up for themselves. It would be seen as defiance if they did not follow their parents, even if they communicate their message with respect. Anyway, to protect myself from their influence, I have cut off my relationship with them. I don't want to deal with people I have absolutely no respect for. But the kids and Khaled still visit them regularly," Hana said.

"I don't blame you. I understand and respect that, Hana. I would have done the same if I were in your shoes. But you need to understand your in-laws' behavior. They only did that because their environment shaped them to be that way. They don't know any better," Mrs. Magda said.

Mrs. Magda and Hana's conversation ended when they heard Maher's voice call out for them.

"Yes, Maher. The food is ready and I'm going to serve it in a few seconds! You can head to the dining room now," Mrs. Magda called.

The three hungry men greeted Mrs. Magda, Hana and Saneya as they finished setting the table. It was funny how all were so eager to eat the food fit for royals.

After their guests left, Mrs. Magda showered and changed into her comfortable clothes. She was eager to read her students' papers. She felt that this was a great opportunity to learn more about them. But that was wishful thinking from her end. Reality struck hard as soon as she read the first paper, which was Ossama's assignment. She could not make it past the first paragraph – she could not understand a word! The essay was a melting pot of grammatical errors. It had run-on sentences, verb tense, subject/verb agreement and noun/pronoun errors. It was obvious that Ossama had not understood, let alone applied, any of the rules of grammar. This was beyond depressing. How could these students not know how to write proper sentences? Were they not in the best school in the region? How had they passed all the quizzes, tests and exams in the past?

"Ugh," she sighed as she looked towards Maher, hoping to catch his attention.

When she realized that she had failed in her first attempt, she tried again. "*Ugh,*" she sighed again, much louder this time.

"Huhhh... You said something?" Maher asked her, with his eyes still glued to the TV.

Relieved to have gotten his attention, Mrs. Magda exclaimed, "Yes! Maher! This paper is a catastrophe! And it is an insult to the academic institution that prides itself on offering a high quality program!"

It was at that point that Maher finally looked at Mrs. Magda. He hoped and prayed to God that she would not get herself worked up anymore. He dreaded the thought of participating in an endless discussion at this hour of the night. He wanted to watch the *Cairo Today* TV show in peace. He just wanted to keep up-to-date with the current events in the country, and then sleep.

"What's wrong, dear?" he asked wearily, while seeking God's mercy.

"*This* is what's wrong!" she exclaimed while pointing at Ossama's paper. "The poor boy! He is sixteen years old and he cannot even write one proper sentence. I don't understand how anyone can consider this school the best in the region. This school has everyone fooled! They believe that this is 'the best education that money can buy', when in reality the students can't even write and express themselves, let alone think! You know that many students in Dubai know how to write better than this. And the schools they attend charge a quarter the tuition price of this school. Ugh!"

"That's sad, Magda…" Maher said, unsure of what to say next.

"Yes, Maher, it is. I don't think I will grade the other papers. I'm going to call it a night. I want to go to school early tomorrow to work on my presentation," she said.

"I think that's wise. Getting worked up over something you cannot control will drain you. I will follow you soon. Good night, dear," Maher said, relieved by the miracle that had just happened.

"Yes. I totally agree. Good night, Maher," Mrs. Magda said.

CHAPTER SEVEN

Maha's Home
Sunday, August 29, 1999, 5:09pm
Cairo, Egypt

Maha arrived at home around 5:00pm. And she was *so* hungry. In fact, she had dreamed of her mom's Negresco on her way back from Cross Country practice. She'd always had a soft spot for it. Nothing could ever compete with it. Mind you, it was essentially little more than pasta and cheese; but there was just something special about the chicken cubes, mixed with that sauce. It was a sauce that no other in the world could compete with. It was a graceful melange of bechamel and cheese topped with nutmeg. And it was the nutmeg that made it just right.

The first thing Maha did when she passed through the main door was walk into the kitchen and ask Mary to prepare the food for her. She then went into the living room to greet her parents, Ayah, and Maya. They were in the midst of a heated debate about Amr Khaled's credibility as a Muslim cleric.

The story behind this man was incredible. Amr Khaled was a simple accountant who happened to lead a strong religious movement in Egypt. Ironically, however, he had no background in Islamic theology whatsoever. How this man was able to pull it off was beyond any sane comprehension. Normally Maha would have loved to take part in this conversation, but she was feeling a little bit off and couldn't seem to understand why. She thought that her 10km run during practice would've made her feel better. But it didn't. In fact, after thinking about it, she realized that she had been feeling off ever since last week. And it was strange that the 10km run didn't make her feel better, because it usually did. Maha loved nothing more in the world than to run. She had the endurance and patience to last the longest of distances. She was a great runner because she knew how to pace herself. She could go on and on over any course without feeling the need to stop. This was true off the course as well. Everybody seemed to know this about her – except for Maha herself.

She left her family, passed the dining room and walked through the hallway into her room. Picking up the Sony Discman player on a side table perpendicular to her desk, she played her favorite CD of the moment. She turned up the volume on the two black speakers and heard Usher's voice. "This is what you do… This is what you do," Maha sang as she bounced to the beat of the song. She then booted up her computer and tried to connect to the internet, but it took a while. Her dial-up connection wasn't working, because her mom was using the phone line. After five minutes, the line was free and Maha was able to connect online. She checked her Hotmail account and turned on her MSN messenger. She found Sultan, Laila, Yusuf, Fahmy, Yasmine, Menna and Noha all online. She changed her status to "Away" because she wanted to take a shower and have her dinner, and didn't want anyone to think that she was ignoring them on purpose.

After she showered, she went to the dining room, where Mary set her dinner. She skipped the salad and headed for the Negresco with full force, not even noticing how fast she was eating. Her mother interrupted her solitude.

"The food is not going to run away, Maha! Slow down," she exclaimed, surprised at Maha's overindulgence.

"I'm hungry, mommy! I ran a ten-k for practice today," she wailed.

"I understand, dear. But that doesn't mean that you have to shock your digestive system like that. Take your time. Chew your food," she said.

"Fine," Maha said, annoyed that she couldn't have a few minutes free of criticism.

"Good! I'm just worried about your health, and gobbling up food like that is not healthy," she said.

"Ok. I get it," Maha replied.

"Ok. So tell me, how was your day at school today?" her mom asked.

"It was fine, I guess. Just a few issues with Laila. But it will pass," she said.

"Yes, it will. I know it's a difficult time for you, trying to adapt to all these changes, but I want you to know that I am proud of you. You are strong. And always know that we have all been there before. You are not alone," she counselled her daughter.

"I know, mommy. But it's painful that my values are different from everyone else's. It keeps me from having strong bonds or moments to share with friends. Like, I don't enjoy clubbing. I prefer to stay at home and read a book. I don't want to have boyfriends, because it's not in line with my family values. I don't want to sneak around and lie to everyone all the time. Nevermind cousin Fahmy, who will not allow it. He always reminds me that guys at our age date girls for fun. In fact, he once told me that a guy will never date a girl he has strong feelings for," Maha said.

"Well, to some extent, that is true. Few people I know who dated during their school or college years got married," her mom confirmed.

"Isn't that hypocritical, then? I mean, for guys to date girls they actually don't love and not date the ones they love," Maha asked. She remembered how Yusuf had given her the 'good girl' lecture after one of her friends dated Hossam, a serial dater with a passion for robbing girls of their innocence. Hossam had learned from his older brother the 'playa' ways at a very young age. In the seventh grade, he'd started showing interest in Maha. Because he knew that she loved reading, he approached her many times to ask her if she could go with him to the bookstore to help him find a nice book to read. Maha was flattered that he sought her recommendation.

But when Fahmy and Yusuf heard of it, they wanted to protect Maha from him, and guys like him in general. So Yusuf crushed Maha's belief in true love. He had a *talk* with her that shattered her hopes of finding it. It was the most heart-breaking and embarrassing conversation Maha had ever had in her life. She remembered his words clearly: "Don't believe a guy who wants you to take him to the bookstore. Don't *ever* believe that he wants to read a book! Trust me, he doesn't! Guys like Hossam *don't* read books!" In fact, she remembered everything about that conversation. Yusuf had approached her during lunch break, and they had stood together on the curve of the 400-meter track. Maha had never seen Yusuf that upset in her life. She hated nothing more in the world than to disappoint him. It made her heart palpitate when he was upset. So he ended the *talk* with the values of 'good girls': They don't date. They don't go out 'til late. And they stay like that 'til they marry their fate. Even though at the time she didn't understand the power that his words would have on her, she had promised Yusuf she'd never disappoint him. Her word was her bond.

Only time and the years that followed proved how strong Yusuf's influence was on her. Many guys had asked to go with her to bookstores. And she'd always refused. There was one who'd even tricked her into going with her and her friend to the bookstore. And on the day, she was surprised to find out that it was just the two of them. He told her that her friend had already gone with him on another day. Little did Maha know that it was all a lie. Later, when she found out the truth, she made sure to distance herself from people like him. Because of this, Yusuf was never disappointed. Maha also never dated or stayed out 'til late. But she was not really so keen to wait and marry her fate.

"It is hypocritical, if you look at it that way. But when you look at it in a different way, then no, it's not," her mother replied.

"How, mommy? It's so difficult to see beyond the hypocrisy!" Maha exclaimed, remembering Hossam the hypocrite.

"Look, Maha, there are many contradictions in our society. There are many issues, flaws and problems. But you must know in the midst of all this chaos, it is up to each individual to stand still and stay grounded. A person can only achieve this when they know their values and commit to them," she explained.

"I don't get it. What do you mean by this?" Maha asked.

"What I mean is that it should not matter to you what other people are doing, as long as you know your values and who you are. Just be yourself! Even if it means you have to be alone," she said.

"Ok... I kind of get it now. I need my own moral compass to help me navigate through this year," Maha said.

"Exactly," her mom smiled.

"Well then, maybe I should know what my values are in the first place. That would be a good place to start," Maha said.

"I guess so. And let go of what does not work for you or serve you. Trust the process, Maha," her mom advised with an 'everything-is-going-to-be-fine' tone in her voice.

"Thank you, mommy. This conversation has made me feel much better, for some reason," she said, realizing that she really loved nothing more in this world than her mom and her family. Whenever she tapped into her family's unconditional love, she realized how irrelevant everything else was. Her family was her heart.

"Anytime, my dear!" she said, hugging her daughter.

"Ok, well, I'd better get started on my homework. I have to write a five-hundred-word essay about the Arab-Israeli conflict," she said while rolling her eyes.

"Oh no! Well, you'd better get started soon before your dad finds out about it. You know how he gets all worked up about this topic! He'll give you one of his long lectures and you will not hear the end of it," she smiled.

"I wouldn't want that to happen now at all, mom!" Maha chuckled as she hurried off into the hallway to her room.

When Maha checked her computer, she found that she had around 30 messages. They were from Sultan, Yusuf, Yasmine and Noha. She was grateful that she had received none from Laila. After skimming the messages, she realized that Sultan and Noha needed her help with a major issue. Yasmine wanted to remind her of Menna's birthday party at Coco Jungle next Thursday. And Yusuf wanted to ask about their history homework.

She answered Yusuf's message first. *I'm about to start my paper,* she typed. *I didn't get a chance to do anything yet because I came back home late from practice. How about u?*

I just finished mine, his reply appeared on her screen. *Let me know if u need help with anything – even though I am sure you don't need it!*

Haha. U r hilarious Yusuf! Thank u 4 making me laugh! I was in dire need of this, she smiled as she typed back.

I know. I'm glad ur laughing, he replied.

U know!?! What is it that u know? she asked.

I know enough to know that u were in need of some comic relief, he typed.

I'm sure of that. U do know everything, after all :)

Haha. I wish. Now I will leave u to get started on your homework because I need to get going to my soccer game, he typed.

Thank u. Good luck in the game.

Thanks. C u tomorrow, he replied.

Peace. C u, she typed.

She then answered Yasmine's message and told her that she would be joining the group of girls on Thursday. Maha didn't mind the change. She was hoping that going out would help lift her spirits. Then just as she was about to message Sultan, she found a new message alert from him.

Are u there? he typed.

Yes. I just got to my computer a little while ago. What's going on? she typed, not understanding what Sultan wanted from her – especially after ignoring her like that in the morning. She had begun to notice an obvious pattern, though. He was quite talkative when it was only the two of them, but he avoided her in public. It was almost like he didn't want anyone to know that they were talking. He was acting as if Maha was his little big secret.

What took you so long? I've been wanting to talk to you all day, he typed.

And y didn't u? U saw me at school today! U have my number! U can call me u know like u did yesterday, she retorted.

I know. I'm sorry. I've just been going through major issues with Noha since last nite. I didn't mean anything bad, he apologised.

Oh ok. So what's happening? Maha asked, confused by him and not knowing what to believe anymore. She realized the effect he had on her was not good. He made her moods fluctuate. He had a hold on her emotions. And she was really starting to dislike that hold. Their friendship had changed; she had to get used to that.

I don't know, Maha… ever since Noha started school… she has been acting strange, Sultan said.

R u serious!?! It's only the second week of school, Sultan. There is a lot of adjusting to do, Maha typed.

Oh please, Maha! I'm not so sure about that! Sultan argued.

Take it easy, Sultan. Sometimes people adapt in different ways to change, Maha typed. And just as soon as she sent that message to Sultan, she found a new incoming message from Noha.

Can you please tell Sultan that everything is fine between us? He'll only believe you at this point, Noha typed.

I don't know what makes you think so. But sure, I'll let him know, Maha agreed.

Maha realized that her friendship with Sultan was only an advantage to Noha when she was in need of her help. At that moment, that weird feeling crawled into her gut again. Maha realized that she could not continue playing that role anymore. Sultan and Noha's relationship took a toll on her – things were always complicated between them. And Maha could not handle being stuck in the middle of it all the time.

Thanks. Ciao, Noha typed.

Anytime. Peace to u, Maha responded.

Ok, sis. I guess u do have a point, Sultan had replied in the meantime.

I know I do! I better get going now, bro. I need to finish up my paper for tomorrow, Maha typed.

Ok. Thank u M, Sultan replied.

Don't mention it, Maha typed as she admitted to herself the truth about the status of their friendship. In all honesty, it was now distant and broken. The former was because of Noha. And the latter was because of Laila. Maha didn't understand how a friendship so strong could wither away like that. It used to be as smooth as 90's RnB, but most probably the vibe just got lost along the way. Not that it was a good or a bad thing. It had just never been found.

Maha gazed at the blank document on her computer screen for a few minutes. She couldn't get her mind to focus on the assignment for history class. She was in need of help. She had to write a 500-word open letter to Ehud Barak, the Prime Minister of Israel, and she didn't know where to begin. At that point, Maha knew that listening to Tupac's "Changes" could get her in the mood to focus. And it wasn't because the song was an international hit sensation, or because Tupac was a lyrical genius who could refer so insightfully to the plight of black people in America. It was more than that. Beyond the form of the words, Maha understood the spirit of the meaning behind them. For wasn't the plight of any human being the same? Wasn't all suffering the same, after all? And regardless of race, creed, and social class, didn't everyone want to be loved for who they were? Was there a difference between an African American and a Palestinian struggling to make a living? Wasn't it the same struggle, but a different battle? Despite this suffering, Maha knew that God would reward them. She could see the oneness beyond the differences. She could relate to the song because she heard that beyond the pain of Tupac's words, he had hope in humanity.

Maha played the song. And two minutes and 53 seconds into it, she heard the words that set her soul on fire:

> *We gotta make a change...*
> *It's time for us as a people to start makin' some changes.*
> *Let's change the way we eat, let's change the way we live*
> *and let's change the way we treat each other.*
> *You see the old way wasn't working so it's on us to do*
> *what we gotta do, to survive.*

And just like that, things changed for Maha. She knew that she was more than ready to write.

> *Dear Mr. Barak,*
> *I am glad for this opportunity to communicate with*
> *you. To be honest, at first, I wasted so much time concerned*
> *about the best way to write this letter to you, and I got*
> *stuck. I wanted to find ways to convince you to see the*

Arab-Israeli conflict from the Arab perspective. I was seeking your empathy, for you to be compassionate towards our struggle. But in doing so, I lost my way.

I researched the history in full detail, and with the knowledge I gained, I became confused. I didn't understand how previous leaders could be so careless about important information that determined the fate of millions of people, or even how they could make important decisions based on little or non-existent knowledge. Do you know that Theodor Herzl did not know that Arabs lived in Palestine? He published the "Jewish State" and insisted that your homeland be Palestine in oblivion.

Do you not know what the first Jewish settlers admitted when they arrived in Palestine? When they noticed the Arabs, Max Nordau, Herzl's collaborator, realized the truth. He said: "We (the Jews) were committing an injustice," (Quicksand, 19).

Do you know that in spite of all this, Zionists overlooked that fact? They wanted to have Arabs "fold their tents" and then "silently steal away" the land. "After all," Zionists believed that Arabs had "all Arabia with its million square miles," and that there was "no particular reason for the Arabs to cling to these few kilometers."

Sad but true, Mr. Barak: injustice begets even more injustice. Even a Zionist agent was in a state of grief after land sale negotiations. He heard "the sad melody of the Bedouin men and women who gathered by their sheik's tent." Their "songs were lamenting their bad luck, which was forcing them to leave the cradle of their homeland," (Quicksand, 21).

Also, is it not the British Imperial Strategy that made this conflict worse? Their double undertaking of the Balfour Declaration and the Palestine Mandate was a mess. It provoked the collision between Arabs and Israelis (Quicksand, 38). Balfour's "lamentable ignorance, indifference and levity" wreaked havoc. How could he promise that Palestine would become as "Jewish as England is English" (Quicksand, 31)? In the meantime, he worked to legalize their temporary rule of Palestine. Well, at least until the Arabs were fit to stand alone. Is it no wonder that the Israelis and Arabs are still in conflict until today? It is clear that both sides have not recovered from this brutal betrayal yet.

Your history has been full of contradictions ever since. How can you, the people without a land, do unto others what has been done to you? You have endured the pain of being expelled by Europeans out of Europe. Now you do the same thing to Palestinians. You expel them out of their homeland! You use force and weapons on a people and children who can only throw stones at you. Are you even aware of the size and abilities of your opponent?

Like I said, I got stuck, lost and confused in completing this task. In retrospect, I feel fortunate that happened, because now it is clear to me why. I tried to search for the possible good that this conflict could be serving my people, for the greater good and humanity. Then it occurred to me that your existence and your injustices have become a major driving force: because of you, millions of people worldwide are uniting for a just cause. And it is because of my hope in humanity that I believe that change will be inevitable. And if it does not start with you, it will with one of your successors.

So why not be the change?

"Hey, Maha! Did you finish your homework?" Ayah asked.

"Yes. Thank God! I thought it would take forever!" Maha said.

"I miss my school days. They were the best days of my life," Maya mused.

"Best days? Are you kidding me? I can't wait until this year is over. It has been an awful nightmare and it's only been two weeks," Maha said.

"Well… It's a nightmare for you because you are going through so many changes," Ayah conceded.

"But not everyone has a stressful senior year," Maya said.

"Well, lucky them," Maha grumbled, rolling her eyes. She noticed that weird feeling creep into her gut again.

"What's wrong, Maha? You don't look ok," Ayah asked, concerned.

"Umm, I don't know. It might be heartburn or something. But there is this feeling that comes and goes. It's been going on for the past week," she admitted, looking troubled.

"It might be because of the stress of all the changes you are going through. I'm sure you're ok," Ayah tried to reassure her.

"Yes. You are right, Ayah. I used to get that feeling when I got married and stopped talking to my family. It was one of the hardest times of my life!" Maya said, remembering the pain that she had endured during the first few years of her marriage.

"It's just a few changes. Nothing dramatic. I just ended my friendship with Laila. And with Sultan, I guess. I just have to adjust to the fact that things will never be the same again…" Maha felt her throat knot up and tears started to well in her eyes.

"Oh come on, little sis! Please don't…" Ayah pleaded.

"I just don't understand why I'm feeling this way. I am fine. I'm fine. I guess I'll need some time to adjust. But I know that everything will be fine. I did everything I could to be the best friend possible to both Laila and Sultan. But I guess when something dies, it dies," Maha said.

"It's ok, Maha. Everything will be fine. People come and go. Cherish the great memories you share with Laila and Sultan. As much as you have been a good friend, they have been good friends, too. Well, to the best of their abilities," Ayah added.

"I guess so. I can't say much about Laila, because she is who she is. As for Sultan, I don't know, it's weird," Maha shook her head.

"I know. We've all been through this, Maha… Take it easy" Maya advised her.

"You are right. I guess I should. I feel like I want this to be a year of solitude. I'm even thinking of not going on the class trip in December," she admitted.

"Oh no, don't do that! Maha, these are the best days of your life! And a piece of advice from me to you: you can never solve a problem by avoiding it," Maya responded.

"That's so true, Maha! If anything, avoiding things make things worse. Think things over so you don't regret anything later," Ayah agreed.

"Why would I regret it later?" Maha exclaimed.

"Little sis, please take it easy and let's talk about it tomorrow. I just know that you would not want to miss out on an event like this. This might be the last time you'll all be together," Ayah said.

"Well… Ugh, I don't know, Ayah. I don't know what feels right anymore," Maha muttered.

"Take your time and think about it. Now, you need to rest. Good night, dear," Ayah said.

"Good night, Maha," Maya chimed in.

"Good night, girls. Thank you for your support. I needed this," Maha smiled.

"No worries," they both said.

CHAPTER EIGHT

Streets of Cairo
Monday, August 30, 1999, 7:15am
Cairo, Egypt

Mrs. Magda gazed out of her window as Sayed maneuvered his way through the streets of Cairo. The city was beautiful in the morning. It was so quiet, and its silence made its history come to life. It was suddenly apparent in the architecture of buildings and the structure of roads and bridges. Even though it was run down, its vulnerability made many people care even more. While Air Supply's "All out of Love" played in the background, Mrs. Magda realized how a deep breath and more heart could change a life. In these few minutes of peace, Mrs. Magda could be herself without having to worry about anything.

As she took a deep breath and opened up her heart to the world, she saw love that morning. She saw it in the smiles of two street children helping each other roll a tire down the opposite side of the road. She saw it in the kiss a mother gave to her infant while begging for money. She saw it in the eyes of a cart vendor as he sold fool and tameya to hungry customers. It amazed Mrs. Magda how, despite everything, these people could still be happy. They had no safety and security, yet they could smile and care for each other. It was ironic how one could have nothing, yet have everything at the same time. Mrs. Magda's life changed that day when she realized she was wrong. She was wrong to think that Egypt needed to develop the Western way. It was obvious to her that morning that what Egypt needed was for its people to develop it in its own way.

This made Mrs. Magda remember her childhood, and how tirelessly she had to endure listening to her parents discuss and argue with each other about Egypt's future. Of course, her mother was all for Egypt embracing Western ways of modernization. Meanwhile, her father insisted that the modernization of any nation did not mean that it had to become Westernized. In fact, he refused to accept that ludicrous idea. Mrs. Magda was too young to understand the real issues behind these discussions. It was not until after she had graduated from university that she appreciated her father's wisdom in advising her to stick to her roots, learn her language, and embrace her culture. It helped her to survive her first working experience as a French teacher at the Lycée in Cairo. Even though she had been working at a French school, most of the teachers were of Arab origin, and the dominant culture amongst the teachers was Arab. Mrs. Magda had trouble fitting in at first. The other teachers would make fun of her because she did not speak Arabic fluently. This troubled Mrs. Magda, because she could've made fun of their broken French and English. But she didn't. She decided to take the high road. And after she accepted the fact that she was different, things changed. All her colleagues appreciated, respected and loved her for her uniqueness. In fact, many became lifelong friends.

"Madam, we've arrived," Mrs. Magda heard Sayed say.

"Oh, yes. I didn't realize."

"No problem, Madam."

"Ok, so you can go back home now and take Maher to work. Oh, and please see if Saneya needs anything for the house. I forgot to leave her money, so tell her she can put it on the tab at the supermarket,"

"Ok. I will do that"

"Great. Thanks Sayed. See you at three."

"Ok, Madam."

"Bye."

As soon as Mrs. Magda walked into school, she saw a group of girls huddled in a circle on the field next to the middle school building. She needed to pass by them to cross the field and get to the high school building. And she wished she hadn't when she heard the most obnoxious conversation they were having.

The group of girls were making a list of the names of the people they wanted to make fun of. Two of the girls seemed to be the ringleaders, and were directing short songs for each person.

"Oh, you know what! We can take the melody of 'It's a Small World' and make up a song for Stephanie," one girl said.

"Yeah. We have to mention that she smells. And that she can't date anymore guys 'cause she's already dated all of them," another snickered.

"Oh, oh! And how about we say that she thinks she's so cool because she can have boyfriends," another chimed in.

"Wait! Wait! Let's mention that she not only dates Americans, but Egyptians, too," another added.

"Yeah, like seriously. Why does she *do* that?" one girl sneered.

"And of course, when an Egyptian guy dates a popular American girl like her, they get all up in everyone's grill thinkin' they gangsta. They play the 'I don't wanna be a playa no more' dilemma," another one said.

"It's like, seriously… they're such losers. They also get caught up in the whole 'hate playin' but love the game' melodrama," another one added.

"Whatever happened to gentlemen? Real men? Have they gone extinct or what?" another girl asked.

"They're endangered, dear. You'll never find them in a place like this, that's why you don't know of any," her friend told her.

"Sad," the girl who asked the question responded.

"Why? It's not like you can date anyway. Well, not unless you don't care about what people say. Or you are a halfie, or your dad is cool," her friend said.

"Well, I'm none of the above. And my dad is *so* not cool. He's so Egyptian, respectful and proper," she responded.

"It's strange you say that. You know, my great aunt was talking to my mom yesterday, and she was like, talking to her about protecting me from the Western corrupting values. She believes that the way people live their lives in the West is unhealthy and the source of all illnesses."

"That's so close-minded and biased," one girl answered.

"Well, many people from the West agree with that. They're making changes so that they can live a more holistic life – be it in their food, sleep, relationships, exercises and even spirituality. They are starting to borrow many practices from the East, like yoga and meditation, to have healthier lives," another one said.

"True. And many are starting to downsize and live a more green life," she added.

"Oh, well. Let's get back to our song about Stephanie. 'Cause she's far from going green," the ringleader sniggered.

Mean. Very mean. Extremely mean, Mrs. Magda thought to herself as she walked past the girls and overheard their conversation. What a generation of cognitively disconnected people. Who in their right mind speaks like that, let alone have a group of agreeable friends enable it? And *why*? Why were students at school so cruel to each other? Where had all the nice and good people gone? Those kind of people seemed to be endangered in these new and upcoming generations. The fake and superficial students did not seem to surprise Mrs. Magda anymore; the loyal and genuine ones did, though.

CHAPTER NINE

American School in Cairo
Monday, August 30, 1999, 7:31am
Cairo, Egypt

Maha walked into school dragging the weight of the world on her shoulders. She slumped. Gravity pushed her down. She could not resist its force. When she walked towards her locker, she found Sultan standing by the kiosk. He was hanging out with Mahmoud, Ossama, Yusuf and Fahmy. A few steps from them stood Laila with Yasmine and Menna. Maha was in no mood to engage in small talk with any of them, so she decided to take a detour. She headed towards the high school building to find any excuse to escape the crowd. She needed to find something to do until class started. As she walked up the stairs, she found Mrs. Magda's classroom door open, and her teacher inside. Even though she was clueless about what it was that she wanted to talk about, she was so relieved to see her. She hurried in.

"Hi, Mrs. Magda," Maha said as she entered her class.

"Oh! Hi, Maha!" Mrs. Magda said, turning away from the computer screen to greet her.

"I hope I'm not interrupting," Maha said.

"Oh, no! Not at all. I was just working on a proposal, but I have plenty of time for it. Tell me, what brings you here?" Mrs. Magda asked.

"Nothing much. I just wanted to talk to you. I'm trying to avoid hanging out with my friends downstairs," she admitted.

"Sure, Maha! I'm happy to talk. But first, can I ask why it is that you don't want to be with your friends downstairs?" Mrs. Magda asked.

"Well, they are so annoying! There are so many changes going on. I've lost two of my lifelong friends in just a week. There has been so much tension ever since. I guess things will calm down once the new dynamics amongst the group settle. Also, I'm confused about whether or not I should go to the winter social in Luxor and Aswan in December. My sister tells me I might regret it if I don't. But I don't see how I can enjoy myself with people I can't stand in the first place. I get that we are all childhood friends. But I can't stand the social pressure! They have such FOMO!" Maha complained.

"FOMO?" Mrs. Magda asked, bewildered.

"Yeah, they have this constant fear of missing out! I swear it makes them all reek of desperation!"

"Hmm. It's interesting that you say this! Some people, Maha, live their whole lives and don't realize this. They don't know that social pressure makes them act the way they do," Mrs. Magda said.

"I know. It's strange, Mrs. Magda. The sad truth is that I realize how much this pressure affects me, but I don't know what to do about it. Hanging out with them has become such a waste of my time. And you know, I didn't realize until recently how much I hate to waste things. I know God doesn't appreciate wasters," Maha said.

"You're right. But I promise it will all work out. Give it some time, and you will know," Mrs. Magda advised.

"What do you mean?" Maha said.

"What I'm trying to say is that in time, you will know what you need to do. You will only know when you are ready to accept the changes that will come along with it. I understand that there is so much pressure on all students, and especially on Egyptians at this school. That's why it is difficult for many of you to speak up. This age is a difficult stage in anyone's life, and the environment that you are in is not helping at all," Mrs. Magda said.

"Really? How so?" Maha exclaimed.

"Well, let me try to find a way to make it easy for you to understand. Ok. Take the example of an American, Indian and Japanese person of your age. Let's say that each of them lives in their home countries. In general, what do you think their issues are?" Mrs. Magda asked.

"The normal things that most people go through at my age. They have to deal with the stresses of academia, universities and standardized tests. Also, the pressure of friendships, family and relationships, that kind of thing," Maha speculated.

"Excellent! Now I want you to know this. Egyptians at this school have to go through all of these issues and even more. They have to deal with being in an environment that rejects the values of their home country. The American in America, Indian in India and Japanese in Japan speak their language at school. They learn about their culture and history. They do not live in in the midst of major contradictions. Their family culture is more or less like the dominant culture at school and within their community. Now *that*, Maha, is privilege. Unfortunately, Egyptian students here are oppressed. You all are in an environment that is harsh towards your roots. This is an issue, because at this age, you need to form your identity," Mrs. Magda explained.

"But Mrs. Magda, this does not hold true only for us. I mean, that's how it is for all Egyptians who go to international schools, whether they follow British, French or even German curricula. All the people I meet from other schools do not speak one word of Arabic. They want to have nothing to do with being Egyptian or even Arab. You can see it in the pursed lips of people trying to speak in a British accent. Or the aloof behavior of those in French schools. Let alone the intellectual elitism of the people in

German schools! None of these students want to have anything to do with their Egyptian roots. And those who do, have to do it in the opposing extreme!" Maha said.

"Oh, my! And I thought that it was the false promises of the American Dream that had you all fooled into letting go of your roots! Wow! This is tragic. And so brutal. There is a dire need for change!" Mrs. Magda declared, looking heartbroken.

"I guess so. I mean, I agree. Especially after you explained the whole privilege and oppression issue. Things are much clearer to me now," Maha told her teacher.

"I'm glad they are. And so to get back to the initial point of our conversation, I guess what I'm trying to say is that you are dealing with too much already! And you have to be aware and mindful of your abilities," Mrs. Magda said.

"I understand now. I'm so grateful I got the chance to talk to you. You know, nobody speaks like you do. Everybody I talk to tries so hard to be the voice of reason. But with you, it's different. It's more from the heart," Maha said. She was glad that she felt much better than she had earlier that morning.

"Oh, Maha! I appreciate that you think that! I'm glad I talked to you as well. You are unique yourself. And I can't do anything but encourage you to be the best that you can be," Mrs. Magda said.

"Thanks, Mrs. Magda! Well, anyways, I have to go now because I don't want to be late for class. See you in class tomorrow," Maha said.

"Sure. See you," Mrs. Magda smiled.

As soon as Maha walked out of Mrs. Magda's room, she hurried down the stairs. She wanted to get to her Chemistry class in time. She zoomed to her class, jumping down three steps at a time. She was oblivious to everyone and everything around her. Even the textbooks she carried were literally slipping from her fingers. As she descended the first flight of stairs and turned down the next, she collided straight into someone's head. The books slipped from her hands, and she lost her balance while trying to grab onto the person's arm for support. As she pulled hard on their sleeve to right herself, she suddenly realized that it was Sultan she had bumped into.

Ugh! Oh my God! It's Sultan! Maha thought to herself. She could feel her heart pound, stomach flip and that weird feeling creep into her gut again. She had never been this close to him before. She found she could not overcome the intense smell of his 'Cool Waters' cologne.

"You were in my way," Maha blurted out after regaining her balance.

"You can thank my arm, then, for saving you from what could've been an awful fall," Sultan teased her. He knew how stubborn she was about admitting she was in the wrong.

"I wouldn't have needed it if you hadn't been standing there in the first place," Maha snapped back.

"Admit it! Oh, come on, just tell me that you planned this so that you could fall into my arms," Sultan goaded.

"Ugh! Eh! You are so arrogant! Only you would think and say something ludicrous like that. I swear you need help!" Maha shrieked in retaliation, wanting to provoke him back.

"*I* need help? I'm the one who needs help when you can't even admit that you bumped into me by mistake?" Sultan exclaimed. He forced himself to contain his smile that he knew provoked her.

"Whatever," Maha said dismissively, trying to act aloof to cover up the fact that she realized that he did have a point.

"Yes! That favorite word of yours that you always say when you're stuck," he said, gesturing the peace sign.

"Fine. I get it. Forget about it," Maha gave in.

"Say sorry first."

"*Sorry?* What for?" Maha said, thinking that Sultan had really gone insane.

"For being so obnoxious," he said, teasing her again.

"Ugh," Maha sighed, realizing that he knew just how to press her buttons. "Dream on."

"Dream what?" Sultan smiled slyly. He stepped closer to her, took her arm and twisted it. "Say sorry."

"How dare you? You loser. You think you're funny. I'll tell on you. I *swear* I'll tell on you," she threatened. Her face had turned red and she thought that he had crossed the line.

"No, you won't. Say sorry or have mercy," he said.

"In your wildest dreams…" As she spoke, she felt real pain shooting through her twisted arm. "Ow… *Ow…*" she cried and broke her arm free of him. She put her arm between her legs and lowered her forehead to touch her knees. During those few seconds, Maha had come up with a master plan to leave without saying sorry or even 'mercy'.

"Maha! Are you ok? Look at me… I was just joking…" he said apologetically.

Maha was relieved to see Sultan panic. She lifted her head and said gleefully, "Well, your sense of humor sucks!" She laughed to see that Sultan wasn't too happy about being fooled.

"It ain't over till its over, Maha. I will get you," he promised.

"Ha! Only in your wildest dreams, buddy," she retorted.

Maha then realized that she was already 10 minutes late for class. Ms. Jackson would have marked her absent by now. "Oh, no! I didn't realize the time, Sultan! We are so late for class! I'm sure our teachers would have marked us absent by now," she wailed.

"Yooo ohh! I can't afford to have absences in French class," he said. "Well, you know what? We might as well not go to class now. I mean, considering we're already absent!"

"I think so, too! I am not in the mood to do any of Mrs. Jackson's chemistry experiments anyway," she said.

"Let's go outside and hang out, then! There must be a few people who have flex now as well," he said.

"Strange of you to suggest that. But cool. I just need to print out my history homework at the computer lab, and then I'll join you," she said.

"Great! See you in a bit," he said while walking out.

"See you," she said.

When Maha finished printing her assignment, she went outside to find Sultan. She saw him with a few guys hanging beside the kiosk. Some of them had flex, while others had skipped class. It was so common to have people skip class in senior year – it was considered more of an act of coolness than it was of rebellion.

Maha found Sultan and the guys he sat with immersed in a conversation about their plans for the weekend. They were deciding whether to go to Upstairs, Downstairs, Crazy House or Coco Jungle. Maha decided to skip that conversation. There was something about the names of such places that bewildered her ability to reason. So she decided to hang out with Leena, Sylvia and Mariam, who were sitting near the group of boys.

"Hi, Maha," Mariam and Sylvia said at the same time.

"Hi, girls! What's up?" Maha said, noticing that Leena looked awfully sad.

"Nothing much. Leena is just a bit upset that Selim is dating Thalia. It's been only two days since he and Leena broke up," Mariam explained.

"Oh! I'm sorry, Leena! What happened? Are you sure it's true? Or is it just some lame gossip?" Maha asked.

"It's true, Maha. Selim called me last night to tell me. He thought I should be the first to know," Leena said, rolling her eyes.

"What a strange thing to do! I've never heard of anyone doing anything like that in my life," Maha said.

"Like, *seriously*," Sylvia chimed in.

"He is *so* weird, Leena! First, he gives you that ultimatum. Then he breaks up with you because you decided not to give in to his ultimatum. Then he calls you to let you know that he has a new girlfriend!" Mariam gasped.

"Ultimatum? What ultimatum?" Maha asked.

"Last week, he gave me an ultimatum, saying that we could not continue together the way we were anymore. He wanted to do more than just hold my hand. So I told him that it would be difficult for me, and that it was important for me to honor my self, my culture and my religion. So he ended the relationship, and he's dating Thalia now," Leena said.

"Well, if you ask me, sometimes losing people is not really a loss. In fact, good riddance! Guys like him are usually difficult to understand. They have complex issues. They try to be all liberal and Western because it's cool, when at heart they are as conservative as SeSayed. No need to waste your time trying to understand someone like that, because they can't even understand themselves," Maha said.

"Easier said than done, Maha. I've been in a relationship with him for two years! How is it so easy for him to just move on like that?" Leena wondered sadly.

"Maybe he hasn't moved on, Leena. Maybe he's just trying to replace you. Maybe that's the only way he knows how to cope. It's the way he plays the game," Maha suggested.

"Leena is not a game. This whole 'playa play on playa mojo' cool-dude crap has got to stop," Mariam said. "And to be honest, I think the issue is not only with Selim and Leena. I believe that this is a problem with everyone in our generation and society. As girls, our society expects us to be respectful, have limits and not date guys. But at school, the trend is the opposite. To be cool is to be the popular girl who has many boyfriends. It's the same thing for guys as well! They grow up learning that the good girl is someone they marry and don't date. But at school, that would make them terminal losers. To be cool at school, guys have to be playas. It's twisted. We oscillate between the two extremes.

And it's no wonder many people end up losing their way. It's so confusing!" she continued.

"Os-aa what?" Sylvia asked.

"Oscillate. Like to consistently swing back and forth between two things."

"Oh ok, gotcha! Well, you're so right," Sylvia agreed with her. "And the sad truth is, when girls and guys develop real feelings for each other, they get stuck as well."

"Why?" Maha asked.

"Because they can't do much about it. They either deny their feelings or keep it on the down low. Those who rebel and go forward with their relationships will never hear the end of it from their parents, cousins and friends," she added.

"So what are their options?" Maha asked.

"To be friends," she said, shrugging.

"Why?" Maha asked.

"Because what else can they do?" Sylvia asked.

"I don't know," Mariam sighed.

"I think the best option is for them to be friends, I guess," she said.

"That's too complicated, though. I don't think a guy and a girl can be real friends," Mariam declared.

"I think they can. Just as long as intentions are clear between them, and they both respect each other," Maha said.

"That's easy for you to say, Maha. Everyone in this school is like your brother because of your cousin Fahmy. Nobody can mess with that," Mariam said.

"Well, I don't know… But I *have* known most of the guys since elementary and they really are brothers to me," she conceded, realizing for the first time in her life how blessed she was to have her cousin and their friends respect her as a sister.

"To be honest," Leena said, "I'm just finding all these issues too confusing! I think it's best that no one dates while at school.

People need to get their priorities straight, and focus on their academics and pursue their passion. Because it won't get any easier after graduating and going to college. Then there will be a whole different kind of pressure. So it's best to make the most of school years and keep it light."

"Oh, don't remind me! The pressure to get married is something I'm not looking forward to," Mariam groaned.

"Same here," Leena and Sylvia said.

"I'll make sure that I'll never let it get to me," Maha said, feeling overwhelmed by all this talk.

"Oh well! Let's leave it at that, because break time has already started. Time to prepare for the next class," Leena said.

"Yes. I'd better get going because I don't want to miss another class!" Maha said. "Bye, girls."

"Bye, Maha," the girls said.

CHAPTER TEN

American School in Cairo
Monday, August 30, 1999, 8:02am
Cairo, Egypt

Mrs. Magda spent the rest of her morning working on her presentation. She was happy when she finished it. She was confident that it would help her persuade Mrs. White to make this new change at school. In the meantime, she emailed the presentation to Salwa to get some feedback.

> *Dear Salwa,*
>
> *Hope all is well. Kindly find the presentation attached down below.*
>
> *The main aim of my presentation is to address the changes needed to create a mindful curriculum at school. The school must ensure the students' healthy development, wellbeing and learning. To achieve this, professionals must commit to ensuring their social, emotional, and physical development. They cannot continue to focus only on the cognitive development of students. Gone are the days when the belief was that students should simply study, memorize and learn to pass exams and tests. What good is all this knowledge to a person who does not have the emotional*

wellbeing to speak? Or to communicate his/her ideas? Let alone succeed in their personal life and relationships.

Also, in the presentation you will find that I have covered all aspects of Arabic Calligraphy. I mention the benefits of having it as a core requirement at school. I also point out that it will extend the learning experiences of students beyond the technical knowledge they currently acquire. It will offer a holistic discovery of the art and cover its historical and spiritual aspects. This will nurture the physical, creative and spiritual development of students. Also, learning two languages will enhance their cognitive abilities. Bilingual education offers many advantages, including maximizing cognitive flexibility and executive function abilities. This will also help to create a bicultural environment at school.

Moreover, the good news is that these changes involve little cost. It will only necessitate the salaries of two or three teachers. Students will be responsible for getting their own resources for the course. This includes handmade reed pens, writing ink, special paper and custom exercise sheets.

Finally, I'm positive, adamant and keen to achieve this goal. I do believe that this will be the first step in the right direction to creating positive change here.

Waiting for your feedback.
Warm wishes,
Magda

As soon as Mrs. Magda sent the email, she decided to go to the staffroom to share her ideas with a few teachers. She grabbed her mobile phone from her Louis Vuitton handbag and headed towards the staffroom. When she arrived, she found a group of teachers engaged in a casual conversation, discussing their weekend plans. As soon as they noticed Mrs. Magda, they greeted her. This took her by surprise; it was difficult for her to approach the other teachers, as she felt her veil created a cultural barrier between them. But what Mrs. Magda didn't realize was that it was her own thoughts that made her feel that way. She avoided these kinds of friendships, because it reminded her of the pain behind most Arabs' inferiority complex, and the sense of grandiose behind most Westerners' superiority complex. It was also too tiring for Mrs. Magda to justify to Westerners the values of her culture. Why was it that some people did not feel the need to justify their culture, religion or even the color of their skin, while others were ostracized for those very things?

"I hope that you will have an easier time settling in this week," Mrs. Stone said. She gestured for Mrs. Magda to sit next to her.

"Yes, the first month is usually the hardest. I remember mine was difficult," said Mr. McMan.

"Oh, ok! It's good to know that I'm not the only one," Mrs. Magda smiled as she joined them.

"Oh no! You're so not alone. I remember after my first week I wanted to end my contract!" Mr. McMan assured her.

"Oh, yes! I remember. It was quite dramatic with you," Mrs. Stone recalled.

"End your contract! It must have been an awful experience for you to reach that point after just one week! What happened?" Mrs. Magda asked.

"Yes, it was! I had a group of six Egyptian boys in my class, and they were just what spoiled brats looked, dressed and behaved like," Mr. McMan said.

Mrs. Magda felt like the world had tipped over. Mr. McMan's words had shattered the tiniest shred of hope she had to restore equity and social justice in this school. How could such a thing be possible if the professionals themselves were judgemental and biased? How could Mr. McMan speak like that about his students? Mrs. Magda went silent, and all she could do was listen and wonder how an educated man could speak like that.

"Granted, all the teachers know that the Egyptians at school have issues, especially the boys. They always get themselves in trouble," Mrs. Stone cut in. "But the group that Mr. McMan had were the leaders of bad influence."

It was obvious that this conversation troubled Mrs. Magda as she cringed and took a step back. It was humiliating for her to engage in such a conversation. How could Mrs. Stone and Mr. McMan not hear themselves speak? How could they not understand that it was their ignorance that was the bad influence? And that it was their own assumptions that kept them from maximizing the learning potential of their students?

"I don't understand any of this… Why do you speak like this about your students?" Mrs. Magda asked.

"Let me explain it all to you," Mr. McMan said. "But first, before I fill you in about the incident, let me brief you about the Egyptian students at this school. Trust me, you will thank me for this one day, the same way I thanked the teacher before me when he told me all this."

"Oh, really… I'm all ears," Mrs. Magda said, anticipating what Mr. McMan would say.

"Know this: the Egyptian students at this school are amongst the most privileged in the country. They come from big families. They are sons and daughters of the country's biggest politicians, businessmen, thinkers, writers and artists."

"And?" Mrs. Magda prompted.

"These students are used to getting what they want, when they want it. It doesn't matter to them how they get it. And that's what the teacher before me explained. They are spoiled. They act like brats and have no respect for the rules. They will egg your car if they don't like you. Trust me."

"Egg my car? What are you talking about?"

"They did that to the teacher before me. He walked out one day after school and he found out that his car had been egged!"

"What? Oh my! What happened then?" Mrs. Magda gasped.

"The school did an investigation and discovered that some Egyptian boys had done it during their lunch break. Anyway, that teacher left after the incident."

"I can imagine. But still, just because some Egyptian boys did that, does not mean that *all* Egyptians are like that," Mrs. Magda argued.

"I get what you mean. But when most issues like that are caused by Egyptian boys, you can't help but generalize."

"I'm sorry, but why does no one wonder whether it is the environment at school that provokes them to do this kind of stuff? Has no one considered that perhaps your expectations of them are causing them to behave like that, like some kind of self-fulfilling prophecy?"

"Well, listen to my story and you tell me."

"Ok, sure…"

"When I first arrived, during the second week of school, I announced that there would be a short quiz on the Cold War the following week. The Egyptian boys did not like the idea of that. They got upset. They did not want to study for it, so they tried to convince me to postpone it. They even had their parents complain to the administration about me. They said I was unreasonable," Mr. McMan said.

"So for the whole week, they made Mr. McMan's life hell. They were rude to him. They engaged in side conversations during class. They were late to class. It was a catastrophe," Mrs. Stone added.

"Eventually, when they realized that I was firm on my decision, they plotted a way to steal the quiz from my desk drawer," Mr. McCan continued.

"This sounds like a major drama," Mrs. Magda said. "How did you find out that they stole the exam?" she asked.

"After I graded the papers, I realized that they aced my quiz. And I couldn't understand how they did when most of them were on academic probation. I knew there was something strange about it. So I went with my hunch and interrogated them, and I found out that one of them stole the quiz," Mr. McMan explained.

"We still don't know how they did it, even today. There are many versions to the story. Some people say that the boys approached one of the janitors and bribed him with EGP 1,000. They apparently asked him to steal the quiz for them while cleaning the classroom," Mrs. Stone said.

"That story makes no sense," Mrs. Magda argued. "I mean, how would a janitor who doesn't read English know which paper to steal? Also, how did the boys know exactly where the quiz was being kept?"

"I'd never thought of that," Mr. McMan admitted. "I'm sure they had a way of doing it. These boys can master any means of destruction."

"But these are big allegations that you are making, Mr. McMan! Do you know anything about these boys? Their family life, relationships, hobbies and even interests?" Mrs. Magda asked.

"No, I don't. But most professionals at this school know. Egyptian students are destructive, spoiled and arrogant," he declared.

"What do you mean by *they know*? And even if it is true, why have the professionals not questioned why this is only applicable to the Egyptians as opposed to the other nationalities at school?" Mrs. Magda asked.

"What I mean is that everyone knows that most of these students can get what they want, when they want it. Life is easy for them! Half of these students will not have to work hard to earn a living after they graduate from here. Life is, to some certain extent, pre-destined for them," Mr. McMan said.

"I beg to differ. One of the fundamental reasons why Egyptian students are struggling is because of the environment at school. Everything about it aims to annihilate the Egyptian culture. They are taught to reject their roots, culture, language and religion. How could you not expect there to be any feelings of hostility, resentment and anger from their end? How could you not see or understand that, as a professional in the field?" Mrs. Magda asked earnestly.

"Hmm... Interesting. I never looked at it that way," Mrs. Stone said, looking a bit confused.

"Then what do you think the solution to the problem would be?" Mr. McMan asked.

"These students need to feel respected. The Arabic language needs to be included in the curriculum. The administration must dedicate more effort to making this school more bicultural!" Mrs. Magda said. "And to be honest, I think I have an idea that will be the first step in resolving this situation."

"Oh! Wow! If that's the case, let me tell you that you have my utmost support," Mr. McMan promised.

"Yes, mine as well!" Mrs. Stone added. "You will be making a lifelong dream of many teachers come true."

Mrs. Magda appreciated their positive feedback. She felt more secure and confident to make this change happen soon.

"All I need is your support and your commitment to ensuring the wellbeing of all the students here. This change will only be possible when I have that from all the professionals at the school," she said. "I still want to talk to more people about my idea."

"Sounds great! We would love to hear about it, but we have to go now." Mrs. Stone and Mr. McMan excused themselves, saying they had to prepare for the next class.

As they both walked out, Mrs. Stone glared at Mr. McMan and rolled her eyes. When they reached the corridor outside of the staffroom, she whispered to him, "Oh, she is such a naive fool! She doesn't know what she's getting herself into. And to be honest, I think what she's doing is pointless. This is an international school with an American curriculum. Professionals, families and students either accept that or they don't. They have to adapt to us, and not the other way around. Is it not enough that we are doing our best to educate Egyptians here? They should feel blessed!"

"Well, times they are a-changing! Let's wait and see what will come out of all this," Mr. McMan responded.

At that same moment, Mrs. Magda noticed the head of security and janitors standing in the corner of the room. They seemed to be arguing about something. Mrs. Magda was curious to find out what the issue was and offer some help.

"Hi," Mrs. Magda said as she walked over to them. "I'm the new Theory of Knowledge teacher. My classroom is right next to the second flight of stairs. I've seen you all before, but have never had the chance to talk to you until now."

"Hello, Madam," Sherif, the head of security, greeted her politely. "Welcome to the school. Hope you will enjoy your experience here. You know, you are the first Egyptian to teach a core class in the history of this school, and this makes me and the rest of the Egyptian staff proud. Before, the school would only hire Egyptians to teach Arabic, French or P.E. But now, we are all so happy that things have changed!"

Mrs. Magda was glad to hear that as she felt a strong bond with the other Egyptians working at school. "You should know that you also make a great contribution to the school – it could not function without you," she told them, wanting to remind them of their importance as well.

"That can't be true!" one of the janitors exclaimed. Mrs. Magda noticed that the name badge on his uniform identified him as Ahmed. "Because if it was, then how come we're so underpaid and not appreciated by everyone at school? Nobody even recognizes us, and when they do, they treat us like we are charity cases. They use us just to make themselves feel good by donating leftovers, worn-out clothes and old belongings to us. We work hard, Madam, and we don't want people's pity. What we want is simply what is just for us and the amount of effort we put into our work! We perform our dawn prayers here and we leave after our evening prayers. It takes us an hour to commute to and from work. All this, and we make only three hundred Egyptian pounds a month."

"I'm sorry to hear that. Have you tried talking to the administration about this?" she asked, her heart wrenched by the seemingly endless injustices that plagued the school.

"Talk to the *administration*? That's wishful thinking, Mrs. Magda. They'll tell us to go find another job somewhere else. They know that there are millions of people who could replace us," said Ahmed, shaking his head.

"Well, not if you all unite together and make your point as a group. I promise to support you all to the best of my abilities, if you ever decide to do something," Mrs. Magda said.

"Thank you for this! You know, Mrs. Magda, most of us are believers, and the mention of God is enough for us to put our trust in Him. When we see his signs, it makes our faith stronger, and that makes us unshakable," Ahmed told her.

"I hear you, Ahmed. And keep it up. Because at the end of the day, a person without faith is like the desert without sand," Mrs. Magda said. "By the way, is that what you were arguing about earlier?"

"Oh, no! We are arguing about the soccer event that is taking place on Thursday for the Day Beyond Walls. We are facing the same problem that we face every year, and we don't know how to resolve it this year because it is too complicated," Sherif replied.

"What is the issue?" Mrs Magda asked.

"Well, the issue is that the coach had to select twenty students in a draw to take along with the school's official soccer team to a slum area close to Heliopolis. The purpose of this event is for the children to look beyond their differences, and learn to cooperate with each other by playing the game. The students will play in several matches with those living in the slum," Sherif explained.

"That sounds like a great idea. That's an excellent example of community service! But I don't understand, why would there be an issue?" Mrs. Magda said.

"There is an issue because of the twenty students who were selected in the draw, fifteen are Egyptian," Mr. Sheriff said.

"Ok, and this is a problem because…?" Mrs. Magda asked.

"From your answer, I can tell that you haven't met any of the Egyptian students' families yet," Mr. Sheriff said.

"No, not yet. Why? What does this have to do with the issue?" Mrs. Magda pressed.

"Well, Mrs. Magda, it looks like I need to explain to you what most of these people are like," Mr. Sheriff said.

"Sure. Please do," Mrs. Magda replied, perplexed.

"Most of these people want to have nothing to do with our roots, or being Egyptian. It is so extreme that they have completely disconnected from what it is to be human," Mr. Sheriff said.

"I'm sorry, but I still don't seem to understand," she said with an apologetic look on her face.

"No worries. It's a difficult and disturbing reality to understand," he said. "For them, it's shameful to speak Arabic. They behave as if they have hidden French, British or American origins, when in reality that couldn't be further from the truth."

"They boast at any opportunity about the fact that they have a passport, link or family lineage that connects them to any of these countries. They appreciate Western values more than ours. They don't teach their kids anything about our culture, history, language or religion," Ahmed added.

"All they do is encourage their kids to be the best in a sport, or the most popular in the school, or have the highest grades in class. They don't do this for the wellbeing of their kids – their intention is to gloat about it to their friends," Sheriff said.

"Are you sure about this? How do you know all this?" Mrs. Magda asked.

"From the kids, of course. They tend to talk to me a lot, especially when they have to wait for hours at the front gate until their parents or drivers pick them up. Some end up taking taxis home, which they always find humiliating," he said.

"Humiliating? Why?" she asked.

"Because they consider it a sign that their parents neglected them," he said.

"Anyways, to get back to the point," Ahmed continued. "The issue with the Day Beyond Walls event is that most of the Egyptian mothers are getting hysterical about their kids going to the slum area. Some want to have their kids vaccinated. Some don't want to have their children take part. Some want to join the group to ensure the safety of their children. They want to take hand sanitizers, perfumes, colognes and air fresheners," he explained, biting his lip, and Mrs. Magda could tell that he was trying so hard to keep a straight face.

"*What*? Is this a joke?" Mrs. Magda exclaimed.

"We wish. Now, in order to try and contain all the drama surrounding the issue, Mrs. White agreed that the parents can join on the field trip. She had the support of Mr. Marron, the principal of the middle school, and Mr. Schwartz, principal of the elementary school," Ahmed continued.

"Ok. This will be good for them, then. It's obvious that they need an experience like this," she said.

"*Good*? Who are you kidding? Once they got their approval, these people came up with a list of demands," Sheriff scoffed.

"Demands?" she asked.

"Yes – they want to have a doctor and nurse on the trip just in case anything happens. Also, they want to bring a catering service to provide lunch, snacks and drinks. One mom asked for a whole carton of sanitizing gels, wipes and face masks. Another one asked if she could take some of her used stuff to donate to the families of these children. One even asked for body guards and security personnel. And this is just a few of the things on their list," Mr. Sheriff explained.

"Just a *few? What?* Who are these people? Do they not live in Egypt? Do they not see this everyday? Do they not interact with these people?" Mrs. Magda said incredulously.

"*Huh?* These people don't see that kind of thing. They know nothing about that world. And the sad thing is that every year we go, the people living there get offended by these families' behavior. You know it's in our culture that even if we don't have much, we will do everything we can to properly host and feed guests who are visiting. Families there put so much effort into preparing meals. They make koshary and molokheya with chicken to offer to students, staff and teachers. But they always get rejected. It hurts their feelings, because they end up feeling 'inferior'. This then provokes the boys into playing aggressively in their games, especially with this one kid named Khalifa. He is so talented, he can beat our whole team. He is untouchable," Sherif said.

"Wow! I'm shocked!" Mrs. Magda said, shaking her head.

"Maybe if you're not busy that day, you can join us," Sherif suggested. "I have to be there to ensure that communication goes well between the two groups. You being there would really benefit us, especially with the families at the slums. They will not be aggressive with you. I believe that they will respect you because you are veiled."

Taken aback by his comment, Mrs Magda said to him, "I'd love to join. But I hope that people do not judge me because of my veil. I am who I am, and that should be the case regardless of what I'm wearing."

"I didn't mean to upset you. I was just saying that the families could relate to you more because of your veil, because they too are veiled. They cannot relate to the moms who wear tight, revealing clothes and nine-inch high heels. They try so hard to look cool, casual and grounded. Not that there is anything wrong with it – I'm just saying that it's provoking. Such extremes are sickening to these families, especially because they struggle to have basic things like electricity, water or even food," Sherif said.

"Yes. True, Sheriff. When you think about it, we don't have much in the world. That's why family means everything to us," Ahmed chimed in.

"Yet, you know something, you look so much more content than many of the people who have more," Mrs. Magda told them. "Everything in life is a test. What makes us all equal, regardless of our differences, is that none of us know what will happen next. Life as we know it today may change completely tomorrow. Let's appreciate what we have now. Anyways, I would love to join you on Thursday."

"Great! I'll arrange for that! Thank you, Madam," Sherif said.

"Don't mention it, Sheriff. I have to go now. See you on Thursday," Mrs Magda smiled at them warmly.

"Ok, see you then," Sherif and Ahmed said together.

Mrs. Magda walked back to her classroom and packed her things. She was so relieved that she was going to go home, eat the food Saneya had made, and have a quiet night with Maher. She wanted to check on her vegetable garden and read a book, and then go to sleep early.

As she walked out of school that day, Mrs. Magda could not help but realize how well things were working out for her. She felt confident that she would be able to achieve her goal soon, especially with the support of Salwa, the teachers, the security personnel and the janitors.

The next day, Mrs. Magda checked her mail in the few minutes remaining before class started. She was glad to have received an email from Mrs. Salwa congratulating her on a job well done with the presentation. She said she thought it was thorough, credible, relevant and persuasive, and wished her the best of luck with her meeting with Mrs. White next week. Mrs. Magda was grateful for Salwa's positive support and guidance at this point.

Her few moments of solitude came to an end when the students walked into class. She saw Laila snub Maha and close the classroom door in front of her. Mrs. Magda sensed major tension between the two.

"Good morning, class! How are you today?" Mrs. Magda asked cheerfully, hoping to change the mood in the class.

"Fine," they all replied.

"Well, ok... If you say so," she said.

"Yeah, well, not Laila and Maha," Mahmoud amended.

"Take a chill pill, Mahmoud!" Laila cried out.

"Say that to yourself, Laila! You're crossing the line," he retorted.

"Hey! Hey! What is going on? This is no way to speak to each other. We can resolve the problem, whatever it is, after class. Ok?" Mrs. Magda intervened.

"Fine!" Mahmoud and Laila said together.

"Now, let's get started with class. So first, let's discuss your questions. Then we'll talk about the significant discoveries throughout history, and assess their impact and contribution towards knowledge," she said.

"Yes, Mrs. Magda," Ossama said, thinking about his participation points.

"Great, Ossama! But before I begin, I just want to take a minute to talk about your papers. I have decided that I will not grade them now. Your papers had many grammatical errors, so I want to give you all a chance to rewrite them at the end of the term. From now on until then, I expect you to read for thirty minutes and write a journal entry of at least two hundred and fifty words every day. You are free to choose whatever it is you want to read. It can be a book, an article or even lyrics to a song! The point is, I want you to read and write. I want you to take note of grammar and see how people use or break the rules to express their ideas. I will collect these journals at the end of term, and using the I.B. rubric, I will grade both your papers. This is so you can see your own progress. Any questions?" Mrs. Magda said.

"No. It's clear," Ossama said while the rest of the students nodded their heads in agreement. They were all annoyed by the fact that they had to do daily homework for class. However, the thought of writing about songs and lyrics intrigued Maha. She loved reading lyrics, and always made an extra effort to understand the meanings of songs.

"Ok, great! So let's begin with you, Ossama! Tell us the questions you came up with," she prompted.

"Sure, Mrs. Magda. The first question is personal. I want to know, what are the practical skills I need to help me live a life that is in line with my family and cultural values? The second question is more about conformity. I want to understand the reason why there are many contradictions in our society. If religion preaches to us to be true to ourselves, then why is it so difficult to pursue passions like music? If love is so important in life, then why are there many people living loveless lives, be it in their professions or in their relationships?" Ossama asked.

"Wow! These are quite thought-provoking questions," Mrs. Magda replied.

"Ohhh man!" Mahmoud interjected. "My questions are the same as yours! That must say something about our struggles, bro!"

"Yo, this is dope," he said. "It's obvious neither of us have much say over our lives."

"I hear you! The only question I have that is different from yours is about decision-making. I want to know, what makes a wise choice wise? And how can I make sure that all my decisions are wise?" Mahmoud asked.

"Excellent question, Mahmoud!" Mrs. Magda exclaimed, anticipating a great discussion.

"My questions are different, Mrs. Magda," Laila interrupted. "I want to know, what do I need to do to marry the man of my dreams? After I get married, how can I get pregnant without getting fat? And after I have children, how can I maintain an active social life and take care of my kids at the same time?" Laila asked.

"Interesting questions, Laila," Mrs. Magda replied. "You know, many women struggle with handling stress from these life changing events."

"Are there people in this world who don't struggle?" Maha interjected. "I mean, it's obvious to me that both men and women struggle and suffer!"

"Excellent observation," Mrs. Magda said.

"That's why my questions are a little bit different, Mrs. Magda," Maha spoke up.

"That's fantastic, Maha. It's fine to be different," Mrs. Magda said.

"Well, I would like to build a toolbox of practical skills to help me face life's different challenges. I want to find out ways to overcome negative emotions like anger. I want to figure out how to forgive, and how to maintain mental strength and agility. And last but not least, I want to know what love is," she said.

"All your questions relate to gaining more emotional intelligence," Mrs. Magda observed.

"Uh huh," Maha agreed.

"Ok. Well... I think we should group your questions under main themes. For example, Mahmoud and Ossama's questions relate to the theme of individuality and conformity. Laila's questions deal with women and the issues they face, be it motherhood, body image or social pressure. Maha's questions revolve around the theme of emotional intelligence. I will create a question from each theme, and as a group, you will research the answers and present them to me in class next week," Mrs. Magda said.

"Hmm, interesting," Ossama said.

"I don't know how I feel about working with Maha," Laila objected.

"Well, you are going to have to address your issues before you start, because this is a group project. I do not want your issues interfering with this. Are you both willing to put this aside for now?" Mrs. Magda asked.

"Yes," Laila said.

CHAPTER ELEVEN

"I guess so," Maha conceded, trying to escape the humiliation that she felt in front of Mrs. Magda. It really mattered to her that Mrs. Magda appreciated her. Maha had always aspired to be at the top in all the classes that mattered to her. She couldn't care less about the classes that didn't interest her. At this point, she started to realize that TOK more than mattered, and she worried that her beef with Laila was giving her a bad image in front of Mrs. Magda.

"Good. Then we will talk through your issues after class," Mrs. Magda said.

"Ok," they both agreed.

"Now, give me a minute to think about the three big questions for you," Mrs. Magda said.

After a few minutes of reflection, she wrote the questions on the whiteboard:

1) Why is it a struggle for people to be themselves in any society worldwide?

2) How has body image affected girls, women and mothers worldwide? What kind of impact has it had on their relationships?

3) Which practical skills will you put in a toolbox to help you face all of life's challenges?

"You are to use nine different resources. Your resources must include both Western and non-Western perspectives. You will use a minimum of three resources for each perspective," Mrs. Magda instructed.

"This is so challenging," Mahmoud said enthusiastically. "I can't wait to get started on this."

"Me, too," Laila agreed. "In all my schooling years, this must be the assignment that I'm most keen to work on."

"Me, too," Maha said, thinking about her toolbox and wishing that her life had come with a written manual. There was nothing that she wanted to do more than to fast-forward through this part of her life.

"I'm glad to hear that you are all engaged and enthusiastic to learn," Mrs. Magda said. "Now, let's get started with the second half of our discussion, before we run out of time. So, can anyone define the word 'discovery' for me?"

"Well, yes. The definition of discovery is easy. It is 'the act of finding or learning something for the first time'," Mahmoud said.

"Good!" Mrs. Magda said. "So can you give me an example of a great discovery?"

"I think one of the greatest discoveries in history was finding out that the earth was round and not flat," offered Maha.

"Excellent, Maha! On that basis, can you tell me who was the first to find out this information?" Mrs. Magda said.

"Of course, it was none other than Galileo!" Laila blurted out. "Before him, everybody thought that the world was flat."

"Really? Is that so? Tell me, according to whom was Galileo the first man to discover this?" Mrs. Magda asked.

"According to the Western perspective," Mahmoud said.

"Yes," affirmed Mrs. Magda. "So what does that mean?"

"It means he was the first person in the West to learn about this information. But that does not mean that nobody else could have made this discovery before him," Maha said.

"Right on!" exclaimed Mrs. Magda. "Just because people in the West believed for centuries that the world was flat does not mean that it was. And it also does not mean that nobody made that discovery before them. In fact, historical texts reveal that this truth was discovered in Ancient Egypt, long before Galileo. Eratosthenes, a scientist, was the first man to discover that the Earth was round."

"Wow! Ancient Egypt? Talk about the West being a few centuries too late," Ossama chortled.

"This is so aggravating, then!" Maha said. "If everything we learn is from a Western perspective, how are we expected to learn the truth? Or even be aware that there are different perspectives? This is so Orientalist of the school! I'm so shocked."

CHAPTER TWELVE

American School in Cairo
Tuesday, August 31, 1999, 7:42am
Cairo, Egypt

At that point, Mrs. Magda took a moment to observe how the class reacted to Maha's statement. She did not want to see them get stuck the same way many Arabs had done before upon discovering the truth of how dominant the Western perspective was in the world. Many Arabs fell into a cycle of negative emotions when they realized how suffocating the Western perspective was, as it gave no room for any other perspectives to breathe. Many have been deemed extinct, and the very few that remained were endangered. This struggle was still taking place in every home in the Arab world. Every family had been plagued by the fear of losing their members to the struggle between pro- and anti-West. On whatever side a person fell, though, the sad thing was that they usually became extremist in their views. Mrs. Magda did not wish this for her students, because she herself had endured the pain of losing so many people to either side. The Western wannabes completely disconnected from their roots. They created new identities that made them more Western than Westerners. Those against the West, meanwhile, became tangled in the roots of a distorted Arab identity from the dark ages.

After a long pause, Mrs. Magda asked, "Why do you find this aggravating, Maha? Knowledge is power, after all. The knowledge that you're gaining is empowering you."

"I don't know what you mean," Maha said. "I'm too confused and overwhelmed by all this. How in the world can I be empowered?"

Maha's response confirmed to Mrs. Magda what she had already predicted, and she decided not to pressure her.

"Ok, Maha. That's no problem," she assured her. "Does anyone else understand what it is that I'm trying to say?"

"Yes," Ossama said. "You're trying to empower us. You want us to see and act beyond the limitations inflicting the Arab World for the past century. As a people, we can't seem to move beyond our anger, the anger that we've inherited from our ancestors. We blame others for the atrocities that afflict our schools, homes and communities. We act like victims, because we feel we have no choice but to react to atrocities. We lack the knowledge to help us own and take responsibility for our actions and move forward. This can help us understand what is happening"

"And what do you think is happening?" Mrs. Magda asked.

"I don't know. I wish I knew," Ossama admitted.

"I think I know," Mahmoud said. "I think it's a test. It's a test of faith and patience. Many pray to God and seek his guidance. These prayers give millions hope, patience and faith. I think that's how we've survived so much injustice in our own homeland."

"Interesting, and what else?" Mrs Magda prompted.

"I think God's guidance has strengthened our faith and hope. This is what has kept us going. It is in our blood. We hope. We feel. We pray. Few Westerners understand our way of life. In their societies, knowledge became divorced from religion centuries ago. In the West, many disregard religion on the basis of what Karl Marx said: 'Religion is the opiate of the masses'. Mainstream education promotes this perspective in many young minds. Religious people are not held in high regard.

The stereotype is that they're poor, ignorant and backwards," Mahmoud explained.

"And how do you feel about this?" Mrs. Magda asked.

"I agree with it," Laila said. "All the poor people just regurgitate information that they don't even understand. They obey orders only."

"What do you want them to do?" Mahmoud retorted. "Live in extreme poverty and not know how to feed or shelter themselves, and just be cool about it? Do you not understand that religion, faith and hope is all they've got? And that it's powerful enough to help them endure and suffer anything?"

"They should work hard. Hard work pays off. But they are so ignorant, unreliable, lazy and greedy," Laila bit back.

"Do you realize what you just said? Do you really believe that's true? How can you think that hard work is what separates the poor from the rich? How are these people expected to work hard when they do not have job opportunities?" Maha cried indignantly. "It is privilege and circumstance that determine this. Take yourself as an example. Think about all the *hard work* you did to get here, and you will see the truth. It is nothing more than your privilege that has given you the opportunity to get an education like this. Privilege got you here, Laila. And by the way, this is true not only for you, but for all of us. Hard work did not get any of us here. Privilege did."

"And the sad thing is, we think it's a privilege to be in a school like this. We waste so much time learning theoretical knowledge that we'll never use," Ossama chimed in.

"You're so right, Ossama! I agree! Theoretical knowledge is by no means applicable in the real world," Maha exclaimed.

"What do you mean by that?" Mrs. Magda asked.

"I mean, there is such a huge gap between theoretical information and practical experiences. Any theory can be challenged, because there will always an exception to the rule. Theories are not absolute, yet we study them as if they are," she continued.

"Hmm, interesting!" Mrs. Magda responded.

"So then why do schools torment students with useless and inaccurate information?" Mahmoud asked.

"It's because that's part of the system," Maha said.

"Ok, so it is obvious this needs to change," Ossama declared. "In fact, I think the whole education system needs to change. It would be nice to have schools cater to our needs and wellbeing, rather than the opposite."

"That's an excellent point, Ossama! I think in order to move forward, schools need to make many changes as well! And on that note, we're going to have to end the discussion here, because class time is up. I want you all to enjoy and make the most of your experiences on the Day Beyond Walls. See you next week!" she said, reminding herself to address the issue with Laila and Maha before they left. "As for Laila and Maha, would you like to talk to me about any of your problems?"

"No, thanks," they both said.

"It's all forgotten," Maha added.

"And I hope forgiven, too," Mrs. Magda replied.

"Hopefully," they responded.

As soon as the students left, Mrs. Magda took a moment to reflect on what had happened in class. She had not expected the discussion to turn out the way it had.

She got out her journal and wrote down everything that had taken place, and realized to what extent the students engaged in the discussion. This was an excellent example of self-directed learning. It was such an eye-opener to everyone, including her. Mrs. Magda was content with that. Also, it reaffirmed the need for the changes she aspired to make in the school. She could not wait to meet Mrs. White on Sunday.

CHAPTER THIRTEEN

American School in Cairo
Tuesday, August 31, 1999, 9:10am
Cairo, Egypt

Mahmoud, Laila, Maha and Ossama walked out of the high school building. As they headed towards the kiosk, they made plans to meet up for their project.

"I think we should meet for half an hour today after school," Mahmoud proposed.

"Sounds good," Ossama said.

"Yes, that works fine for me," Maha agreed.

"Sure, me too," Laila affirmed.

"Perfect! Let's meet up beside the kiosk and then we can walk to the library together," Mahmoud said.

"Ok. See you all then," Ossama said as he dropped his bag beside the kiosk and got out his ID card so that he could go off campus for his lunch break.

"Are you going out for lunch?" Mahmoud asked.

"Yeah. I want to go to Kimo market to get a sandwich and some chips," Ossama said.

"Great! I'll join you! I'm craving the turkey sandwich from there," Mahmoud enthused.

"Yeah man! I'm craving the TLT, too," Ossama said. "Girls, any of you want to join us?"

"Thanks, Ossama! I prefer to hang out on campus," Maha said.

"Boys, I'd love to join you," Laila said.

"Good! Let's go," Mahmoud said.

"Where are you guys going?" Menna asked as she walked up and joined in on the conversation.

"We are going to Kimo," Laila responded.

"Fantastic! I would love to join you, too," she said as she got out her ID card from her black Jansport.

"Ok, let's walk out from the front gate," Ossama said. He started to make headway to the front gate and the rest followed him.

As soon as they walked passed the gate, Menna opened up the small pocket of her Jansport. She got out a pack of Marlboro Lights and an eccentric silver metallic lighter.

"I've been dreaming about this all day," Menna said as she lit her cigarette. She inhaled the nicotine and puffed out a big cloud of smoke.

"Tell me about it! I'm so relieved Maha didn't come. It would have been impossible to smoke around her," Laila said.

"I don't see why," Mahmoud said.

"Yeah! There is no reason for you to hide the fact that you smoke from Maha," Ossama chimed in.

"Oh, please! She makes a nun look like a devil. She is so self-righteous. I know she would start preaching about how we are sinning," Menna said.

"I think you are dramatizing this a bit," Mahmoud said.

"Well, I'm just not that comfortable with her knowing that I smoke! And I would like to keep it that way," Laila said.

"Suit yourself!" Mahmoud shrugged. They all arrived at Kimo market, dubbed the coolest supermarket in the city. The shop was evidence of the power of trade in the 20th century. Located only five minutes away from school in the midst of the desert, it had an abundant reserve of American goods. Brands like Kool-Aid,

Oscar Mayer, Kraft, Campbell and Sunmaid raisins overcrowded its shelves.

"I can't join you inside because I haven't finished my cigarette. So can you please get me a TLT?" Laila asked, getting an EGP 10 note out of her wallet to give to Ossama.

"Sure! Anything else, like juice or Pringles?" he asked.

"No, thanks," she replied.

"Can you get one for me, too, while I stay behind with Laila?" Menna asked Ossama, handing him another EGP 10 note.

"Sure!" he said as he walked inside with Mahmoud.

Once inside the supermarket, the boys headed towards the deli. They were happy to find Mohammed sitting on the chair behind the fridge. He sipped on his Al arosa tea and ate the last bite of his white cheese and tomato Fino sandwich while he listened to Shaaban Abdel Rehim. His curly hair was hardened from the overdose of gel he'd applied that day.

"Hey hey, Mo," Ossama and Mahmoud said. "What's up, man? It's been a long time."

"Hey hey, ya maaan! I'm fery fery good!" he greeted them, smiling and getting up out of his chair. "So what you want today?"

"We want the usual, of course! The best TLT in the world, man!" Ossama replied.

"Yes! Yes! Right away," he said.

"Ok, but please make it four sandwiches – we have two of our friends outside," Mahmoud added.

"Ok! Ok! In ten minutes, all finish," he promised.

"Yes! Did you see the Ahly and Zamalek match?" Mahmoud asked.

"Yes, Ibrahim and Hossam Hassan are ex'slant!" Mohammed enthused.

"Yes! They are the kings!" Mahmoud agreed.

"But Zamalek are very bad! Why zey go out of match after four minutes in April? All ze fans were mad. And my fazzer-in-law, yoooo," Mohammed whistled.

"Hahaha! Tough times with your in-law or what?" Mahmoud asked.

"Yeah, man! He was mad when Ayman Abdel Aziz did what he did in that game! He was until zey win za cup in Mayo," Mohammed said.

"Haha! That's hilarious, man! He must be quite intense," Mahmoud said.

"Yes! I no see him for many monses," he said. He wrapped the sandwiches in Clingfilm and gave them to Mahmoud and Ossama.

Mahmoud laughed again as he took the sandwiches. "Mmm, I can't wait to eat this. It looks amazing! Thank you!"

"Yeah, man! Thank you," Ossama said.

"Any-tyhum guys! See you!" Mohammed smiled.

"See you!" they called as they walked out of the supermarket.

Ossama and Mahmoud could not believe their eyes when they got outside. They saw Laila and Menna standing right where they had left them, still smoking cigarettes.

"Are you still smoking the same cigarette we left you with ten minutes ago?" Ossama asked.

"No," Laila responded, clearly a little ashamed. "It's a new one. You took a long time, so I figured I could have another one."

"It took us long? What are you talking about? It only took us ten minutes!" Mahmoud said incredulously.

"Oh, please! Can you stop acting like you're my father? This is only my second cigarette today," Laila defended herself.

"Fine. Whatever. But I'm just letting you know that this is no good for you at all!" he said.

"Thanks for the advice. I'll keep it in mind. Now can I have my TLT, please? I'm starving!" she said.

"Here you go," Ossama said as he gave the girls their TLTs.

"Thanks," they both said as they salivated over the sight of their sandwiches. They unwrapped the Clingfilm and started to devour them.

"So, you wanna go back to school?" Menna asked.

"Sure!" Laila and Mahmoud agreed.

"I think I'll go meet up with the rest of the guys at Bandar. I'm in the mood for a shisha and there is enough time for me to do that before next class," Ossama said. "I'll walk with you back to school and continue on my own from there." He estimated that he had enough time to go to Bandar, because it was only five minutes away from the back gate.

"Are you sure you will have enough time to do all that?" Menna asked.

"Yeah, sure! And even if I'm ten minutes late for next class, it shouldn't be a problem," Ossama said breezily.

"Sure," Menna said. And that was the last of that. Words were silenced by their hunger. Peace prevailed on their way back.

As soon as they arrived at the front gate, they said their goodbyes to Ossama. Mahmoud decided to shoot some hoops with Yusuf and the rest of the guys. Menna and Laila stayed behind to smoke their third cigarette of the day.

Laila, Maha, Ossama and Mahmoud were happy to find each other at the kiosk, and glad that the day had come to an end. It was so draining for them to endure four 90-minute classes a day! It was torture, especially those classes that did not interest any of them. For Laila, it was Science, Math and History that held no interest for her. For Maha, it was Math, while Ossama disliked Science. Mahmoud was utterly bored by English. So it was no surprise that they all agreed to have a 10-minute break before going to the library.

As they loitered near the kiosk, Yasmine walked up to Maha and asked her, "Are you going home now or will you stay after school?"

"I'm staying after school for a while," Maha told her.

"This is divine intervention, Maha! I need to stay after school, too. So can I catch a ride with you back home?" Yasmine asked.

"I don't know why you keep asking, Yasmine! I get tired having to respond to the same question all the time! *Yes*, Yasmine! You can catch a ride with me," she laughed good-naturedly.

"Hahaha! You know I'm all sensitive about being the *scrub*," Yasmine said.

"Hehehe! I get it, scrub," Maha teased.

"You know I'm no scrub!" Yasmine retorted.

"Yes, Yasmine, I get it! Let's meet up here at around four," Maha suggested.

"Fantastic! I need to get going now," she said in a hurry.

"Ok! Bye," Maha waved. When she turned around again, she saw Laila and Sultan out of the corner of her eye, engaged in a deep conversation.

"So there you are! I've been looking for you everywhere," Maha heard Yusuf say. She quickly turned her gaze away from Laila and Sultan.

"Yes! I'm here," Maha said with a smile. "What's going on?"

"No, nothing… I just needed your help with something, but it's all good now."

"Are you sure? Cuz, I'm happy to help."

"Yes! If I get stuck on research work again, I'll make sure you help me out," he promised.

"Good! I'm going to the library now to do some research myself, for a project for TOK," she told him.

"Oh no way! Enjoy," he said.

"I'm sure I'll have a blast," she rolled her eyes.

"Ugh! Say that again! I guess I'll get going now and leave you to your research. By the way, are you going to Menna's birthday on Thursday?" he asked.

"Yeah! Why?"

"No, nothing. Fahmy told me to ask you if I saw you around today. He was looking for you all day and didn't get the chance to do it himself," he explained.

"Ok. No problem! Are you guys going?"

"I don't know yet. But we might pass by."

"Sounds great!"

"Ok! Bye now!" he said.

"Bye, Yusuf!" she replied.

Maha turned around and saw Mahmoud and Ossama getting ready to go to the library. She hurried to join them.

"Wait for me, guys!" Maha called.

"Ok! Hurry up!" Mahmoud said.

"What about Laila?" Ossama asked.

"Can't you see? She's still talking to Sultan," Mahmoud said.

"Laila!" Ossama shouted "We're going to the library now!"

"Fine," she said, her eyes still glued to Sultan. "Take a head start and I'll join you in a few minutes."

"Ok," he said.

"Whatever," Mahmoud muttered. "I hate group work for just this reason. I always get stuck with at least one person who is never as eager or as committed to do the work as the rest of the group!"

"Give her a chance!" Ossama said. "She might prove you wrong."

"Well, whether she is serious about this or not, I think we should divide the work between us. Each person should be responsible for their part. If she does her part, then great. If she doesn't, then she is the one who will get affected and not us," Maha proposed.

"I think that's a great solution!" Mahmoud said.

"Me too," Ossama agreed.

They sat around a wooden desk in the library and decided to wait for Laila for another few minutes before getting started. But she didn't show up.

"Please, let's get started. I can't waste more time," Mahmoud said.

"Yes, let's do that," Maha agreed.

"Her loss, I guess," Ossama said.

"It sure is!" Maha said. "Anyway, how should we divide up the work?"

"Well, we have three questions and we are four people," Mahmoud reminded them.

"I think each one of us should choose the theme related to our initial questions," Ossama proposed.

"Ok," Mahmoud agreed.

"In that case, Ossama will address issues about individuality and conformity in societies worldwide. Laila will cover the issues women face, including motherhood, body image and social pressure. I will answer the questions on emotional intelligence, and which skills can help us face life's difficult challenges. What about you, Mahmoud?" Maha asked.

"Well, since we have to provide three different perspectives for each answer, I can be responsible for answering one perspective from each question. So for example, I can do the African perspective for Ossama's question, Western for Laila, and Arab for yours. What do you think?" Mahmoud suggested.

"I think it's a great idea, Mahmoud. But then you'll be answering three questions and not two, like the rest of us," Maha pointed out.

"Well, if one of you does the intro and the other the conclusion, I think it will be fair," he said.

"Sounds great," Ossama said.

"What about Laila? She'll be doing the least work," Maha asked.

"I think that's best for now, Maha. You know, sometimes being fair can set us back," Mahmoud replied.

"I couldn't agree more!" she said, thinking that this was the best way to ensure her peace of mind. Laila was starting to become more of a nuisance than a friend to her. It irritated Maha that

Laila was spending time with Sultan, as if he were her lifelong childhood friend. Laila's talent at pretending helped her put on a great show. Maha had seen the terrible ending of many like her before. Loserville was their final destination. The school ensured this by becoming the perfect stage set for trashy ways.

"Me, too," Ossama chimed in.

"Ok, now that that's done. When should we meet again? And what should we prepare?" Maha asked.

"Let's have our research complete before we meet on Saturday. We can set up the presentation then. And let's meet on Wednesday to research, Saturday to set up and again on Sunday to review it all," Mahmoud suggested.

"So should we have the bullet points for our slides all ready before Saturday then?" Ossama asked.

"Yes, and let's aim for one slide per perspective," Maha said.

"Excellent! Sounds great and doable!" Mahmoud agreed.

"What sounds great and doable?" they all heard Laila's voice from behind them.

"Oh! So you finally decided to show up!" Mahmoud said.

"I was looking for you everywhere in the library. I'm so sorry I'm late!" Laila said.

"It took you thirty minutes to look for us?" Mahmoud asked in disbelief.

"I'm not sure how long it took, Mahmoud. But it did take me a while! Anyways, did I miss out on much?" she asked.

"Yes… We actually just finished up right now," Maha said, relieved that she didn't have to spend a second longer with her.

"All you have to do is answer the question about women and the issues they face, like motherhood, body image and social pressure," Ossama told her. "Then you have to discuss how this affects their relationships. You should choose two perspectives, because Mahmoud will do the third. We'll meet on Wednesday to do the research. And Saturday to do the presentation, so have your bullet points ready! Then we'll review everything on Sunday."

"Hmm, ok! So where will we meet on Saturday?" she asked.

"We can meet at my place at 12:00pm," Maha shotgunned first, because the last place she wanted to go to was Laila's house and have to suffer her obnoxious attitude.

"Sounds good," Mahmoud said.

"It's fine with me," Ossama agreed.

"Me, too," Laila said.

"Great! I'd better get going. Yasmine must be waiting for me at the kiosk," Maha said as she stood up and packed away her stuff. "Alright! See you all tomorrow! Bye!"

"Bye," they all said.

"Maha! Finally! I've been waiting for you forever!" Yasmine exclaimed as Maha approached.

"Yes, and…?" Maha prompted, giving her a look that said, 'Are you *really* going to pressure me about being late?'.

"Ohhhh! Don't give me that look!" Yasmine said.

"And you don't give me that tone," Maha responded, smiling. "Now, I need to get something to eat before we leave! I'm starving and exhausted and I need something from the kiosk to give me an energy boost!"

"Fine! I'll get something, too. But please, whatever it is you are going to get, don't let it be the Salt and Vinegar Chipsy! I can't stand the smell of it," she demanded.

"You're lucky that I'm not in a Chipsy mood, then! I'm more in a Bimbo one. I swear, Yasmine, nothing in this world can beat the perfection of the Bimbo. Forget Godiva, Lindt and all that gourmet crap. Everything about Bimbo is just so right! The ratio of chocolate to biscuit is perfection. The quality of the chocolate, the shape and freshness of the biscuit… Ugh! I *need* to get me some now! What do you want?" Maha asked.

"I'll have the same, of course!" she grinned.

"Hi Aziza! How are you?" Maha greeted the lady behind the counter at the kiosk.

"I'm good. You?" Aziza asked.

"Good! Yasmine and I are hungry, and we'd like eight Bimbos, please," Maha said.

"*Eight*? Are you joking?" Aziza asked incredulously.

"No! Four for me and four for Yasmine," Maha confirmed.

"Fine! Whose tab should I put it on?" Aziza said.

"Mine," Maha decided.

"No, no, make it on mine," Yasmine said.

"Hmm, choose one, girls!" Aziza said, starting to get irritated.

"It's only EGP 2, Yasmine, don't make a fuss about that! That's literally like 75 cents!" Maha said.

"Fine! Thanks Maha. But next time it's on me."

"Respect! And just as a heads up, know that it will be the Salt and Vinegar Chipsy next time," Maha teased as she waved goodbye to Aziza.

"You think you are so funny! But in reality your humor is far, far from amusing," Yasmine retorted. They walked through the back gate and headed towards Maha's car.

"Who said that I ever aspired to be funny?" Maha asked.

"I definitely didn't! But I'm just claiming something about our 10-year friendship. I'm the funny and wild one and you are the prudent and wise one," she declared.

"Ugh! Here we go again with that broken record of yours that doesn't stop! And I have the straight thick black hair and you have the curly brown hair. You want to have straight thick hair and I want curly! Can we *please* get over it and move past this! We are seniors now, Yasmine! We're not the two little girls on the bus anymore!"

"Get over it? What? Are you kidding me? Trying to act all mature and all! I will never forgive you for your thick black straight hair!" Yasmine screeched.

"Fine. Suit yourself! I forgive *you* for being funny!" Maha retorted.

"Hahaha! Nice come back!" she laughed.

"I know!" Maha said smugly as they got into the car. "So, what are we going to listen to today?"

"Hmmm, CD or mixtape?" she considered. "Actually, let's do mixtape! There's a song I want to hear. Well, not the whole song…"

"I know, the intro only…" Maha smiled.

"You get me, Maha!" Yasmine exclaimed.

"I do, Yasmine. After ten years of a friendship like this, I'd be a fool to not understand you. This is in spite of our drastic differences."

"You know, Maha, sometimes I don't know how we are even friends!"

"You're not alone. I ask that same question all the time. We have nothing in common. I mean, not even our genre preference in music. The one interest we're both passionate about is completely different!"

"I know. Like I love soft rock, house and dance, and you are into soul, R&B and hip hop. Worlds apart!" Yasmine agreed.

"I think it just is what it is," Maha mused.

"Me, too. I believe that our friendship would not exist had it not been for our love of music… And the bus," Yasmine smiled.

"Haha! True! Yes, the bus. Remember how we used to pray everyday for Shadi to miss the bus?"

"Hahaha! Yes! He was always bugging you, Maha."

"I know. He was like my sworn enemy. I was so happy when he graduated three years ago."

"Yes. It gave us a chance to work on our song and listen to music without him bothering us," Yasmine agreed.

"Haha! Yes! You know something, you are right. Without music, we would not be friends," Maha said.

"And that would suck! Because like Nietzsche, I believe that 'without music, life would be a mistake,'" Yasmine quoted.

"Hahaha! And you know what else?" Maha said as she took control of the sound system and rewound the mixtape.

"What?" Yasmine prompted, already anticipating the song that Maha was going to play.

"Dancing, too," Maha declared as she hit play and the intro of Lionel Richie's "Angel" began to play.

"Ooohhh Maha! My favorite intro! I have to get into position for this," she said. She tried to flip her hair, rolled down the windows, sat back and took her hands to the center of her heart. She then extended her fingers up into the air to the beat of Lionel Richie's words as he sang, "*I just want to tell you all the things you are and all the things you mean to me.*" She repeated the movement of her hands again, this time with a look of pain plastered on her face as she attempted to evoke the hidden sentiment of the lyrics. "*When I find myself believing there's no place to go. When I feel the loneliness inside my heart.*" Yasmine prepared herself for the intro of the bass and drums as she heard the lyrics that followed. "*You're the answer to my prayer, and you're with me everywhere, you're my angel, my miracle, you're all I need tonight!*" She raised her arms and extended them outside the window, repeating the movement incessantly.

Meanwhile, Maha laughed so hard her stomach muscles hurt. She could hardly sit up straight from the pain of the laughter. She rocked back and forth while trying to gasp for some air. Just as she tried to take a deep breath and move away from the steering wheel, from the corner of her eye she saw a car driving slowly beside her. She realized that it was a Porsche Carrerra, and in it were two guys laughing at Yasmine.

"Uh-oh, Yasmine! You know what else Nietzsche said?" Maha asked.

"What, Maha? What's the problem?" she said as she lowered the music.

"Nietzsche said: 'And those who were seen dancing were thought to be insane by those who could not hear the music!'"

"What do you mean?" Yasmine asked.

"I mean, Yasmine, that there are two guys laughing at us in that Porsche Carrera. And we are bumper to bumper," Maha said.

"What! I can't believe this! Woohooo!" Yasmine said.

"I know, me too! But don't worry, I can call Fahmy if we can't get away," Maha reassured her.

"Get away? Call Fahmy? Are you *crazy*? You're so prudish! I can't believe that there are *two* guys in a *Porsche Carrera* in the streets of Cairo, and they are following *us*! When do you see a car like that in this country, ever? Let alone one that's following us!" Yasmine said excitedly.

"Oh my God! I can't believe you. Your words are hurting my ears! There is no way that I will *ever* let disrespectful guys like them follow us. I have to find a way to get away from them," Maha said. She pressed the gas and swerved out into the other lane to have the Carrera pass her.

"Oh, no! I can't believe you're doing this! I can't believe you're going to get all MacGyver on me and run away from them," she wailed.

"What do you want me to do? Stop and wave?" Maha asked in a sarcastic tone. She saw the guys in the Carrera finally pass her.

"Whatever, Maha! You are such a party pooper!" Yasmine complained.

"Well, Yasmine, don't jump to conclusions, because it's obvious that your 'party' ain't over yet," Maha said as the Carrera swerved ahead of her into her lane and slowed down.

"Oh my God! He is so smooth! I can't believe this is happening!" Yasmine said as she grabbed her cap and sunglasses from her bag.

"Oh, please! I can wax that loser in a second," Maha declared. She couldn't believe Yasmine was trying to 'style up' for the guys.

"Here you go again, getting all MacGyvered!" Yasmine said.

Maha tried all her tricks out on the guys with no luck – she couldn't escape them. She started to panic when they neared Yasmine's home.

"My last chance is this last traffic light before the main intersection by your house, Yasmine! These guys are stressing me out!" Maha groaned.

"I'm sure you will not have a problem with that," Yasmine said.

"What do you mean by that?" Maha said.

"I mean, you always find a way of getting out of things," she said.

"Hehehe! I know," Maha said as she neared the traffic light, making a point to stay behind the Carrera. "He has four directions to choose from, and I just hope he's not going to take a right that leads to Bliss Street!" She prayed for a miracle, wishing that God would guide them blissfully away from Bliss Street.

As soon as the traffic signal turned green, the girls saw the Carrera take a left, distancing them far away from each other.

"Thank God for that!" Maha said, relieved, as she took the right turn to drop off Yasmine at the end of Bliss Street.

"This is such a downer! I missed out on what could have been the best moment of my life. Now instead, I have to go upstairs and do homework. What luck! Homework is such a waste of paper!" Yasmine moaned.

"Please Yasmine, hurry on! I want to go home."

"Fine, fine," Yasmine said. "But one last thing: music and car rides, Maha…"

"What about them?" Maha said.

"We wouldn't be friends if it weren't for music and car rides," she smiled.

"Haha! Tell me about it, Yasmine!"

"And life would be a terrible mistake without both," Yasmine continued.

"Hahaha! It would be for sure! Now can you hurry up and go so I can listen to my *music* on my *car ride* back home. You know I don't like making *mistakes*," Maha said.

"Hahaha! Nice! See you tomorrow!" Yasmine waved.

"Bye," Maha said as she turned up the volume and listened to Mark Morrison's "Return of the Mac". She waited until Yasmine left and then made her way home in a hurry.

CHAPTER FOURTEEN

Mrs. Magda's Home
Tuesday, August 31, 1999, 9:11pm
Cairo, Egypt

Mrs. Magda sat with Maher in their garden, listening to Dalida's "Helwa Ya Baladi" and "Ahsan Nas" while she sipped on her Arabic coffee and he slurped his Turkish one. Maher was such a Turkish coffee addict. He could easily have five a day. He loved everything about it, especially the taste, the smell and how it gave him a kick of energy.

"You know, Magda, there is nothing I love more in the world than sharing these moments with you right here," he said.

"Oh, my... What's gotten into you? The sweet sound of Dalida and Egyptian nationalism, or what?" she smiled, touched by his sincerity.

"Yes. And this place... It's been my home since I was eleven years old. These four walls have witnessed so many things, from heads of state, ministers, politicians, businessmen... and even secret hidden walls within the walls, if you know what I mean."

"I totally know what you mean. Your father was a very well-respected man."

"Yes, I know. He went down in Egypt's history as a brilliant officer who served with his heart and soul."

"He was so loyal."

"Yes, and he sacrificed his safety and security for it. I was never allowed to walk without bodyguards. I had bodyguards all the time, protecting me at school, home, the club, movies, and everywhere else I went."

"He wanted to protect you and your half-brothers and sisters," Mrs. Magda observed, admiring how fearless Maher's father was in his duty to protect his country and family.

"True… Though I'm not sure about my other half-brothers and sisters whom I discovered after he passed away."

"Oh, yes. I can imagine how shocking that must have been for you," Mrs. Magda said, trying to empathize with him.

"Yes, it totally was. You want to know how I found out?"

"How?"

"I was walking in the club one day when I suddenly found this young little kid running to me, yelling my name out. When I talked to him, he told me he was my brother."

"Oh, that must have been tough."

"To be honest, I didn't believe him at first. But then I met his mom and learned that it was true. I couldn't believe that my father had married again, and kept his wife and kids a secret from us and everyone else."

"I wouldn't have either, if I'd been in your place," Mrs. Magda said, trying to play the scene out in her head.

"Well, I guess the good thing is that I got to know them better."

"Yes…"

"Madam… Madam…" they heard Saneya calling from behind them.

"Yes, Saneya?" Mrs. Magda replied.

"Is it ok if I go over the bills with you before I leave for my weekend?"

"Yes, sure. Wait a sec, I'll go get my agenda from inside."

"Ok, and I will get your dinner and bring it out here."

"Great."

After a few minutes, Mrs. Magda walked back outside to the garden and found Saneya setting up dinner. That night, they were having Egyptian baladi bread, white feta cheese with tomatoes, black lentils and green salad.

"Thank you, Saneya," Mrs. Magda heard Maher say.

"My pleasure, Sir."

"Ok, I have my agenda. We can go over the bills now."

"Ok, Madam. But first, can I ask that my children come and wait for me inside? They are waiting outside in the street for me."

"Of course. Tell them to come in. I can't believe that you made them wait outside like this! Go get them, please. I have some sweet treats and books for them," Mrs. Magda said as she turned around to go back inside to get some of the candies, chocolates and biscuits she had stored beside the dining room.

When she walked back out again, she saw Saneya's four children, Ehsan, who was 21, Ahmed, who was 18, 14-year-old Mohammed and Doaa, who was 10. Even though Mrs. Magda had known Saneya for decades, she'd never had the chance to meet her kids, especially when she'd lived in Dubai and visited Cairo only for short stays. Mrs. Magda was surprised to see them dressed in Western clothing. Ehsan carried a Gucci replica handbag and wore tight blue jeans, a fuchsia top and a white head scarf. Ahmed and Mohammed wore baggy black jeans and fake Polo shirts. Their hair was gelled back carefully. Doaa wore a flowy pink fake Polo dress as well. It was then that Mrs. Magda realized that it wasn't only the Egyptians at her school who were affected by the epidemic desire to become more Americanized or Westernized. It was obviously affecting many people in the country, regardless of their age and social background.

"Hi, Tunt," the children greeted her.

"Hi," Mrs. Magda responded, relieved that they weren't forcing an American accent. "Look, I got you all some sweet treats and books. Enjoy them please, while your mom and I finish up some last minute stuff. You can sit anywhere in the garden." She was glad to see them happy. She practiced regular charity work not only because it was mandatory in her religion, but also because it made her feel so good.

"Sank you, Tunt! Sank you ferry much," they all said.

"You're most welcome!"

Saneya had a huge smile on her face when Mrs. Magda turned around to look it her. It made her really happy to see that.

"Ok, Saneya... You're ready?"

"Yes. I got stuff from the supermarket worth EGP 50, the butcher for EGP 200, and the vegetable seller for EGP 150. He was nice enough to give us a whole bag of apples as a gift."

"Well, then you know that he ripped you off with the other stuff if he did that," Maher interrupted.

"Oh, not at all. He always likes to give us gifts all the time," Mrs. Magda said. "But sure, you're right, he is expensive. But to be honest, the quality of his fruits is so much better than the others."

"That's very true, Madam. The other sellers around the neighborhood sell fruits and vegetables that are inedible."

"If you say so," Maher said.

"Ok, great. Thank you, Saneya, for all you help."

"Anytime, Mrs. Magda."

"You know, tomorrow we will have the kishk with chicken and the Egyptian baladi bread. We can also have some green salad. What do you think, Maher?"

"It sounds delicious, dear."

"Ok, that's easy, Madam. We have all the ingredients, so I don't need to buy anything tomorrow."

"Great. Then I'll give the money to Sayed tomorrow so he can settle all this."

"Ok, Madam. Do you need anything else from me today?"

"No, thank you. Go home with your kids now. It's already getting late."

"Ok. Bye now," she said. "Come on, kids. We're leaving now."

As the kids walked towards Saneya and out of the house, Mrs. Magda looked at Maher and gestured to him that they start eating their dinner.

After a few minutes of eating in silence, Mrs. Magda rolled up the sleeves of her 100% pure Egyptian cotton Mobacco sweatshirt and ate the cheese and bread in complete contentedness.

At that moment, Maher looked at her and admired everything about her. When she caught him doing that, she understood that what she saw in his eyes and what she felt for him was love, the kind of love that was so deep it had no end. They both smiled at each other and finished their dinner in silence.

CHAPTER FIFTEEN

Maha was glad that the day had come to an end. She walked out of the high school building for a quick break before her meeting with the rest of the group. When she reached the kiosk, she saw Menna standing by herself and staring at her cell phone.

"Hey, Menna," Maha said.

"Hi, Maha! Yasmine told me you are coming to my party tomorrow. I'm so happy."

"Yes, I am. I can't wait!" Maha exclaimed.

"Me neither! I need a break from all this stress. It will be so much fun. I'm going all out, Maha! Like, I'm going to get my hair done. Like, I'm going to put full make-up on. Like, I'm even going to wear a short red dress with fabulous stilettos that my mom got for me on her last trip to London!" she enthused.

"Oh, wow!" Maha gasped, astonished by the intensity of Menna's prep plans. "Wow! You've made all these plans for tomorrow. I didn't realize it was that big of an event!"

"Oh my, Maha! It's so big! I even suggested that some of the girls come over before heading there! Please join if you can," she said.

"I would've loved to, but I already promised Leena, Mariam and Sylvia that I'd meet up with them. On second thought, why don't we all meet up before going?" she suggested.

"Sure! Sounds great! Call me so we can plan."

"Will do," Maha said. She waved and headed towards Mahmoud and Ossama. "See you tomorrow!" Even though she stood far away, she could tell from the corner of her eye that major drama was going down between Yusuf, Sultan, Laila and Menna.

Menna turned around and saw Laila standing nearby, in what seemed to be a deep conversation with Sultan.

"Laila," Menna said as she walked towards them. "I can't believe this! Maha is coming to my birthday tomorrow! What a bummer! We'll have to watch out everything we do. We won't be able to smoke, drink or even have fun with the guys. If you know what I mean…"

"That's awful!" Laila groaned, making a sad face at Sultan.

"It's not going to be that bad! And anyways, not everyone going tomorrow smokes and drinks," he said.

"Are you kidding? It's going to be *terrible*! With Maha around, the whole outing is going to be so dry! She's so self-righteous about everything. She's such a party pooper and so uptight. I wish she would loosen up a bit. Like seriously, alcohol, cigarettes and even drugs would do her some good," she said.

"Hahaha, you're so funny," Menna giggled at Laila. "I think so, too."

"I don't see you agreeing with me or laughing, Sultan," Laila said bossily.

"I just never thought of her like that," he said, trying to force a laugh.

"This must be the lowest conversation I've ever heard!" Yusuf interrupted suddenly. "You think you are so cool because of your parties, VIP lists and your millions of so-called friends, when in reality you are a *loser*. How dare you talk about Maha like that?"

"What's gotten into you, Yusuf? How can you speak to Laila like that? Maybe it's you who is in need of a cigarette or a drink, and not Maha," Menna teased. It was immediately obvious, though, that she had failed in her attempt to lighten the mood.

"You know what, Menna? You're so right! I shouldn't have spoken to Laila like that, because I don't like to speak to people who are like her in the first place. Your voice was just so loud, everybody heard your conversation," he said as he started to walk away.

Sultan caught up to him and pulled him aside. "What's up, man? What's gotten into you? Why did you speak to Laila like that? Calm down!"

"Calm down? What's gotten into *you*, hearing them diss Maha like that and shutting up about it?" he demanded.

"I'm not doing anything, cuz. I respect that everyone has an opinion…" he said.

"Hey, hey… What's going on, guys? Is it true what Menna and Laila just told me?" Yasmine interrupted them.

"Chill, Yasmine, seriously," Yusuf told her. He turned back to Sultan. "And that's not respecting someone's opinion, Sultan. That's you being cool with two-faced cheapos!"

"Wait, *what*? What are you saying, Yusuf? You know people are entitled to keep their thoughts about other people private. I keep my thoughts private about everyone!" Yasmine said.

"Yeah… And when your actions contradict your private thoughts, that makes you the most sane, balanced, respectful and credible person, right?" he asked sarcastically. "This is insane! And you try to give me advice? *Ludicrous*!"

"Look, whatever. I'm just telling you that you can't keep on fighting with everyone about this. Then you'll end up losing everyone and you will have zero friends," Yasmine said.

"So what? I'd rather have no friends, and walk alone, than have friends like you," Yusuf said to Yasmine. "Sultan, I'm warning you, these girls mean trouble. And their two-faced ways should be the least of your worries. So watch you back!"

"Ok, whatever. Leave me out of this, Yusuf! I have nothing to do with this," Sultan said. "Anyway, I have to go now. I don't want to be late for Noha." He was desperate to escape the uneasy feeling that had overcome him.

"Bye," Yasmine said as she walked towards Laila and Menna.

"Let's go to the back gate," Menna said to Laila and Yasmine. They all understood that this was code for their long-awaited ciggie break.

"Yes, please let's go! I'm in dire need of one," Yasmine said.

Maha, Mahmoud and Ossama walked over to the library at the same time Yusuf walked away from Yasmine, Laila and Menna. The three were excited to start their research.

"Ok, so let's get started," Mahmoud said. "We should have Arab, Asian and North American perspectives for Question One."

"Yes, for my question, too," Ossama said. "I'll do a keyword search for individuality and conformity, and take my lead from there," he continued as he got up and headed towards the computer.

"Good luck!" Maha said. She tried to force herself to look engaged. "Now for my question..."

"Yes, but first, I wanted to check if you are ok?" Mahmoud asked quietly.

"I'm fine. Why would you think otherwise?" she asked.

"I don't know. I just get the feeling you're upset, and I think that it might have to do with Sultan and Laila getting closer," he said.

"Oh no! Never! I'm getting used to it. I mean, I've adapted already. Like, I'm strong enough not to let it affect me... Tell me you know what I mean so I can stop talking," she babbled, feeling a little embarrassed.

"I know what you mean. And I want *you* to know that it's ok if you're upset. Fallouts happen all the time, you know."

"I know. But not with me, Mahmoud. I believe and have faith that there is a reason why this has happened to me. And whatever the reason is, I know it's for the best."

"Wow! That's so accepting of you. How did you come to believe that?"

"Hmm, yeah… Well… I know you're not going to judge me, so I guess I don't mind telling you. I started to read the Quran and there was this one verse that changed my life. I understand now that this will take a lot of self-control and patience from me," she explained.

"You started to read the Quran? Wow! Which verse?" he asked.

"Yeah, I did. But please don't tell anyone. I'm afraid everyone will judge me. The life changing verse is: *But perhaps you hate a thing that is good for you; and perhaps you love a thing that is bad for you*," she quoted.

"Nice. And so true. First, I want to tell you something that I couldn't tell you before. I'm so happy you are distancing yourself from Sultan. He's such a loser. He talks, talks and only talks. He never walks his talk. What is happening to you is good for you! Believe it! Second, I want you to know that no one will judge you," he assured her.

"Oh, Mahmoud, *puhleeez*! Are you kidding me?" Maha scoffed. "*Everyone* will judge me. When Yasmine found out, she didn't stop making fun of me and told me that I was '*eww religious*'. She called me all kinds of names, like fundi, you name it…"

"That's not cool. But don't pay any attention to her. She's so confused herself," he said.

"Whatever. I can't do anything but let it go. I just don't want to put up with that kind of disrespect! I mean, I respect everyone and their right to believe in whatever it is they need to believe in to make them good people. I deserve that same kind of respect!"

"Of course you do. You're just a rebel. And you gotta know that nobody is going to be cool with you rebelling like that."

"Hehe, it's funny when you put it like that, Mahmoud! I guess I *am* rebelling by embracing my roots, culture and religion! Who knew that not wanting to be the Americano Westernized 'It' social butterfly popular mean girl would make me a rebel! I never saw it that way."

"Well, you're an inspiring rebel to me."

"And you're hands down the most awesome and real bro in the world," Maha smiled, realizing that she and Mahmoud were almost always twinning it, especially in the values and principles department. They were identical in that regard. "So, anyway... back to life and reality... For my research question, I think we should focus on African, Arab and Asian perspectives. What do you think?"

"I think that's great! I'll choose the African one," he said.

"Great! And I'll do the rest."

But after about 40 minutes of computer research, they realized that they could not find any resources on non-Western perspectives. All the information available was from a Western perspective. Ossama found one source that discussed the perception of self in Asia, but even though someone from Pakistan had written it, the research method adhered to the Western perspective. This revelation came as a shock to the three of them.

"I can't believe that I can't find any information whatsoever. The only thing I found that was interesting had nothing to with the assignment. I discovered that yoga did not originate in India. Its true origin is in Ancient Egypt, and it was known as Kemetic yoga," Maha told them.

"This is so interesting," Ossama said.

"How have we taken all the information we've learned for granted for so long? I thought everything we learned was 'right'. Seriously, I wouldn't know how to tell the difference between credible and non-credible information. All these years, I thought yoga was an ancient Hindu tradition," Mahmoud said.

"It looks like you're right, Mahmoud! We have to question everything passed on to us, man," Ossama said. "Even this school's education."

"It's so strange that we are considered to be in one of the best schools in the region. I mean, it preaches values of diversity, democracy and equality, yet this library does not have one book that supports any other perspective. Everything supports their perspective only," Maha said.

"I know. What's that all about? " Mahmoud asked.

"It's called bias education, Mahmoud," Maha told him.

"But how is this possible? How could we not have known about this earlier? I mean, we've been at this school since elementary!" Mahmoud exclaimed.

"We have been miseducated," Ossama declared. "Umm, what do they call those systems that control everything you learn, read, etcetera?"

"Totalitarian," Maha said.

"Yeah, yeah, we learned that in history class last year. We were taught that Russia and China had the shrewdest totalitarian regimes!" Ossama said.

"Oh yeah, and remember Mao Tse-tung's 'Little Red Book'? It was his means to control the minds of his people," Maha reminded them.

"Yeah, well, at least he was upfront about his intentions," Mahmoud said.

"Yeah, unlike the deception we've been living. We're being fed the same perspective over and over again, camouflaged in thousands of books with different titles and covers!" Maha said.

"Oh crap…. This *is* crap! Crap crap," Ossama said.

"This can't be true. We are supposed to be at the best school. Nobody can be better than us," Mahmoud said incredulously.

"This is awful. They might as well have their 'Big Black Book of Orders' with straightforward demands. Number one, hate your culture. Number two, be humiliated by your origins. Number three, don't be proud to speak your language. Number four, scrutinize your religion. Number five, don't believe in anything you cannot see. Number six, be ashamed of your family's roots. Numbers seven, eight and nine, love everything Western, mainstream, popular and cool! Number ten, be cool!" Maha rattled off.

"Oh no, this can't be. My head hurts…" Ossama said.

"Me too, man," Mahmoud said miserably.

"I feel like I'm going to throw up!" Maha said. "We have to let Mrs. Magda know about this before the weekend. Just so it's not last minute if we leave it till Sunday."

"Yeah! Yeah! Let me take care of that. I'll email her later tonight and fill her in on everything," Ossama offered.

"Fantastic! So let's put our plans on hold until she responds," Mahmoud said.

"Great! I'd better get going now. I don't want to be late for my dad. I have to sit with him and discuss my university plans," Maha said.

"Oh, ok! Good luck with that," Mahmoud said. "Ossama and I don't have to deal with any of that pressure. Our only option is the American International University here."

"You know, Mahmoud, it's one of my options, too! You never know, you might find me joining you guys next year," she told them.

"You know, it would be nice if we were all together next year," Ossama said.

"Hmm, I'm not sure about that yet," she said smiling. "Ok, bye now. Oh, and if I don't see you tomorrow morning, I hope you both have a great time at the Day Beyond Walls. See you at Menna's birthday later."

"Will do. Good luck to you, too. See you," they both said.

Maha breezed through the traffic on her way back home. It amazed her how leaving just five minutes before rush hour changed the course of her day. Yasmine did not get a lift with Maha that day, and she was relieved. She was in dire need of peace and quiet. It gave her so much solace to have the freedom to just be. And with a little Boyz II Men playing in the background, Maha felt that she could not ask for more.

Once she arrived home, she saw that her parents, Ayah and Maya were just about to start lunch. The food looked so good and the house smelled so nice. Maha was so happy to be home in time to have lunch with her family. It was so difficult to manage this during Cross Country Season, as she had practice three times a week – Sunday and Monday after school, and Wednesday early morning.

"Wow, mommy! The food looks good!" Maha said as she passed by the dining table.

"I'm glad you think so, dear. Hurry and wash up and join us," she said.

"Ok... Give me five minutes!" She hurried through the living room and hallway, and into her room. She turned on her computer and connected to the internet. She then washed up and changed her clothes, and ran back out to the dining room.

"Somebody looks hungry," Ayah said, smiling at Maha.

"If you're talking about me... I'm not! I'm starving and famished. Both at the same time," she declared. She contemplated which dish to start off with. Everything looked so delicious – the salad, basmati white rice, colcasia, and even grilled chicken, sauté vegetables and homemade oven chips.

"Mommy, what is colcasia in English?" Maha asked as she served herself from each dish.

"It's taro, dear," her mom replied.

"Hahaha," Maya interrupted. "Take it easy on the food!"

"Yes, Maha! The food is not going to run away! I don't understand this change in your eating habits, " her mom said, looking concerned.

"Please, leave me to enjoy my taro in peace," she said.

"Fine… So tell us, anything new happening at school?" Ayah asked.

"Yes… Well, a few things, actually. I had to work on this project with Ossama, Mahmoud and quote-unquote Laila for our TOK class. We had to answer questions using three different perspectives, be it Western, Arab, Asian, European, African etcetera," Maha told them.

"That's excellent, dear. I'm glad that your school promotes anti-bias education. This is what the future of learning is all about, especially with the advent of technology. Many more people will become well-informed," Maha's dad said. He was glad that the school promoted high quality, relevant education.

"That's wishful thinking, baba!" Maha said, realizing that she was about to burst her dad's bubble.

"Why?" he asked, concerned.

"Because when we started doing our research, we could not find one book that voiced any non-Western perspective! Not *one*!" Maha exclaimed.

"*What*? That cannot be possible," he said.

"Trust me, it is!" she assured him.

"This is disappointing! You know, Maha, maybe this is a good time to talk about this. But I've been thinking about your choices and options for universities next year, and I've even talked about this with your mother. I need to be honest with you, dear. I'm not comfortable with you traveling for university, be it in the US or Europe," he told her.

"*What*? Baba, are you serious? How could you change your mind like that? I thought we had a deal; I got the grades that will get me into a top school! I got them! You can't tell me this now, just as I'm about to apply to universities," Maha said as tears welled up in her eyes. She couldn't believe that her father was backing out of their deal. She'd made it with him way back in her freshman year: if she got above a 3.8 cumulative average, she could go to any university in the US. She couldn't believe that after she'd finally decided on Parsons, he was changing his mind, just like that.

She knew that that she wanted nothing more in the world than Parsons. She'd made the decision after she'd taken their summer course in Paris. It had been six weeks of pure bliss for Maha. Even though she was on her own, she could not have been happier with all the learning and artistic inspiration. She'd visited every single museum in Paris, and studied every painting in detail. It took her 14 full days to finish up the Louvre. She'd memorized every corner in the place. She knew that this was how she wanted to spend the rest of her life. She was so intrigued by art and its history, and unlearning incorrect information about it. It was not until taking the Parsons course that Maha had learned that the real forefather of cubism was Braque, and not Picasso. How could she let an opportunity like this go? Besides, the prospect of going to Parsons was the only thing that helped her put up with everything going on around her! It was her light at the end of the dark tunnel! How could her father do this to her? She felt betrayed!

"I know we made a deal. Trust me, I regret doing this. I feel awful that I have to. But I know that to ensure your wellbeing and healthy development, it's best for you to stay here. You can attend the American International University," he told her.

"My wellbeing and health? You are already destroying me! How can I ever be fine here when I know I can have a better future abroad?" she wailed. She knew that no institutions in Egypt could possibly offer high quality Art History degrees like Parsons, especially the English-speaking ones. And thanks to the school, studying anything in Arabic was not even an option. *What kind of 17-year-old Egyptian did not know how to speak, write or read in her own language?* Maha wondered angrily. The kind that went to ACS, where they deprive, punish and downgrade Egyptians who speak in Arabic or write in their style.

Maha remembered how in fourth grade, her teacher sent her to detention for a whole week just because she said 'yes' to her friend in Arabic at the end of class. The crime was that it was rude to speak in Arabic because she – the teacher – did not understand the language. Maha had felt awful that day. She couldn't believe she'd been treated that way just because she spoke in her own language. She swore that she never, *ever* wanted to be humiliated like that again. That was the night that she buried her language and never spoke a word of it again. And if anyone asked, she would say that she didn't understand her language. She also remembered how in tenth grade, her English teacher had downgraded her essay because she'd written it in an Arabic and not Western style. "Stop going on and on, describing things. It's very *Arab* of you. Keep to the point. Make your sentences short. Support your points. Keep it Western," were her teacher's exact comments. It was so degrading to be an Egyptian in that school, even though they were living in Egypt. Most Egyptians did not have the courage to admit this truth. Instead, like clowns, they covered up their true colors.

"See, this is just one of the mindless beliefs that this school has brainwashed you with. You have to know that there is more to life than just academia, universities and careers," her father told her.

"What could be more important, baba? You're going all Mussolini on me and my future! I can't handle this!" Maha cried, letting the tears roll down her face. He was the one who had *put* her in that school! He *knew* everything! He knew the truth! Why was he just deciding to deal with the truth *now*? Maha was angry. She did not respect people who could not keep their word. She hated what Ben Harper called 'empty promises softly heard'. *Ugh.* The sequences of events in her life were like knots impossible to untangle. First, losing Laila. Second, losing Sultan. Third, not going to the university of her dreams to fulfill her life-long passion. What else could there be? *Isn't it just* lovely *how the so-called best year of my life is turning out?* Maha thought bitterly.

"I understand you're upset! And you know what, this might not be the best time to talk about it. Maybe we should do it later, when you are calmer," he suggested.

"No, please! Tell me! Don't leave me hanging like this. What could be more important?" she asked again in complete desperation. She wished for a miracle to wake her up from this nightmare.

"Your family is more important. Your identity. Your roots. You live in a bubble, and you know nothing about your culture, language and religion. This is a huge concern for me," he said.

"But you put me in that school and this is how my environment has shaped me," she protested.

"Yes, and I regret that, too. That's why I want to fix my mistake. I want you to go to university in this country, to see the real Egypt and Egyptians. I don't want you to go to university abroad and become even more disconnected. Then you will never be able to live in your own homeland."

"Don't worry about me disconnecting, because I'm already shutting down," she said bitterly.

"That's what you think," Ayah interrupted. "Ask me. I'm seven years older than you, and I was in your situation before. I saw what happened to the people who graduated with me in my class and travelled abroad for university."

"Well, what happened?" Maha asked.

"Well, for starters, most of them can't ever live in Egypt. In general, they became extremists. Many were destructive. They abused their freedom and got into drugs, alcohol, partying and extramarital relationships. Also, some disconnected from their family and cultural values. These people only value the Western way of life. They are poster children for identity crises. They walk, talk, work and eat everything Western. They even act like Westerners, especially when they come back and visit. They try to act all Egyptian, so they pretend to like Egyptian things.

But even going to the most local Koshari eatery in the country cannot mask their deeply Westernized ways. Because the reality is that they don't want to have anything to do with the country," she said.

"Eww! I'll *never* be like that! I myself can't stand Americanized or Europeanized Egyptians. They tick me off. These people should do Egypt a favor and never come back," Maha said.

"That's what you say now, Maha! Believe it or not, all these people said the same thing that you are saying now. You don't know to what extent the environment can shape you," she warned.

"Well, what about the other extreme?" Maha asked.

"The others got involved in extreme religious groups. Some did it for political reasons," she said.

"But why would someone educated ever do something like that?"

"Because religious extremism has nothing to do with education," Maha's dad interrupted.

"Then what does it have to do with?" Maha asked, getting frustrated.

"It has everything to do with a sense of belonging and the yearning to connect and be a part of a group that represents a cultural identity," he said.

"Ok, so I get it. The rise of Muslim extremism is a response to the Western attempt to dominate the world by forcibly spreading their culture, language and perspectives in our own homelands for centuries?"

"Exactly!" Maha's dad said.

"Then why are Westerners so blind to that fact?" Maha asked.

"That's the question of the century, Maha!" her dad exclaimed.

"Anyways, to get back to what I was saying," Ayah interjected. "I think it's important that a person gets to truly know themselves before traveling to live abroad. One has to understand the values they hold and stick to them."

"I get it now. So does that mean there's a chance for me to travel for my Master's degree, then?" Maha asked, hoping for some good to come out of this. She wanted to have something to look forward to that would ensure she had a way to leave this country – for there was nothing that she wanted more than to be out of it.

"I don't want to repeat the same mistake, Maha, and make empty promises. But when I feel you're grounded, strong, wise and responsible enough, then yes… I will consider it," he said.

"Ok," Maha said.

She then ate her kolkasia and basmati rice in the peace that she had initially wanted before all of this melodrama and disappointment. Ayah and Maya changed the topic of discussion to marriage. It was a subject that interested many Egyptian women, especially those in their twenties. Maha didn't pay any attention to their discussion at first, because she was preoccupied with that weird feeling that crept into her gut again. That soon changed, though, as she heard Maya tell an inspiring story of an Egyptian woman named Lisa who attended some of the meditation workshops with her. She seemed to have defied all the odds in redefining cultural taboos.

"Wow! What a strong woman! Good for her that she honored herself," Maha's mom said. "I can't imagine what it must be like to be married to someone for ten years, have so many miscarriages, and then find out that her in-laws set up her husband to marry someone else and have kids in secret."

"What a coward! He should have been candid with Lisa," Ayah said.

"See, this is what I don't get! I think if Lisa and her husband were not under pressure from his parents to have kids, none of this would have happened," Maya said.

"You are right, there is so much pressure on young couples right now to have the perfect job, house, kids, life, the whole package" Ayah agreed.

"But you should know that none of that really matters in a marriage. Marriage needs trust, love, faith and respect in order to survive. It needs two healthy minds willing to build a positive life together," Maha's mother said. "And not expect to get everything they want on a silver platter."

"Unfortunately, so many of our friends are marrying for the package. They make a list of the qualities of their potential partners and divide them into pros and cons. And based on the number of checks and x's, they decide if the person is suitable or not. Remember Elham, when she stayed one afternoon writing up that list with Zainab for her fiancé? After she tallied the x's and found that they were more than the checks, she ended her engagement that same night," Maya said.

"*What*? That's sad!" Maha said in disbelief, feeling shocked about how shallow and superficial her society had become.

"No wonder there are many divorces," her mom said.

"Yes, both men and women are so concerned with their images that they forget themselves. With men, it's a competition of who can get the highest income, have the best house, cars, wife, kids and all the rest. With women, it's another kind of competition. It's all about who can get the latest handbags, clothes and shoes and go to the most parties. Yeah, that's just the case with our friends Amr and Noha. Their relationship is so fake, they make plastic look real. He's always name-dropping and people-pleasing everyone to climb his way up the social ladder. And Noha is always traveling to keep up to date the latest trends, just so she can go supermarket shopping with her Chanel bag," Maya said cynically.

"Yes, the trend is that both men and women forget themselves. There are men who are disrespectful to their wives and cheat on them. There are some who sleep with prostitutes. There are some who don't care much about their families. They don't spend time or money on them. There are some who even beat up their wives. At the same time, there are many women who marry their husband's bank account. Some of these women try to get pregnant fast, because according to tradition, it's supposedly the best way to keep a man. Especially if the wife bears her husband a boy. Unfortunately, when they do, these women feel entitled to be demanding! And those who don't marry for the bank account look for other benefits, like social privilege," Ayah said.

"Ugh… That's sad. Does anybody marry for love in this society?" Maha asked.

"Hmm, good question… I think few do," Maya said.

"I don't understand how people stay in loveless marriages that they cannot bear. It's like they lead double lives and sell themselves to live a certain kind of life. It must be so draining," Maha said.

"It's so true. You know, Maha, the source of all physical illnesses is unhealed emotional pain," Ayah said.

"People have to empower themselves. They have to understand themselves and others," Maha's mom said. "I'm happy to hear of stories like Lisa's, even though it's awful what she went through."

"You know what, Tunt?" Maya asked.

"What, dear?"

"I heard that she might be getting remarried soon, to an unrequited love of hers from her past," Maya revealed.

"Oh, really? Isn't it strange how life unfolds? I'm interested to find out what happens with that."

"Me, too," Ayah said.

"I hope nothing but the best for her. She deserves it," Maha's mom said.

"Me, too. This story about Lisa has restored my faith in humanity," Maha said. She pushed back her chair to get up and head out of the dining room. "Excuse me, everyone. I'm going to go and rest in my room for a bit."

"Ok, dear," her father said. "By the way, everything will be fine, Maha! I know it in my heart. And mark my words, one day you will thank me for making this decision."

"Sure," Maha said. "I hope so."

What she really wanted to say was 'whatever', which was the perfect word to reflect the sense of apathy that had overcome her. But she didn't. She stayed quiet, because she couldn't care less anymore.

Maha went back to her room and checked her MSN messages. She found 10 messages from Ossama, Yusuf, Mahmoud and Sultan.

Ossama just wanted to let her know that he'd written the email to Mrs. Magda and that he was waiting for her response. He'd update her whenever he received any feedback. Yusuf wanted to check in on her and ask her about where she was going for Day Beyond Walls. Mahmoud wanted to know how the college discussion went with her dad. And Sultan had breaking news that he did not divulge.

Maha thanked Ossama first. Then she wrote to Yusuf. *I'm goin to Awladi orphanage tomorrow. How bout u?*

I'm goin to Zabaleen or the garbage people community in Moqattam area. It should be interesting, he typed.

Oh wow! I can't wait to hear all about it, she typed.

I can't wait to hear about yours as well.

Great! Talk to u tomorrow.

Peace, he typed as he signed off.

Then Sultan sent her a message *U there?*

Yes! What's up? What's the breaking news? she asked. She was still feeling weird about the status of their friendship. She didn't understand why Sultan preferred to communicate with her only on MSN, when he did not even say hi to her at school.

It's over between Noha and me for good! he typed.

I'm sorry to hear that, Sultan. Hope you're ok. And you never know, maybe after some distance you'll get back together again.

Not this time, Maha. It's over for real. And I'm fine. I need to move on. I need to have a new start in my life.

Good for you, Sultan, she typed.

Thanks.

See you! Bye, she typed.

Bye, Maha, he responded.

Then she replied to Mahmoud and told him about what went down with her dad.

I'm so sorry to hear that! But I must admit that I'm happy you'll be with me in university next year! he typed.

I'm quite overwhelmed now so I will not be able to share your happiness, she typed.

Oh come on, Maha... It will be fine. How bad can it be? Remember what you told me today? "But perhaps you hate a thing that is good for you; and perhaps you love a thing that is bad for you," he reminded her

Well, it's obvious to me that my heart seems to have no sense of right or wrong these days, she typed. *It is obvious that I'm loving everything that is bad for me... I don't know how I can ever trust my heart again!*

Hehehe... Don't worry about it. Trust the process. Perhaps everything you're upset about is good for you for later and not now.

Perhaps... she typed.

Ok. So I have to go now. I'll see you tomorrow at the party.

Inshallah, she typed.

CHAPTER SIXTEEN

American School in Cairo
Thursday, September 2, 1999, 6:42pm
Cairo, Egypt

Mrs. Magda arrived at school early on Thursday morning. She wanted to check her mail before heading out on the field trip. She read Ossama's email and found it difficult to digest. Her heart burned. How could the school not own at least *one* non-Western perspective book in the library? She wrote back to him and told him not to worry about it, and that they would discuss what to do next in class on Monday. She also thanked him for taking on the responsibility of informing the rest of his classmates. She then hurried out of class and to the front gate to meet Sherif.

To her surprise, when she arrived she found a dozen black Grand Cherokee cars at the front gate of the school.

"What is this all about?" she asked Sherif, pointing to the cars.

"It's all for the field trip today. Some parents organized to have these cars follow the school bus to the slum area," he explained.

"What? How could the school allow this?" she asked.

"Well... Because of Mrs. Samar. She is a member of the Parents' Association and she happens to be the cousin of the wife of the Minister of Education. So you can imagine all the parents' demands were met as soon as she got involved," he told her, rolling his eyes.

"Oh my, that happens at this school as well? What about all the effort wasted on preaching and teaching students about integrity? This school is one huge contradiction!" Mrs. Magda exclaimed.

"I think you're being kind when you call it a contradiction. The administration is manipulative and two-faced. They take so much from tuition, school store expenses, the cafeteria, facilities, and trips. And unlike expats, Egyptians pay from their own money. The irony is that in spite of this, they are the least respected. Well, except if the Egyptian is an important person, like Mrs. Samar. Other than that, we cannot do anything about it. The students can't either because the administration is so powerful, and this makes it difficult for anyone to speak up. So silence has become a common language that many speak here," Sherif said.

"Yes! Everybody is trying to fit into the dominant culture. It's obvious that silence is the only way to help people achieve that. It's so sad that the Egyptians at this school suffer from a heart-wrenching and mind-boggling identity crisis! The irrefutable truth is that no matter how hard they try to escape, they cannot deny their roots. They will never be whole, complete, centered or balanced individuals. They will always be missing something, and it will affect them in a negative way."

"Certainly," Sherif agreed.

"It all depends on each student and their family culture. Some might seek their escape through drugs, alcohol or even dropping out. Others may become extremists in whatever it is that gives them a sense of belonging – fanaticism, asceticism and even materialism are some examples. Let me tell you, Sheriff... I worry for these students."

"I know, it's sad," he said

"And that's just one part of it. The other part is that the school does *not* maximize the learning potential of all students. I was in shock when I saw the quality of my students' writing. Unbelievable! How has this school managed to maintain its reputation?

Especially when the reality falls so far short of expectations! Also, there is no bicultural environment at school. They don't even teach Arabic or religion to Arabs living in an Arab country. They don't have a single non-Western perspective book in their massive library! They don't even have a prayer room for all the Muslim staff! Is there *no* respect? No sense of humanity? I don't get it! Does a person have to be American or at least Americanized to get any kind of respect around here?" Mrs. Magda preached. She was aware that she was not engaging in a discussion or dialogue with Sherif; this was a one-sided monologue. She needed to vent like never before. She couldn't bottle up her feelings anymore. It provoked her that Egyptians *could not* be themselves at school.

Unfortunately, at that point, a mom walked towards her with her nose up in the air and interrupted them. Mrs. Magda choked from the amount of perfume that wafted in the air around her.

"Excuse me," the mom sniffed. "Please carry these bags to the first black car on the sidewalk. Then please empty out the boxes." She gestured to Mrs. Magda to pick up the bags.

Mrs. Magda was almost insulted by her behavior. She wondered if people like her even knew what humility was. But Mrs. Magda knew better. She knew that this woman was acting out of complete ignorance. She most probably thought Mrs. Magda was the help just because she wore a veil. Most people from that social background believed that veiled women were just that. In order not to feed into the drama, Mrs. Magda wisely and politely clarified her position.

"Sorry. I won't be able to help. I have a problem with my back and my doctor advised me not to carry heavy things. I'm only allowed to carry light-weight stuff, like my students' papers," Mrs. Magda explained as if she were talking to a 2-year-old child. She wanted the mom to get the point that she was a teacher at the school.

"Oh! Are you a teacher here? At *this* school? I'm so sorry! I'm surprised. I didn't know that the school had hired a veiled teacher. My daughter Nooshie never told me," she said with slight embarrassment.

"Maybe that's because I do not have Nooshie in my class," Mrs. Magda suggested.

"Yes, maybe. So will you be coming with us on the field trip?" she asked.

"Yes, of course."

"Excellent! Can I ask you a favor, then? Can you please explain to the moms of the boys at the slum that they don't have to offer us lunch? Please tell them that we've had a heavy breakfast and that we will eat our lunch later. My friends and I cannot eat their food. We just can't stomach all the fatty carbs that Egyptians eat all the time!" she said.

"Oh, I didn't know that you are not Egyptian. You would've had me fooled, because you look like a typical Egyptian," she said, not understanding how the mom could speak like that. What was wrong with the way Egyptians ate? And why was she talking about Egyptians as if they were the Other? Why was she being so elitist? It was degrading and downright rude! Mrs. Magda felt herself getting angrier by the minute. She could not *stand* people like this – fake people with no acting skills made for a terrible show that Mrs. Magda could never put up with.

"What?" the mom asked as her face turned pale. She looked as though she had just been gravely insulted.

"What?" Mrs Magda asked with pretend innocence, knowing that at this point, she was not this mom's favorite person in the world. She'd caught her in the act, and people like her did not like to get caught.

"Nothing. Yes, you're right, I am Egyptian. My name is Nagwa," she said.

"Nice to meet you, Nagwa. If I get the chance to talk to any of the moms there, then I will let them know," Mrs. Magda said, relieved to know that she had been right all along. She was glad that she had cut through the crap – she had no tolerance for this kind of act anymore. And she was no fool not to notice an act like that.

"Thanks. Anyways, I have to get going. I need to find somebody to put this stuff in the car," she said, trying to find a way to escape the conversation.

"Good luck!" Mrs. Magda said. As soon as Nagwa had walked off, she turned back to Sherif. "Sorry you had to endure that conversation."

"Oh please, don't say that. To the contrary, I'm so happy that I did. I'm so impressed with how you handled it," he said.

"That's kind of you, Sherif," Mrs Magda smiled.

She then turned around and saw the front gate filling up with many Nagwa-lookalikes. The wax figures at Madame Tussauds looked more real. They all dressed the same. Their clothes, bags, shoes and even sunglasses were heavily etched with logos and monograms. This was the ultimate battle of the brands, where each of them, like soldiers, was at the mercy of their rank. The victors of the mission were those whose shopping had clearly carried the highest price tag. Mrs. Magda didn't understand their world – the kind of world where people felt the need to hide behind monograms. She didn't understand why was it so difficult for people to buy things to their taste, whether they carried a flashy brand name or not. Were these people too weak to be bare of labels?

"Ok! Well, I'd better get going. I have to go check in on everything," Sherif said.

"Ok... And I need a minute to collect myself," Mrs. Magda said as she walked towards a bench to sit down for a few minutes.

As soon as she sat down, she got her book of supplications out of her handcrafted bag made by the girls in Siwa and prayed. She held the book tight and closed her eyes. She sought guidance, patience, strength and wisdom from God to endure today's events.

She asked God to help her gain the understanding she needed to not judge others as they would her. And wished for everyone to see beyond their vanity.

The yellow school bus, followed closely by the dozen black jeeps, arrived at the slum. It was located next to Kilo 4.5 on Suez Road, behind the run-down Al Grashi Cafe. Near the slum was a vast, arid desert; on the other side was Salah El Din School, a haunted place for so-called academic learning. It was a failed attempt at what was once the dream of high quality, affordable education. Now washed up and hidden behind ruins, it served that purpose to no one, be it the children, teachers or surrounding families. If anything, it had become a strong repellent to children, having diverted hundreds to the streets. Ask any street child and they would tell you that they would rather beg than endure the humiliation of teachers at a school like Salah El Din. Unlike many urbanized areas in the city, in this area parents protected their children by *not* sending them to school.

When the bus parked, the students groaned, moaned and complained. They were in no mood to play against the kids from the slum. They would have rather chilled and listened to their music, for all they wanted to do was nothing. Like, literally nothing.

"Please respect what we have to do today," the coach said. "These kids don't have even 1% of what you have, yet they have more stamina and grit than you. Now get going!"

So the students dropped their Discmans and Walkmans and clambered off the bus. They took a few minutes to arrange their sport bags, water bottles, shin guards and soccer cleats. Mahmoud and Sami were the first to be ready. Mahmoud was eager to try out his new pair of Predators. Nothing could come in between him and his cleats. In fact, he had tucked them into his bed on the first night after he'd bought them. When his mom learned of this the next morning, she cursed the day Mahmoud fell in love with soccer.

He was six when it happened. He realized that nothing in the world could make him happier than playing soccer. It had turned into a mad love by the time he was 10. And now Mahmoud's current obsession was to be the next Zinedine Zidane. He wanted to be the next Arab player to break grounds in the world of soccer.

But with Sami, it was different. In any game, there were those who played for the love of it, and those who participated out of vanity. And Sami was the latter kind of player. He played for everything except the game itself.

"I don't know what I'd do without my Predators. I love my super cleats. I'm so happy that my dad got them for me from London," Sami bragged as soon as he had finished getting ready.

Mahmoud and the rest of the team ignored Sami. They understood that he wanted to boast about his new cleats for the zillionth time. They all found it annoying, because the truth about soccer was that it had nothing to do with the cleats. Anyone who bragged the way Sami did was just spoiled and vain.

At that moment, the boys from the slums appeared from around the bus and started making fun of Sami in Arabic.

"Yay, *yaaay*, my super cleats," Hossam mocked. He grabbed a cigarette from the pack of Cleopatras in the pocket of his torn shorts. He lit it with his Kent matches that folded into a small square, and inhaled the nicotine deeply.

"Oh no, I need to make sure that my jersey matches my shorts and socks. And that my shoe laces are in a bow," Hazem teased. He stood behind Hossam in his grubby shorts and wife beater.

"Oh wait, what about my hair? it needs to be styled. There's a strand of out of place," Hossam continued in a whiny tone as he puffed smoke in Sami's face.

"Stop!" Sami cried as he coughed.

"Haha! You're such a wussy. You can't even handle smoke," Hossam smirked.

"It's not only him! They all are! They can't even play the game barefoot on grass, let alone in the desert," Khalifa interrupted. "When you can play barefoot like us, on this land, then we can call you men. Until then, you are wimps and wussies. And you should stock up on all your shin guards, because we will beat you today and you will get hurt," Khalifa threatened, redirecting the conversation from his friends to Mahmoud, Sami and the rest of the team.

"Oh, my! How are they speaking like that to our children?" Nagwa whispered to another mom.

"I think we should take this up with the administration and counsellor. They are bullying our children. This is a trauma that will scar our children for life," the other mom whispered back.

Mrs. Magda was standing right next to them, and overheard this side conversation. She took a deep breath and exhaled slowly as she walked away to distance herself from any kind of provocative and ignorant comments. Trauma? Could they not see that the real trauma was the living conditions of the boys in the slum? And that their childhoods had already scarred them? Mrs. Magda had hoped that the privileged would one day understand that their role was to help those in need, rather than mock, judge and be biased towards them, but she was continually disappointed.

"Oh, please!" Sami said. "You're just jealous that we have the best team for our age group in the country."

"*Best team?*" Khalifa exclaimed. "How did you ever come up with such a ludicrous idea? I feel so sorry for you. You are clearly delusional."

"We are in the best school in the country, so by default we are the best at soccer as well," Sami responded smugly.

"I don't even go to school, and I can tell that you are stupid and have no brain to speak like that," Khalifa replied.

"Who are you calling stupid, you fool?" Sami retaliated.

"I'm calling *you* stupid, you mama's boy!" Khalifa yelled.

"Ok, this is going to have to stop!" the soccer coach exclaimed, placing himself between the two to stop the argument from escalating.

"Yes, coach, I agree," Nagwa chimed in.

"Please apologize to each other," Mrs Magda commanded. "This is inappropriate!"

"Yes, you're right," Khalifa's mother, Haga So'ad, interrupted. "Just because circumstance make us seem different, doesn't mean that we are."

Haga So'ad's aphorism struck Mrs. Magda like a bolt. Thoughts about the relationship between education, wisdom and common sense jolted through her mind. It was enlightening for her to know that education did not guarantee wisdom and common sense after all – Haga So'ad was proof of that. *Could it be true that some of the world's wisest people were the ones who were not educated?* Mrs. Magda wondered.

"I agree with you," Mrs. Magda said. "Now please, let's move on and start the soccer game."

"Sure," the coach said.

All the boys walked away from the bus and into the empty space. Haga So'ad tried to catch up with Khalifa to tell him to calm down a bit.

"What do you want from me?" Khalifa asked his mom.

"I want you to calm down, Khalifa! I don't want you to get into trouble. I just found out that your brother has gotten himself into big trouble and I don't know what to do. I'm scared about what your father will do to me," she said.

"He can't do anything to you. I'm not a little boy anymore! I'll beat the hell out of him if he touches you," Khalifa promised as he took his last puff. "What happened with Ismail?"

"I don't know all the details. He told me that he bumped into one of the McDonald's delivery bikes. It fell and it's damaged," she said.

"Which McDonald's? Were the police there?" he asked.

"The one on the corner of El Marghany Street. Luckily the police were not there. He ran away as fast as he could. But some of the delivery guys saw him."

"He shouldn't go there for a while. Let him try out new locations in El Nozha for now," he said.

"Yes. He told me he'll do that. But he's upset, because it's such a good location. In two days he was able to collect thirty pounds," she said.

"Let Zeinab go. She's six now and she can manage to clean the cars."

"Ok, I'll do that," she replied.

"But don't tell baba about Zeinab. He will take all her money to get the drugs and shisha," he said. "We need to save as much as we can to build our own kiosk."

"Ok. Now please calm down and take it easy in the game," she said.

"*Calm down*? Don't talk to me like that! I told you, I'm not a little boy anymore. I know what I'm doing!"

"Ok. I'm sorry, I don't want to upset you. I'm just worried about you, that's all."

"Ok, ok, ok," he muttered as he walked away from her and back towards his team.

Mahmoud and the rest of the team set up the two goals using four rocks that they'd found. In the meantime, the other boys enjoyed doing nothing. They liked that the tables had turned; Khalifa, in particular, felt good that other people were doing something for him for a change. The great responsibility of caring for his two siblings and mother had robbed him of happiness. Protecting himself and them from his 80-year-old father was an on-going struggle. It was a terrible pattern that never failed to repeat itself. When his father was not busy selling biscuits for a living, he was getting high and beating his family all the time.

That moment of happiness was not a fleeting one for Khalifa. It extended throughout the entire 90 minutes of the game. Khalifa loved nothing more in the world than soccer. It was his passion. It lit his soul on fire. It was the only thing that allowed him to tolerate and accept the dehumanizing ways of his life. Pet dogs and cats in the West received better treatment and care than underprivileged people living in developing nations. From that point of view, life was a farce.

After the game started, Haga So'ad walked over to Mrs. Magda to talk to her.

"Sorry I didn't get a chance to introduce myself. My name is Haga So'ad, and I'm Khalifa's mom," she said.

"Nice to meet you, Haga So'ad. My name is Magda."

"Nice to meet you, too," she said. "I came over to let you know that my friends and I decided not to cook anything for you today. I'm sorry about that, but we know from past experience that nobody eats our food. We always went to great lengths to prepare the meals, and ended up wasting so much. So this year we decided not to repeat the same mistake," Haga So'ad explained.

"I'm sorry you feel that way. And you don't need to worry about it all. The most important thing is that the boys play a good game and that they have fun. Thank you for being so honest and sincere with me. I appreciate it," Magda said.

"Thank you," Haga So'ad said. She walked back to sit with the rest of her friends.

Mrs. Magda went over to Nagwa and the rest of her group to break the news about the food.

"Oh, good! This is a miracle. I'm so happy and relieved that we don't have to eat their food," Nagwa said. "Now come on, ladies, let's go set up our foldable chairs and umbrellas on that side. It's too hot today."

The moms walked away and found their spot, opposite to where the moms of the slums sat. Mrs. Magda found herself standing in the middle between the two groups. When she looked to her right, she saw the moms from the slums laughing and making fun of the other group of moms. And when she looked to her left, she saw the exact same behavior from the other group. She realized that the two groups were all in and of the same thing. They were mirror images of each other, two sides of one coin. Unlike them, Mrs. Magda didn't want to be a part of any of it, for she understood that it was one coin after all. In an attempt to balance this duality, she stood her ground, even if it meant that she did it alone. And so she stayed in the middle.

The game started, and it was obvious even to the casual observer that the boys from the slums were talented. Their bare feet did not come in the way of their game, for their skills were second nature to them. With them, the ball flowed like water. They knew how to roll with it. It was as if every move had been rehearsed. The boys from ACS, on the other hand, were the exact opposite. They were too mechanical, tactical and rigid. They lacked team spirit. And the disparity between the two teams made Mrs. Magda rethink the definition of success. The boys from the slums cared more about the game than the results, while the boys from school cared only about the final score.

By halftime, the boys from the slums were in the lead with a score of 4-0. The moms from the slums were so happy. They crowded around the boys and cheered for them, reveling in their moment of glory.

"You are a champ, my son," Nafoussa said to Hazem. "That long air ball you did was amazing. It got the goalie so petrified, he didn't know what to do!"

"Yes, boys! That's the way to play! Show them all you've got," Haga So'ad joined in the conversation.

"Haha! We'll show them all right! They won't know how to sleep tonight," Khalifa said. "Their loss is going to hurt so bad!"

"You know, if you win today, boys, I'll convince your moms that we celebrate tomorrow. You can have your weekly shower on Thursday instead of Friday, and wear your new clothes, and we'll take you out!" Nafoussa proposed.

"Where will you take us?" Hossam asked with excitement.

"KFC!" she said.

"KFC? No way! You can take us there?" they all asked in disbelief.

"Yes," she promised.

"So we're going to go inside the restaurant and sit down and eat fried chicken? Is this for real?" Hazem asked.

"Yes! We will all go together!" she said.

"Oh my God! This has been a dream of mine forever. I can't believe it!" Hazem said, feeling a boost of motivation and enthusiasm to win the game.

On the other side of the pitch, Sami was receiving a lecture from his mom, Sherie.

"I'm sorry, this is unacceptable! After begging your father to get you those Predators so that you can play better, *this* is how you play?" she exclaimed in disbelief. "You let some nobodies beat you? This is a disgrace."

"Mom, this is a pointless game. There is no need to waste my energy or ruin my Predators on a game like this with people like them," he scoffed. "I'm saving my energy."

"Saving your energy? Do you think your father would like to hear that as the reason why you lost today?" she asked. "We don't have losers in our family!"

"Fine, whatever! Why do you always make a big fuss about everything?" he said, feeling humiliated in front of his friends by his mom's pushy ways. "It's just a stupid game!"

"No, it is not! Everything counts. *Everything* you do in your life counts! And I'm watching you," she said.

"I know you are," he muttered, wishing that she wasn't and that she would just back off and let him be. He walked away as fast as he could. He couldn't tolerate hearing her voice any more – it was even more annoying than losing the game.

"Sherie, dear, take it easy on Sami," Nagwa said consolingly. "You will push him away like that. Be his friend. That's the way to parent nowadays. The old ways of parenting are so outdated. You have to make an effort to go out with him and his friends and do stuff with him."

"I'm not his friend, Nagwa. I'm his mother," Sherie replied. "It's my responsibility to guide him."

"Yes, guide, but don't control," Lara chimed in. "Find the balance, Sherie. Bringing up boys is challenging for us all."

"You can say that again," she said.

"But it all works out in the end. We have such limited time with them now before they take off and travel for college next year," Lara said. "Enjoy this time with him."

"I guess. I don't know if Sami is ready to travel on his own," she said doubtfully.

"Same here – we don't know if our boys will be able to live on their own," Nagwa said as Lara nodded in agreement.

"I don't think he'll able to do the laundry, iron, cook and clean for himself," Sherie continued.

"You know, I was considering hiring help for him as soon as he settles into his dorm," Nagwa said.

"That's a fantastic idea! I didn't think of that before," Lara said enthusiastically.

"I'll consider it for sure when the time comes," Sherie said.

"*Aaahhh!*" Sami's cry interrupted their conversation.

"Sami, my dear! Are you ok? Oh God, please!" Sherie screamed frantically as she saw Sami lying on the field.

"Oh, poor thing! You're crying now?" Hossam mocked.

"Get up!" Khalifa spat.

"Shut up! I'm in pain, you imbeciles!" Sami moaned.

"You're just pretending," Hazem accused.

"Leave him alone," Mahmoud interrupted, wishing that this game would end soon. He couldn't believe how people's behavior could suck the life right out of a game.

"Are you ok, Sami? Can you get up?" Khalifa mocked, not believing that anyone's pain threshold could be so low.

"Yo, stop it!" Sami said to Khalifa. "Leave me alone! And back off!"

"And if I don't, you'll go cry to your mom?"

The coach arrived to check in on Sami. Everyone refrained from talking, especially Hazem. He wanted to avoid trouble. There were 10 minutes left in the game, and he was adamant that nothing should come between him and his KFC. So he ran fast and took up his position to continue play.

At the end of the game, the boys from the slums won by a whopping seven goals to two. It was a well-deserved triumph.

"See you next year!" Khalifa said gloatingly to the other team as the boys shook hands with each other.

"Sorry, we're not going to be here next year. We are moving on to bigger and better things," Sami replied dismissively.

"Yeah, yeah. Bigger and better, that's all you care about," interrupted Haga So'ad. She couldn't believe what she had heard. *Did they not know that the 'bigger and better' way of life was the source of their misery?* she thought.

"Don't speak to him, mama!" Khalifa commanded.

"Ok," she said.

"Please…" Mrs. Magda interfered. "Stop! Just let it be, Haga. Trust me when I tell you that we all have struggles that we have to overcome." She felt that she had to knock some sense into everyone. Privileged or not, everybody struggled. She wanted to ensure everyone understood that truth.

"I understand that," Haga said, embarrassed by her actions.

"Good! I'm glad this is over," Mrs. Magda said.

"Yes, me too," she said. "Thank you for coming, Madam Magda."

"Thank you for welcoming us. Bye," she greeted her.

"Bye," Haga So'ad responded.

"Team! Let's get going!" the coach said.

As they all packed up their belongings, Mrs. Magda overheard one of the moms from school talking to one of the moms from the slum.

"I have so many valuables, furniture, kitchenware and accessories. They're in a car that's parked over there. Can you come with me, so I can donate the stuff to you?" the mom from school asked.

"Madam, I don't know if you realise, but we live in wooden shacks. We do not have space for rooms, kitchens or even bathrooms. Please give all this stuff to people who have actual homes and space for it all!" she said, looking puzzled and questioning the level of intelligence of the lady.

"Oh, I'm so sorry! I didn't think about that," she said, looking embarrassed.

"Yes, it's obvious you didn't," she said. "I have to go now and catch up with the rest."

"Oh, ok. I'm sure I'll find someone who will need this stuff somewhere else. There are plenty of places like this that plague Egypt."

"I know," she replied, pursing her lips.

CHAPTER SEVENTEEN

Maha arrived home early. She had finished up her volunteer work at Awladi orphanage sooner than expected. The toddlers had settled into their afternoon nap right after lunch. So Mrs. Hamilton, who led the group, had excused all the students to go back home.

Maha didn't mind leaving early. Her experience at the orphanage was overwhelming. It was a struggle for her to hold back her tears. She felt so much love and compassion for the orphans. It troubled Maha that people could just give their children away. Wasn't the greatest love of all that of a mother for her own child? And wasn't giving that child away the biggest betrayal of all? She wondered what it would be like for those toddlers when they discovered the truth about this betrayal. This made Maha realize, with her heart and soul, that family really was everything. She thought that maybe her father was right after all. Maybe the only thing that mattered in this world was family. She had met Shaimaa that day, a student from Sacre Coeur who was also visiting the orphanage for volunteer day. It was the very first time Maha had bonded with someone her age who was veiled. To her surprise, Maha had discovered that she and Shaimaa had more in common than what appearances might suggest. They both had a drive to be a positive force of change for anyone and everyone. This was obvious in how they cared for the orphans.

She walked into her room and turned on her computer. A few minutes after logging on to MSN, a plethora of beeping sounds attacked her ears. They were message alerts from Yasmine, Leena, Mariam and Sylvia. She had received no less than 50, and all were about Menna's birthday.

Maha! Great! U got back from ur Day Beyond Walls! So tell me, what are your plans for today? Yasmine typed.

My plan is to meet up with Leena, Mariam and Sylvia first and then go to the birthday. I hope to be there around 9, Maha responded.

Oh, no! I wanted to go with you and cruise to downtown! Also, I thought we could meet up with Menna and Laila before we go. Do you think you, Leena, Mariam and Sylvia can join us? Yasmine typed.

That sounds like fun! You know how much I love a cruise. Let me check with the rest of the girls and get back to you.

She dreaded having to meet up with Laila and was in no mood to put up with Yasmine's incessant banter, but she couldn't say no to Yasmine. Maha didn't know how to say no. Yasmine knew this very well about Maha, and so she asked her questions in a way that ensured she always got what she wanted.

Maha checked with the other girls on MSN, and they were fine with the new arrangements. So the plan was to meet at Menna's house in Zamalek at 8:00pm. This was great news for Maha, because she realized she had a few good hours to rest and even nap.

Ok, great news, Yasmine. The girls are fine with the change of plans! she typed. *I'll pass by you at 7 cuz you never know what traffic is going to look like at that time.*

Great! I'm so excited for the car ride! Yasmine replied.

Me too :) Maha typed.

By the way, I'm going to the hairdresser now. I want to do my hair and get my nails done. Wanna join? Yasmine asked.

I'll pass! I prefer to take it easy and nap, she typed.

Yeah, then again, you don't need to get your hair done. You don't know what it's like for people like me. We pay real money to get hair like yours, Yasmine replied.

Oh no! Here we go again!! Bye Yasmine! See you @ 7! Maha responded.

Oh yeah, you bet it will keep going! The only time it will stop is when something happens to your hair.

Bye Yasmine! Go to the hairdresser!

Fine! Bye! Yasmine typed before logging off.

Maha always liked to keep the way she dressed simple and natural. She had a deep aversion for tacky trends and vanity. It wasn't that she didn't like to take care of herself, but rather because she believed that less was always more.

Later that day, when it was time to get ready, Maha decided to wear something light in color. But before she started getting dressed, she played music. She softly sang the words to her all-time favorite uplifting song, Cyndi Lauper's "Girls Just Want to Have Fun." *"I come home in the morning light, My mother says, when you gonna live your life right? Oh mama dear, we're not the fortunate ones, and girls, they want to have fun."*

She squeezed herself into her cream-colored pants and snuggled into her green halter-top. She put on her gold hoop earrings and put her hair up in a high ponytail. She moisturized her face and put on some lip-gloss. She then got into her stillettos and grabbed her beige clutch before she walked out of her room. After she passed the hallway, she saw her dad and mom sitting in the living room.

"Oh, wow! You look beautiful, dear," her mom said.

"You know, Maha, you remind me of your mom when she was your age," her dad said, directing a smile at her mom.

"Oh no way! I don't even come close, baba," Maha protested.

"Trust me, you do!" he assured her.

"Thank you, baba," she smiled. "So just to fill you in on my plan, I will pass by Yasmine, then head to Menna's house to meet the rest of the girls. Then we will all go to Coco Jungle. I plan on arriving there around 9 and staying for an hour or two, max. Then I'll be back home, inshallah."

"Sounds great, dear! Whatever you do, don't be late. And if anything happens, please call me," he said.

"And please have fun! You need this," her mom added.

"Thank you so much! I will do. I'd better get going or I'll be late for Yasmine," she said.

It took Maha only five minutes to get to Yasmine's house. She was surprised to find Yasmine waiting for her at the entrance of her building.

"Wow! You're early! That's unlike you, Yasmine. Everything ok?" Maha asked.

"We're both early, you mean! It's unlike you, too," Yasmine retorted.

"Why do you have to be so defensive and have an answer for everything?" Maha asked.

"Hehehehe... I know, it's annoying sometimes," she admitted.

"Only *sometimes?*" Maha asked incredulously.

"Fine, fine! I get it!" she said. "So where's the party at?"

"What party?" Maha asked.

"The music, Maha! The music! What's wrong with you today?"

"It's all in front of you!" she said. "I'm just so tired."

"Well, then maybe this is a good time to bring this up..." Yasmine said.

"What?" Maha asked.

"Well... Some of the girls have concerns about tonight. They want to have some fun, you know..."

"And what's the problem?"

"Well, they don't know how you'd feel or if you'd judge their kinda fun… You get me?" Yasmine said cryptically.

"What do you mean? Get to the point," Maha pressed her impatiently.

"Well, you know you're kind of a good girl. And everyone tries to be on their best behavior around you," she said.

"Best behavior? You're out to make me sound like a strict principal…" Maha said grimly, hating how Yasmine always tried to make her feel – like she was some kind of uptight goody two shoes. It bothered Maha that being honest, healthy and positive was something to be ridiculed. Being productive was not as cool as being destructive – that was the trend at school. And recently, Yasmine's *coolness* weighed Maha's being down. She believed she was *sooo* cool she could afford to do almost anything. Like be obnoxious, rude, loud, disrespectful and hurtful. Meanwhile, in reality, her humor dried up in the sorrows of her troubled life. That was the invisible disguise of Yasmine that had come to light that year. Maha wanted to keep that reality in the dark, because she was the one who could not afford to lose any more friends. The thought of being alone terrified her.

"I just wanted to give you a heads up that many people might not be on their best behavior tonight. And might be like you've never seen them before," Yasmine explained.

"What's your problem, Yasmine? You make it sound like this is the first time I'm going out with everyone. I've known them all since I was a kid," Maha said, not understanding why Yasmine was intentionally making her feel like she'd been missing out.

"I'm not saying that this is the first time you're going out with them. I'm just saying that this might be the first time you see them in a different light."

"Well, whatever it is, Yasmine, everybody is free to do and be whoever it is they want to be," Maha told her.

"Yes, of course, I know you believe that."

"Ok, good. Now please let's listen to some good music until we get to Menna's," Maha said. She took a moment to try and understand Yasmine's intention behind the conversation.

"Don't get mad, Maha," Yasmine said, trying to break the awkward silence in the car.

"I'm not mad, Yasmine. Can you just let it go? I don't understand how you live like this. You never ever let anything go. You hold on to every little thing," Maha said impatiently.

"I just wanted to make sure that you aren't mad."

"Well, if you don't want me to get mad, and you know that asking endless questions gets me mad, why do you keep asking them?"

"Haha, I get it!" Yasmine laughed.

"Good!" Maha said. "So what are we going to listen to? We're going to be at Menna's in about fifteen minutes."

"Let's listen to something…" Yasmine trailed off as she took a moment to think.

"Smooth," Maha said decisively.

"What do you mean? Smooth the song or something smooth generally?" Yasmine asked.

"The song, please, Yasmine – before we get to Menna's!"

"Ok, here you go," Yasmine said, selecting the right track. "This collaboration between Santana and Rob Thomas is smoother than smooth."

"I know. They're both music legends. And the song is supernatural," Maha agreed.

"You know you pun like Big Pun," Yasmine said.

"Hahaha, and you no doubt doubt like No Doubt!" Maha countered.

"Don't Speak," Yasmine said, laughing at the game they had just created.

"Hahaha," Maha laughed. "You're Killing Me Softly, Yasmine."

"Fly Away," Yasmine said, trying to think of a quick comeback.

"Hehehe! I love this game that we just made up!" Maha said.

"Me too! It's like the best game ever," Yasmine agreed.

"Best game ever? I'm not so sure about that. But anyways, it has to end because we've just arrived at Menna's. Can you call her and tell her that we've arrived? I'll call Leena," Maha said.

"Sure," Yasmine said, dialing Menna's number.

After a few minutes of discussion, the girls decided to get out of the car and go up to Menna's, because she and Laila were not ready yet. Leena, Mariam and Sylvia joined them a few minutes later.

"Ok, girls! Menna and I will be ready in five minutes," Laila called. True to her word, five minutes later Laila walked into the TV room, which was next to the bedroom.

"Are you all ready to have some fun?" Menna asked, following Laila into the room.

"Yes!" they all screamed.

They were just about to head off when Menna's mom walked into the TV room behind her, looking upset. "I can't believe how ignorant and backwards your sister's husband is, Menna! He is impossible!" she sobbed. "Can you believe it? He doesn't want your sister to give birth in the US. He is *ruining* my first grandchild's future and he doesn't even know it, that imbecile!"

"So does that mean that the baby will just have an Egyptian passport?" Laila asked.

"No. God forbid. I would never allow that – it would be an insult to my family and me! I'm the fourth generation in my family to hold a dual citizenship. So of course, I will pass that gift on to my grandchild!" Menna's mom said.

"Then what is the problem, Auntie?" Laila asked.

"Don't you get it? The problem is that the baby will be born in Cairo! My mom doesn't want Cairo to be the birthplace. She doesn't want it written on the baby's passport," Menna explained.

"Yes! That's true!" her mother screamed. "I will not allow for it, even if it means risking my daughter's marriage! She will give birth in New York, and that's *that*! End of discussion!" She exhaled a triumphant breath of relief and flounced out of the TV room.

The girls were paralyzed by the awkward silence that filled the air after such a melodramatic incident. Yasmine reminded everyone about the time and Coco Jungle, trying to break the ice.

"Well, then, how about we have something to get us in the mood before we go?" Menna suggested. She went to her dad's bar and, with a flourish, got out a bottle of vodka and some tequila.

"Woohoo!" Laila whooped. "I'd love to have me a drink now."

"Me too!" the rest chimed in, except for Maha, Leena and Mariam. Maha felt like she'd just gotten the biggest shock of her life. She couldn't believe that everyone around her was going to drink. Did they not even realize that they were committing a misdemeanor? Is this what living a double life felt like? Was this what the loss of innocence felt like? Gone were the days when pizza and cake topped the mood barometer of happiness. Now it seemed it was the taste of vodka that condoned the erratic instability of adolescence. Maha felt pressure. She then saw Laila get out a pack of Marlboro Lights from her bag.

"Ok, who wants a smoke?" she asked.

When Maha saw that everyone raised their hands, she forced herself to be in denial. She could not cope with how left out and different she felt from everyone around her.

"Come on, Maha! Have one cigarette!" Menna pleaded.

"No thanks, Menna! I don't smoke," Maha said firmly.

"I know you don't smoke, drink, do drugs, date or even eat junk! That's why we didn't know if we should tell you," Salma said.

"Why wouldn't you want to tell me?" Maha said, wondering what else they kept from her. "I'm totally cool with it."

"Ok, then come on, have one with us," she cajoled.

"Yes. Come on, it's nothing! It's just one cigarette," Laila said.

"I don't know," Maha said uncertainly, feeling her palms start to sweat. There was nothing that she wanted more than to get out of there. But she knew she couldn't. That would bring an end to her already non-existent social life. Feeling clueless, Maha didn't know what to do anymore. In fact, she didn't even know who to trust and believe anymore. Laila? Sultan? Yasmine? Her sister's ex-husband? Even her father? Was it that everyone around her was changing? Or was it that she was the one who was changing? Why couldn't she cope with the feeling that these losses left behind in her heart? Instead she carried the burden of heavy words that pushed her down.

Then she remembered Yasmine's words of wisdom: "When you've got nothing, you've got nothing to lose!" Yasmine would always say that before embarking on something destructive. Little did Yasmine realise that Maha always knew better, that even if you believe you have nothing, you still have something. But that night, none of that made a difference. She couldn't bear the thought of not having any friends. And because of that, Maha walked straight into the line of fire. It was the kind that burned its flames into nothing but thin air.

"Yeah, Maha! And remember, there's nothing wrong with just having one cigarette," Yasmine encouraged her.

"Well… I guess I can just have one cigarette…." Maha said hesitantly.

"Oh! *Wow*! Maha is going to have her first cigarette! This day should go down in history!" Menna exclaimed.

And just like that, Maha fell into the heart of darkness. This was the moment of tragedy, where there was no light in the dark. Despite the lit fire, darkness reigned as Maha took her first cigarette and lit it up.

"Inhale it!" Menna instructed her.

And when Maha did, she felt awful. The taste of the smoke in her mouth was nasty. Her body could not handle it and she coughed profusely. In an instant, Maha felt the world spin and the image of everyone blur. Something awful was happening to her body. She sat down quickly.

"Don't worry. It's not so pleasant at first, but once you get used to it, it's amazing and cool! Only cool people can handle the smoke," Laila said, realizing that Maha was not ok.

Maha was disgusted. She could not imagine how something so awful could be so cool! She tried to take a few more puffs, and soon felt the smoke evaporate her pain. So she took a few more puffs. Maha realized that Laila was right – the cigarette did get better. In fact, it did much more than get better. Maha felt great. It was the best she'd felt since the start of the school year. It was strange how her misery had found the best company, not only for that moment, but for the rest of the night as well. After the girls got their fix, they went to Coco Jungle, and Maha had three more cigarettes that night.

"Maha, you don't have to do this," Leena said.

"Do what?" Maha asked.

"Smoke all these cigarettes. You're not like them. True friends don't bring you down. They pull you up," Leena said.

"I'm not doing it to be like them. I'm doing it because… I don't know… I just need a break," Maha said.

"I understand you need a break. So take a day off. Plan a trip. But this… This is so *not* the way to take a break. Don't get sucked into this," Leena begged her. "This is pure peer pressure getting to you! Please, Maha. Think about what you're doing."

"Thanks Leena. I will. I know… I know… I won't smoke again. It's just for one day," Maha assured her.

"I hope so," she said, looking over at the other side of the club.

"Who are you looking for?" Maha asked.

"Selim. I heard that he was going to be here with his new girlfriend. I want to make sure I leave when they get here," Leena said.

"I understand. I guess this too shall pass," she said.

"I hope so," Leena sighed. "I've got a lot of nonsense going on in my life that I need to get rid of. *C'est vraiment degueulasse!*"

Then a guy approached Maha and interrupted their conversation. She had never seen him before and didn't know his name or anything about him.

"Hi," he said as he came and stood by Maha.

"Hi," both Maha and Leena said.

"From far away you looked like someone I know. That's why I came all the way to say hi. But when I came closer I realized you're not her," he said, directing his comments at Maha.

"No worries," Leena said.

"Let me introduce myself. My name is Ahmed," he said, still looking at Maha.

"Nice to meet you," Leena said.

Maha said nothing. She hated these awkward situations. Thank God for her mom's advice – she'd been the one to teach her how to play 'dumb-to-not-get'. The idea behind this approach was to act *sooo dumb* that no one would want to talk to her. This had saved Maha so many times before, especially when she traveled abroad. It worked like magic. Yet the situation at Coco Jungle required her to act a bit more than the usual. It was the first time that something like this happened to her in Egypt, with someone older who wasn't one of her 'bros' or Fahmy's friends.

"So," he said to Maha. "What's your name?"

"Solly, solly. No sbeakin English," Maha garbled, warming up to play so-dumb-to-not-get.

As soon as Leena heard Maha, she broke into a fit of giggles. She tried so hard to control her chuckles. Maha, of course, got upset that Leena was ruining her cover, so she gave her the coldest stare ever. The unspoken message was to either stay and play the role or walk away. And so Leena, unable to control herself, turned her back and walked away.

"What language are you speaking in?" he asked, looking confused.

She looked him straight in the eye and shrugged her shoulders.

"What language is this?" he asked again slowly. "Arabic, French, Spanish, Portuguese, Russian?"

Maha didn't respond. She prayed that her dumbness would make him walk away and never talk to her ever again.

"Ok, maybe Mandarin, Hindustani or even Swahili?" he persisted.

"Si si si!" she said.

"Which one, Swahili?" he asked.

At that moment, Yasmine walked in and blew Maha's cover by interrupting the conversation. "Oh, Maha! I see you've met my cousin's friend, Ahmed! He's at AIU! Ahmed, this is my best friend, Maha."

Oh, God! Maha could not believe that she was about to make an even bigger fool of herself than she had already. Her cheeks flushed with heat as she blushed. Her palms started to sweat and fidget.

"I didn't know you spoke Swahili, Yasmine," Ahmed said, trying not to laugh.

"Swahili? What are you talking about?" she asked as she looked at Maha's face and tried to figure out what was going on. Suddenly she cracked up. "Oh no, Maha! Don't tell me you played the *so-dumb-to-not-get* exit strategy on Ahmed? Are you kidding me?"

"Maha? Hmmm, what an interesting Swahili name. To be honest, I thought you were Persian at first. But your *'si si si'* threw me off and I thought you might be Spanish," he exclaimed. "I must say, you are quite creative! I didn't see that exit strategy coming."

"No! Please, this is not personal. It's just that I don't..." Her cheeks burned and she looked at Yasmine pleadingly. "I don't talk to complete strangers..."

"You know, you could have told me that from the start," he smiled.

"You think?" she said.

"No, really…," he trailed off, suddenly distracted by the scar on her left arm. "What is that?" he asked, pointing at it.

"It's an infection from a vaccination I had when I was young," she explained.

"No way! My sister has the same exact one!" he exclaimed.

"Really? I've never met anyone…" Maha began, and then stopped because she sensed that he was setting her up to make a fool out of her. She could tell from the smirk on his face and the glare in his brown eyes.

"What is wrong with you two? First Swahili, and now a fake sister? Who are you imposters? I want my friends back!" Yasmine cried dramatically as she waved and walked towards another group of friends.

"Haha!" Ahmed laughed.

"What's so funny?" Maha asked.

"Nothing… I mean, Yasmine is funny," he explained. "So, Maha… Where are you really from?"

"I'm Egyptian," she said.

"Are you are still in school?" he asked, sensing her playful spirit.

"Yes. I'm with Yasmine at school. We're seniors now."

"Oh, so do you know where you are going to for college?"

"Yeah. My father made that decision easy for me. AIU," she said.

"That's good. You know, AIU is not that bad. It's what you make of it, really," he said.

"I guess. Well, anyways, I still need to find out what I want to major in – Art, English, Business or maybe Marketing," she said.

"Wow! What different choices!"

"What's your major?" Maha asked.

"Business… My dad gave me no other option," he said, smiling.

"Hmmm," she giggled. "This is so funny. To say that the society we live in is a patriarchal one is an understatement. It's more like a father-iarchal one."

"Haha! I know, right! What fathers say, goes," he agreed as he inched closer to her.

"Hahaha, and thus spoke the fathers of Egypt," Maha said, not knowing whether Ahmed would get her play on words.

"Touché," he said.

Maha became immersed in what seemed like an endless conversation with Ahmed. Contrary to popular belief about what went down in a conversation between a guy and a girl in a club, Ahmed and Maha were breaking new ground. That night, even though it did not look like it to strangers, they expanded each other's intellectual capacities. And for the very first time in her life, Maha was in awe of this kind of stimulation. She succumbed to a sensation that she had never felt before as she heard Ahmed speak about history, science, politics, current events, arts and literature. Maha had a soft spot for true intellectuals like him. She even transcended the rhythms of the catchy pop hits, like Informer, Hot Stepper, Bombastic and Cher's "Believe", that played in the background. She didn't hear the music. She lost track of time as she fell deep into conversation. She didn't realize that Sultan, Yusuf and Fahmy had arrived. She panicked when she made eye contact with Fahmy and was brought back to reality. She checked the time on her phone, and realized that it was already late and that she had to hurry home. She cut off her conversation with Ahmed and excused herself.

"What? You're gonna leave just like that? How can I see you again?" he said.

"See me again? Are you kidding me?" she said, imagining the look on her dad's face if he were to ever find out something like that. Maha thought Ahmed was crazy to approach someone he didn't even know, and reckless and destructive to ask her to see him again – even though she really wanted to see him again as well. She knew she couldn't. She understood her limits and hoped he did too. Did he not live in Egypt? Was he not Egyptian? Did he not get the memo about 'good girls' and how they didn't date? What planet did he live on? Or was he just playing her?

"Can I at least have your phone number?" he pleaded, as Fahmy walked towards her from behind Ahmed.

"No, no! No phone numbers! Please, just let it be," she insisted, praying to God to get her out of this situation. *Phone number?* Maha thought that Ahmed had lost his mind! She never understood how people had the audacity to disrespect others like that, let alone live with their emotions on their sleeves. She couldn't bear the thought of falling into the trap of leading a double life like so many of her friends did. It was enough that *now* she had to hide the fact that she smoked from her parents. She didn't want to drown in even more guilt. She believed that a life of lying was not worth it. That's what she had learned from her parents. She valued that. She had always wanted to commit to that. But unfortunately, that night the thick tar of nicotine stained that squeaky clean record of hers.

"Maha," Fahmy said sternly. "You're late. Uncle told me that you should have been back by now."

"Yes! I know! I lost track of time. I have to go now," she said as she ran out of that jungle called Coco. She waved goodbye to Fahmy and Ahmed. And that was that.

Maha zoomed back to her house as Tracy Chapman's "Fast Car" played in the background. Luck was on her side, and she made it back in 20 minutes. The streets were empty and quiet. It was 12:20am by the time she walked in. She hated this part of outings. Sometimes she wondered if they were even worth the confrontations she had to endure with her dad afterwards. She took a deep breath and prepared for her walk of shame. She took off her shoes and slowly tiptoed her way through to her room. She hoped her parents would be sound asleep by now. But that would be very unlike her dad and wishful thinking on her part.

"Maha!" her dad exclaimed.

"Yes, baba," Maha said, walking towards him and dreading having to look him in the eye. She worried about getting too close because she reeked of the nasty smell of cigarettes.

"It's 12:20am. We agreed you would be home at 12:00am," he said very sternly.

"I know. I'm sorry. It was a mistake and I promise you it will never happen again," she said, silently opting to never go out again. She hated upsetting her father and was willing to do anything to never be put in such a situation again.

"Good! Because this will be your last chance. You have to understand that with this freedom comes responsibility. You have to respect the limits of your responsibilities," he lectured her.

"I understand. Trust me, baba, it will never happen again," she promised.

"Ok," he said.

"Thank you for the second chance. I appreciate it," Maha said as she turned away and walked towards her room.

"I know," he replied.

As soon as Maha got to her room, she turned on her computer, logged onto the internet and played Mary J Blige's "Not Gon' Cry". She then stepped gratefully into the shower. The smell of cigarettes on her fingers, hair and clothes was getting to her. She couldn't stand it.

When she came back to her room, she read a weird message Sultan had sent her while she was away.

Is everything ok? Are you ok? he wrote.

And it was at that point that Maha broke down. It was the first time in a long time that Sultan had asked about her. Whenever they talked, it was always all about him and his problems. She did not understand anything about their friendship anymore. This confusion was what she could not handle. She yearned for their friendship to be simple and light like it used to be. This irrational side of their friendship troubled Maha, because a life of pure reason was what appealed to her most. She believed that that was part of the problem, and since she could not reason with how she felt about their friendship, she thought it would be best to cut it out of her life. And so she realized that she had no room for Sultan anymore. On that note, she responded to Sultan in a long message:

> *Dearest Sultan,*
>
> *It occurred to me that this is the first time you have asked about me in months. You kill me softly with your lack of words when you see me at school. But you seem to find them when we are on MSN. I guess what I'm trying to say is that this has all been too confusing for me. And I'm at a point in my life where not only do I not want this confusion, I can't handle it either. I prefer to live a life free of it. For wouldn't life be so much better without it? There is no point in trying to rationalize that which cannot be rationalized. And so, since I cannot rationalize our friendship anymore, I've realized that I need to let go and move on to the next, and hopefully less confusing, part of my life. So please, Sultan, just stop contacting me.*
>
> *Before I go, though, I want you to know that I appreciate you so much. To think that our friendship started off as an accident a decade ago makes me wonder – was it ever a coincidence in the first place? We've both come a long way from the little boy and girl you and I used to be. You have been many things to me; a friend, brother, father and even enemy. You taught me things you don't know I learned. You are a master! And your lessons will forever live with me. I can't believe that I'm writing this*

now, but I have to admit it – "I did learn from the best!"
and I thank you for that!
   Please forgive me for everything that I may have done
that might have hurt you. I'm so sorry if I did.
   I wish you a life full of happiness, health and love.
   Warm wishes,
   Maha

After Maha finished typing the message, she reread it a few times and then sent it. It was strange and liberating to let go of the things that did not serve her any longer – even if that meant Sultan. And with a heavy heart that just felt lighter, Maha turned off her computer and went to bed.

CHAPTER EIGHTEEN

Mrs. Magda was so happy when she woke up on Friday morning. She had all the time in the world to sleep in and relax. She and Maher did not have any plans that day except for a lunch event, which was at 4pm in Mansoureya in the countryside. Mrs. Magda was so excited that she had nothing to do until then. Maher was, too. He'd had a difficult week at the bank, and all he wanted to do was enjoy his breakfast and Turkish coffee, and then get ready for the Friday prayers.

"I'm so happy," Mrs. Magda told Maher as they lay in bed, staring at the ceiling.

"I'm happy you're happy," Maher smiled, grateful that he was going to have some peace of mind.

"And you know something," she said. "I feel that a positive change is coming. Otherwise things will escalate if they are not addressed."

"Don't worry about it. It will all work out. Everything works out in the end. Nothing ever stays the same. Change is constant. But as long as your commitment is the same, then all will be well," he said.

"Yes, my commitment hasn't changed a bit. If anything, it's

stronger now than ever."

"I know. You don't need to tell me," he winked at her and squeezed her cheek.

"Hmm, and what are you implying by that?" she asked, fishing for a compliment.

Maher knew her game and usually he liked to play along with her. But today was different. He wanted her to know her worth in no uncertain terms.

"I'm implying that you are a fierce yet graceful woman," he told her, looking at her with great admiration. He had known Mrs. Magda ever since she was 12, and had seen her grow from a young girl into a beautiful and strong woman, now in her forties. He was so grateful to have her in his life. He did not know what he'd do without her. To him, Mrs. Magda was the air that he breathed.

"Oh, no! I can't believe my ears," she purred, blushing at the thought of how that thing called love had brought and kept them together all these years.

The sound of the phone ringing interrupted their moment of intimacy. Not wanting to get up, Mrs. Magda looked at Maher and asked, "Do you want to get it? Or should I?"

Maher knew what she was trying to do, but he did not feel like getting out of bed, either. "That phone call is for you. It's Hana, and I know that she wants to talk to you about today's lunch."

Mrs. Magda knew he was right. Who else would call this early in the morning? So she got out of bed and walked though to the living room of the house. Right beside the door was a rectangular Ethan Allen side table made out of cherry wood. It had three sets of wireless phones on it, and Mrs. Magda grabbed the one that was ringing. As soon as she put it to her ear, she heard Hana already in the middle of her sentence.

"I hope you're not still asleep. Today's lunch is a huge event and all of Cairo's who's who will be there! So you'd better be ready!" she exclaimed.

"I was still in bed, Hana. I'm so exhausted. I wanted to spend the rest of the morning sleeping in," Mrs. Magda said.

"*What*? Have you lost your mind? Do you not understand that there is a huge lunch today? This is the biggest event of the year! I know you're veiled, but you still need to prepare for this event. You need to go to the hairdresser to get your hair, make-up, manicure and pedicure done!" Hana insisted.

"Oh come on, Hana. That's the last thing I want to do today," Mrs. Magda groaned.

"Are you *serious*?" Hana asked incredulously.

"Yes," Mrs. Magda responded doggedly.

"What is this about, Nelly? Are you still holding on to your phobias?" Hana pressed.

"Oh, no! Here we go again," Mrs. Magda laughed. "Hana, this has nothing to do with any kind of phobia, even though I do still believe that beauty centers must maintain high standards of cleanliness. I mean, after all, you do expose yourself to strangers who touch your hair, hands, feet and face," Mrs. Magda said.

"Hahaha," Hana laughed.

"What's so funny?" Mrs. Magda asked.

"Nothing. You're just one of a kind, Nelly."

"Why, of course! I love being myself."

"And I'm so happy you are your self and that you are my best friend."

"Me, too," Mrs. Magda laughed.

"Ok! So I'll meet you at the lunch, then?" she asked.

"Yes. I'll see you then. Enjoy the hairdresser's," Mrs. Magda said.

"Enjoy lounging, then," Hana replied.

"Hahaha! Bye bye," Mrs. Magda said.

"Bye," said Hana.

Maher and Mrs. Magda could not believe that they made it to the countryside location of the event in just 30 minutes.

"It must be because it is a Friday and that we left home early," Mrs. Magda said.

"Yes, I think so, too. I must admit that I enjoyed the drive. And I miss seeing all this greenery. This country is a blessed nation. It has everything – desert, fertile land, rivers, oceans, mountains and oases. It has an historic ancient civilization and one of the world's greatest wonders," Maher said as he drove through the green fields of Egypt's countryside.

"I love Mansoreya. This place reminds me of my childhood and my family. We used to come out here every weekend to take a break from the hustle and bustle of the city. The smell and sight of the morning dew always made me appreciate and see nature as a universal miracle. The functions of nature are so intricate and precise. It's woven into a tapestry of events that make the course of life. Nature is life's greatest teacher. Do you ever think sometimes about how a tree doesn't need to learn how to grow? It just grows," Mrs. Magda said in awe. "I hope you don't mind me monologuing. I want to monologue for a while."

"I don't mind at all. In fact, I want to monologue with you. Can I?" he said with a smile.

"Of course... So now we can collaborate and create our own monialogue," she said, laughing at her attempt to create a dialogue out of their monologues.

"Hahaha. Well, isn't that what we and most Egyptians do, anyway? Isn't that how we speak? We preach and love to listen to ourselves talk," he said with a big smile on his face.

"Indeed. It *is* the Egyptian trademark. I love that about us Egyptians," she said. "But I'll put a twist on it and actually address your comments in my monologues."

"I'm all ears, dear."

"So yes, Maher, Egypt *is* a special country. Which is why somebody has to save it from the identity crisis that is brewing," she continued.

"You are so right, Magda. Egyptians are suffering from a major identity crisis. So many people belong to many different groups because of that. Unfortunately, this has made our society divisive. There are those who disassociate from our culture and want to have nothing to do with it. Then are those who are the complete opposite, and are so rooted in our culture that they want to take us back in time. Between these two groups is a whole range of subgroups. Can you imagine how different life would be if the majority of Egyptians could unite? And respect each others' differences?" Maher asked.

"Yes, we would be ahead of our game," Mrs. Magda responded.

"Exactly," he said. "Oh, it looks like we have arrived. Oh, my! Look at the crowd! I was naive to think that we were going to be the first ones to arrive. I guess we won't have more time for our monialogue today."

"Ugh, I guess not. We can do it another time though, right?"

"Sure, dear."

"Oh my, it's so crowded! It looks like it's going to be one long event! This is going to be so tough for me. I don't know how I will be able to connect with people who are not connected with themselves," Mrs. Magda said, thinking about the amount of effort she was going to have to put in to make small talk. She would have preferred to engage in real talk – that came effortlessly to her.

"It will be fine," Maher reassured her.

"I know it will. It's just not my thing, you know. I don't live in La-La Land like the majority of the people here," she responded.

"You know, it's not their fault that they are like that. Their environment shaped them that way," he said.

"I understand that! But I have limits to what I can and cannot handle. I don't have to be like them just because some of them are the most influential people in the country," Mrs. Magda argued.

"Relax a little and let's enjoy today. Please, Magda. You know I have to be here for work. Our bank needs to have a respectful relationship with the Central Bank. Trust me, I would have preferred to spend the day at Katameya Heights Country Club. But I could not say no to an invitation from the head of the Central Bank," Maher said.

"Of course. I understand. But that doesn't mean that I have to tolerate the circus associated with it," Mrs. Magda said as she nudged him.

"Oh, God forbid! You are never one to put your principles aside, even for a ten-second break!"

"Never ever," she said sarcastically.

"Ok look, we've finally made it to the valet area," Maher said.

"Oh, no! No wonder I detect the smell of decadence. This looks more like a wedding and nothing like a lunch. I can't believe how everyone is so dressed up. Everybody is hiding under layers of make-up. Not a wrinkle or a pimple in sight!" Mrs. Magda said as she thought of the Chloe outfit she was wearing. She personally loved the sophisticated yet feminine style of Chloe clothes. She also loved that Gaby Aghion, the brand's founder and designer and the person who had coined the term *pret-a-porter*, was Egyptian. For Mrs. Magda, Chloe was the symbol of where East met West. She believed beautiful creations emanated from harmonizing the differences between the two.

"Haha, you crack me up, Magda," Maher said, interrupting her thoughts.

"And please do me a favor and look at my wrinkles and pimples," Mrs. Magda said as she tried to squeeze her face to reveal her wrinkles and pimples.

As soon as she got out of the car, she saw Maher waiting for her behind her door. When their eyes met, it was like they were 12 years old all over again. Maher understood Mrs. Magda so well, and she loved that about him. She didn't need to be anything but herself with him. Together, they were solid and strong. They never cared about what people thought. They never let social pressure into their lives. They preferred to be real with each other. They both had soul, and that mattered most to them. Everything else was irrelevant.

"So, are you ready to have some fun today?" Maher asked as he locked his arm through hers.

"Watch me have a blast, love," she winked at him.

When they walked through the entrance of the house, the butler welcomed them inside and showed them the way to the gardens. When they made it through, the first people they saw were Hana and Khaled.

"Hello," Mrs. Magda said as she walked up to Hana.

"Hi! You finally made it," Hana greeted them.

"Yes, we thought we were going to be the first ones here because we left early," Maher said.

"I think many beat you to be a part of the scene, if you know what I mean," Khaled said.

"Oh, please! Khaled, don't get started with that subject or you'll get Nelly all worked up," Hana admonished him.

"I have chosen not to speak about that tonight. I'm going to enjoy myself. I'm taking an official break from lame scene-and-heard issues," Mrs. Magda said.

"Wow! I cannot believe my ears! Who cast a spell on you?" Hana teased. "Please tell me all about it on our way to the ladies' room. I need to check out my hair in the mirror."

"*Spell?* Oh vanity, vanity, please give me a break," Mrs. Magda groaned.

"You said you wouldn't complain," Hana reminded her. "Come on, let's go."

On their way to the ladies' room, which was quite a walk from the lunch area, Mrs. Magda saw Nagwa, the mom from the field trip. Nagwa caught sight of Mrs. Magda as well, and in an instant turned around to give Mrs. Magda her back. Mrs. Magda explained this to Hana.

"Oh, my! How *rude!*" Hana exclaimed.

"It has nothing to do with her being rude. It has everything to do with the fact that she's avoiding me, because I know her truth. I can see right through her," Mrs. Magda said.

"I feel bad for people who are like that. They must be so uneasy all the time," Hana said.

"That's an understatement, Hana. May God help them heal themselves and their wounded hearts," Mrs. Magda said.

They finally made it to the ladies' room and Hana busied herself with fixing her hair. Mrs. Magda, in the meantime, was engaged in observing everyone checking themselves out. These women were obsessive and compulsive in front of the mirror. They could not stop scrutinizing their make-up, hair and clothes in the mirror. Then, all of a sudden, someone rushed into a bathroom stall. The sound of the lady's tears echoed through the bathroom. Yet that did not stop anyone from fixing their hair or make-up, except for Mrs. Magda and Hana. It annoyed Mrs. Magda that they were the only ones who cared enough to ask after her.

"Excuse me, are you ok?" Mrs. Magda asked as she knocked on the door of the stall.

"I'm fine. I just need to be alone," the lady said. Mrs. Magda realized that she recognized her voice, but could not tell who she was.

"Are you sure?" Hana said.

"No, I'm not," the lady said as she opened the door. Hana and Mrs. Magda almost fainted when they saw Nagwa walk out.

"*Nagwa?* What happened?" Mrs. Magda asked.

"Major drama is what happened. My husband is having an affair with a friend of mine. I just found out now. I don't understand, how could they do this to me?" she screeched.

"Are you sure about this?" Hana asked cautiously.

"Yes – he sent a text message addressed to her to me by mistake. He said that he missed her, and that he couldn't stop thinking about their time together yesterday," she started sobbing again.

"What a fool!" Hana said.

"I'm sorry to hear that. This must be so painful. But I'm sure that this happened for a reason. I mean, for you to receive the message like that – it must be divine intervention," Mrs. Magda said.

"Really? What do you think the reason is?" Nagwa wailed.

"I don't know. Sometimes incidents like this happen when it's time for a couple to reassess their relationship, and try to make it work for the better. Others might realize that there is no point in continuing. Whatever it is, have faith that a positive change is coming into your life," Mrs. Magda said.

"But that's not going to be easy, especially because this isn't the first time he's cheated on me. He's done it before. I wanted a divorce, but my mother and grandmother advised me to stay in the marriage for the sake of my children. Now when I look back, I regret not having left him then. What good is it for children when their parents are not good to each other?" Nagwa asked.

"Of course, it's not good for the children," Hana agreed.

"I don't know what to do. I hate feeling stuck like this!" she cried.

"If you want to 'unstick' yourself, you can pray istikahara. I usually do when I'm confused about something. I ask God for his guidance to help pave the way. Whatever way opens for me, I follow," Mrs. Magda told her.

It was at that moment that Mrs. Magda and Hana could see the real work of faith take place. Nagwa stopped crying. She thought for a moment about what Mrs. Magda had said. "That is a great idea! I know my grandmother and mother do it a lot. But to be honest, I never have. I think I will pray later tonight and surrender to whatever it is that will be. Thank you so much," Nagwa said sincerely. "I don't know what I would have done without you. I feel my heart is healing from all that pain."

"Don't mention it at all. It's the least we could do," they both said as they walked out of the ladies' room.

"Oh, life does work in mysterious ways," Hana said to Mrs. Magda.

"Yes, indeed."

"I mean, just to think that you, the person she had snubbed, were the only one to help her with her crisis. That's amazing."

"Yeah, it really is. I guess it's amazing how it all works out in the end."

"I guess it also means that we should take care of how we treat or mistreat people, because you never know, they might be the ones to help us out one day."

"True."

"Now, lets head back and have something nice to eat before the food is gone," Hana said.

"Sounds like a great idea, I'm famished!" Mrs. Magda said.

As soon as they made it back, Mrs. Magda told Maher all about what happened with Nagwa.

"I can't believe it, Maher! These people fill their lives with so many things. Yet they are lifeless," Mrs. Magda said.

"Yes, it is sad but true," Maher said, taking hold of Mrs. Magda's hand.

"I can't wait to get out of here. I want to go home and get into my comfy clothes and read a book."

"Don't worry about it! We will leave soon," he promised.

Mrs. Magda was so happy to hear that. She saw Hana and Khaled getting some food, and so she and Maher decided to follow suit. After scouring the 5km buffet of decadence, Mrs. Magda ended up having some green salad and stir-fried chicken. She always felt overwhelmed by the massive choice of food at grand buffets. It did not make sense to her to do things in such excess.

After they finished eating, Maher and Mrs. Magda hung out with a few friends, and then called it a night. Mrs. Magda was glad when she got into the car. She could not wait to relax for the rest of the night. She also looked forward to the next day. She had no plans but to read, relax and take care of her vegetable garden. This was convenient, as it gave her the opportunity to rest and clear her mind before her early meeting with Mrs. White on Sunday.

CHAPTER NINETEEN

Maha lay in bed trying to recollect everything that had happened the previous night. She felt like she needed a break from the ongoing circus that she lived in. She needed a reality check. She needed to disconnect from all those who were tripping. It wasn't her style to trip like that. And she knew no one could ever change that about her.

Her train of thought was interrupted by her silently vibrating phone. It was Shereen, and she was in no mood to answer. The only thing she was in the mood for that day was to hibernate. But even that seemed challenging. A few seconds later, her phone was vibrating again. This time, it was a text message from Shereen.

Hey Maha. Wassup? Jus wanted 2 know what u're going 2 do 2day. A bunch of us want 2 go 2 the movies. Wanna join?

Ugh! Maha thought to herself. She couldn't believe that she already had to make decisions about her day. Why was it so hard for people to just chill? Why was it that people always had to have something to do?

It really annoyed Maha that she was in a constant mode of having to choose. Decisions here. Decisions there. About university, outings, food, clothes, homework, sports, friends and a million other things. This decision overload was starting to overwhelm her. Maha didn't want to go to the movies that day. And saying no was the difficult part of the decision-making process. Luckily, she had a great excuse, because she had to go to school to finish her projects for the I.B. Art Show at the end of the year. She was supposed to meet Seif there.

Sorry, Shereen. Would have loved to join but I have to go to school today for my Art project. Next time.

She was relieved that she'd gotten that over and done with. She yearned to sleep in a bit more, but even that was not an option when she heard her Nokia vibrate again.

Ok fine. But seriously, wuts wrong with u Maha? u don't go out or hang out wit me or ne of the girls! Do u even have friends n e more?

Maha couldn't believe Shereen's nerve to text her like that! Who did she think she was? Queen of Sheeba? It was so arrogant and self-centred of her, or anyone for that matter, to think like that! So just because someone stops hanging out with 10 or 20 people, it means that the person has no friends anymore? In a world of 6 billion people, that way of thinking would be immeasurable to say the least! Let alone conceited, pretentious and stuck up. This preposterous way of thinking annoyed Maha. It validated how she felt about the group. Because seriously, who in the world *thought* like that?

This confirmed that the decision to distance herself from them was appropriate for her. She could not connect with them anymore. And it was not because Maha felt she was in the right and they were not. It was *not* about that. It was just that it wasn't working for her anymore. It was at that moment that she swore to herself that she would rather be alone in this world than have "friends" like that. She had to let negativity like that go! She knew that she would never fit in with that kinda crowd. And so, her zillionth decision that morning was to not respond to the message.

Fortunately, she still had other great friends, and she texted one of them to arrange to meet up at school later that day.

Hey Seif. How r u? I just wanted to let you know I'll go to school around 1.

Great! See you then Maha! Seif replied.

Maha arrived at school at 12. She wanted to have time to set up her stuff and see how she was going to do her part in a painting of an African mask she was sharing with her friend Khadija. Khadijah was really cool. She was beef-, drama- and judgment-free. And that's what made her everybody's friend, really. When Maha got to the art studio, she saw Khadija's work. She was amazed by the detailed charcoal work of the African pattern. This piece was an ode to Africa. It was meant to acknowledge African art as the source of inspiration for the world's greatest post-modern art movements in the early 20th century. It was an original mask of an African tribe. Maha and Khadija had decided to deconstruct it and represent the essence of the different art movements within it: short brush techniques to represent the influences of Monet and Cezanne; cube-like and deconstructed facial features to reflect the styles of Braque and Picasso; and a mixed hue of colors to capture the palettes of artists like Van Gogh and Seurat.

After deconstructing the canvas, which was twice as tall as Maha, she got her oil paints ready. She decided to work with the greens, yellows, reds, browns and oranges to create the base. By the time she had arranged her colors on her palette and gotten her turpentine and cloth ready, she heard her phone vibrate. She checked it and found Seif calling her.

"Hey, Seif."

"Hey, Maha. Are you at school yet?"

"Yeah, I decided to come early to get my stuff prepared."

"Great. I'm outside with two of my friends. They're visiting for a few days. And Tarek is supposed to be joining, too."

"Oh, ok. Tarek? Tarek from the British school or the German one?"

"Yeah, the British one. How about we go to Greco and hang out for a bit?"

"Sure, no problem. I'd love that. Gimme five and I'll meet you at the front gate." Maha could never say no to Greco. She loved their frappe freeze – the melange of hazelnut and French vanilla made it sublime. It beat any other drink hands down. She loved having her almond and chocolate biscottis along with it. It was something she could literally live on all day, every day.

"Peace."

Maha covered her palette, grabbed her backpack and walked out to meet Seif and the rest. By the time she got there, Tarek had arrived as well. Maha joined them.

"Hey, Maha!" Seif said.

"Hey!" she said.

"People, meet Maha. This girl is one of a kind. You will never meet anyone else like her," Seif told his friends.

"Oh, Seif," Maha said as she raised her eyebrows. "Don't overdo it."

"You know I'm putting it lightly!" he protested.

She laughed and shook her head at him before turning to greet his friends. "Hi, I'm Maha."

"Hi, I'm Lara," one of them replied.

"Ok, nice to meet you. You're from Egypt?"

"Yeah. Well, I am Egyptian, but I live in Dubai. I go to the Dubai American School," Lara explained.

"Oh, ok. I raced at your school a few years back."

"Oh, really! Nice. Yeah, I know our schools are, like, rivals in every sport," Lara smiled.

"We're rivals, too!" Seif's other friend chimed in. "I'm at the American School in Madrid. I'm Adam, by the way."

"Nice. *Hablas español?*" Maha asked.

"*Poquito.*"

"*Bueno,*" Maha said as she felt a sudden wave of positive energy overcome her. It was strange how renewed energy felt so good. It would have never occurred to her how losing something actually meant gaining something. It was funny how endings were beginnings and beginnings were endings in disguise. And just like that, Shereen's provoking text seemed like a decade ago. It was cathartic, how out with the old and in with the new gave new meaning to her.

"Hey, M," Tarek interrupted.

"Hey, T. How are you?" Maha asked.

"Besides the fact that I'm the only odd one out because I do not go to an American school… Very well, thank you," he said with a smirk.

"You know it ain't personal, brotha," Maha teased, attempting to Americanize her already-Americanized accent.

"How can I not take it personally? I'm gutted," he said, emphasizing his British accent.

"Now stop, stop… We go to za Greco now," Seif said, copying the English accent of the average Egyptian.

"So not cool, Seif. There's no need to make fun that way," Maha admonished him.

"I'm not… Well, who am I kidding. You're right and I'm so sorry," he said.

"It's cool."

"Oy, you're so right bro. She is one of a kind," Adam said.

"Oh, well…" Maha said.

"Let's get going, people," Seif said as he made sure to stress his p's to show Maha that he had learned his lesson.

"*Vamos,*" Adam agreed.

They all got into Seif's baby blue Opel car and headed to Greco, which was New Cairo's coolest cafe in town, located right next to Bandar. It wasn't very far away from where they were.

"Hi, how are you?" Maha greeted the cashier when they arrived.

"Great! And you?" the cashier smiled at her.

"I'm fine, thanks."

"How can I help you?"

"I'd love to have a frappe freeze, skimmed milk with a shot of hazelnut and french vanilla," Maha said, remembering the first time she had discovered the place with Leena. They'd experimented with these flavors from the very first time they went, and ever since, it was the only thing Maha drank.

"Ok. Anything else?"

"Yes, please – two almond biscottis and two chocolate ones," Maha said as she started to salivate, eager to drink and eat.

"Great. That will be EGP 20."

"Ok. Here you go," Maha gave the cashier her money, got her receipt and walked to the other side of the counter to pick up her order.

"Let's sit outdoors," Seif suggested.

"I'd prefer that, too. But let me check if either of the two tables are available. You know how they're always occupied."

As Maha walked outside, she couldn't believe her eyes when she saw a couple getting up to leave one of the tables. She jumped towards them to shotgun it. The couple were taken aback by her determination, but that was ok. Maha felt a great sense of accomplishment, and no blank stare could shake that. She left her backpack and walked inside to tell the rest that she'd gotten a table and that all they needed were three extra chairs.

"Perfect stroke of luck," Tarek said. "Now I can smoke my cigarettes."

Oh, no! Maha had completely forgotten about the cigarettes that she'd smoked last night. She suddenly realized that she wouldn't mind having another one. But she could not dare do it in front of Tarek or Seif – she knew they would tell Fahmy, and that would be the end of her. So she decided to let it go.

They all sat together and chatted about their different experiences. Adam's dad had wanted him to check out AIU as an option for university next year. It was the same case for Lara, but she did not have any other option – her parents would not allow her to go anywhere else. Tarek planned to go to London for university. He was hoping to get into the London School of Economics, but any other option was fine with him. His parents felt the same way, just as long as he was going to major in Business or Finance.

At one point, Maha paused and disconnected from the conversation. She looked at everyone and listened to them. Like, *really* looked and listened. And she could not help but realize how they were all the same. In the guise of Americanized accents, attitudes and beliefs, it was obvious that Adam, Lara, Seif and Maha put a lot of effort into hiding who they really were. The same was true for Tarek, but in his case it was his prim and proper accent. They all belonged to schools with acronyms that abbreviated the differences in learning systems – the letter A represented America, B for British, F for French and D for Deutsche. Maha realized how their education system was symbolic of colonialism. Even though the colonial era had officially ended decades ago, it was obvious that that was only true as far as maps and borders were concerned. Colonialism was still alive and going strong, but in this supposedly post-colonial era, it was the colonization of minds and not territories that was the battlefield. Maha, and many like her, preferred the colonial powers their schools were affiliated to more than their own country. They were like their model citizens but with zero benefits. Regardless, their loyalty to these powers was like that of soldiers: unshakable. It was obvious that America led the race in Cairo. It was sad but true that in a generation filled with carbon-copied wannabes, it was almost impossible to find originals: the Egyptians.

Maha's train of thought came to an end when Lara interrupted the conversation and excused herself to go to Kimo market. She wanted to get a phone card to call her parents in Dubai.

"Hey! I'll join you," Maha said, thinking that this would be the perfect opportunity to smoke. She was itching for a cigarette. She was fired up about what she'd just realized about herself. *How could she ever accept the fact that, like the rest, she too was ashamed of her roots?* She got up and headed out of Cafe Greco with Lara. As they walked back towards school, Maha asked Lara for a cigarette.

"Sure. Here you go," Lara said as she pulled out one of her Marlboro Lights.

"Thanks. But please don't tell any of the guys. They'll tell my cuz, and I don't want him to find out."

"Don't worry about it. I won't tell. And if it makes you feel any better, I'm going back to Dubai after tomorrow. So I won't see anyone."

"No, it's cool. Thanks," Maha said. "I'll wait here while you go in and get your card."

"Cool. I'll be back in five minutes."

"Sure. Take your time," Maha said as she got her Discman out to listen to some music. As soon as she put on her earphones and pressed play, she heard the lyrics to Sting's "Englishman In New York":

> *If "Manners maketh man" as someone said*
> *Then he's the hero of the day*
> *It takes a man to suffer ignorance and smile*
> *Be yourself no matter what they say*

These lyrics had taken on a whole new meaning for Maha. Deep down, she knew that this was life's way of guiding her through to find her way. And that day, Maha knew that it would always be forward.

"Hey, sorry I took so long," Maha heard Lara say.

"Don't worry about it. I was enjoying listening to some of my music," she said as she heard her phone vibrate.

"Hello?" she said after she got out her phone from her bag.

"Hey, you girls finished up?" Seif asked.

"Yes. We are walking back."

"Ok, how about we meet up at the front gate? Adam and Tarek need to leave."

"Sure. See you in a bit."

"Cool. Peace."

When they reached the school, Maha greeted everyone as they prepared to part ways.

"Ok, bye everyone. It was lovely meeting you all. Until we meet next year at AIU!"

"Hold on, Maha. I'll come with you and walk you to the art building," Seif said as he waved to the others.

"Great," Maha said as she waited for Seif to join her.

"I'm glad we met up today, Maha," Seif said.

"Me, too. Especially after such a terrible morning… I really needed this."

"Terrible morning? What happened?" he asked, sounding concerned.

"Nothing much! Shereen texted asking if I wanted to join her and the gang at the movies, and I told her I couldn't. Then I received this weird text from her with so much attitude!"

"What did she say?"

"She complained that I don't hang out with her or anyone else anymore. She even asked me if I still have friends!"

"Whaaat!?! Loser!"

"Tell me about it! I swear they are all so socially pressured!"

"No, Maha. Not only that. They're Haters. They hate anything and everything. They're always making fun of people. They're so mean to many people!" Seif shook his head.

"I know, don't remind me. I can't believe I used to be like that. I can't believe I used to entertain this crap!"

"I know what you mean."

"I'm so glad that I don't recognize the old 'me' anymore. It's more peaceful this way."

"I know. It shows on you. You keep strong, sista!" he encouraged her.

"Will do, brotha," Maha smiled as she arrived at the main entrance of the art building.

"Ok. So I'll leave you to your work. Let's talk later," he suggested.

"Sure. See you."

"Bye."

When she walked into the Art Studio and towards her stuff, she noticed a few books with interesting covers, and stopped to flick through them. One of them was an Arabic Calligraphy book. In it were small verses of beautiful stories that she had not known about. The other was Gazbia Sirry's *Lust for Color*. Maha had not heard of her before, so she flipped the pages to discover more about her. At the end of the book, she read a short bio about her journey and career as an Egyptian painter. At the bottom of the bio was a black and white photo of her standing with her arms crossed and holding a cigarette. To Maha, this photo suddenly became the symbol of the intellectual struggle, and the cigarette was its weapon. Maha yearned for nothing more than to live the life of an intellectual. And so, after Maha finished her work that day, she passed by Kimo market and bought her first pack of Marlboro Lights.

CHAPTER TWENTY

American School in Cairo
Sunday, September 5, 1999, 6:05am
Cairo, Egypt

Mrs. Magda made it to school early on Sunday morning to print out her presentation and notes. She wanted to be at Mrs. White's office at 7:45am sharp. She didn't know how she was going to get inside the administration building – the doors only opened at 8:00am – but she walked over to the entrance and hoped for some kind of miracle.

When she arrived, she found her miracle in the form of a janitor exiting the building through one of the side doors. She waved at him to keep the door open, and asked him for directions to the principal's office from there. She was grateful for his help, because she made it to Mrs. White's office by 7:40am. Hala had not yet arrived, so she sat in the waiting area and read her book of supplications and prayed. She sought God's protection and guidance. Five minutes later, Mrs. White walked out of her office and was taken aback to find Mrs. Magda already sitting in the waiting area.

"Oh, hi! I was just going out to open up the main entrance for you. How did you get in?" she asked.

"I found a janitor exiting from the side door, so I asked him to show me the way from there. I got lucky, I guess," she explained.

"Well, great! Come on in. By the way, I asked Mr. Marron, the middle school principal, and Mr. Schwartz, the elementary principal, to join us. They will be here in twenty minutes. I hope that's ok with you," she said.

"Sure, it's no problem at all. I'll start off with my presentation and when they join I can brief them on everything," Mrs. Magda said.

"Perfect!" Mrs. White smiled.

As Mrs. Magda sat down in the principal's office, she realized that Mrs. White looked exhausted. It was the first time she'd looked at Mrs. White beyond her strong and broad physique. Like, *really* looked at her. She noticed the dark circles under her fierce blue eyes and her rigid features.

"Well… Let's get started?" Mrs. White suggested, looking at her watch.

"Yes. Sure. So, first I would like to address the key issues to ensure the healthy development of all students. The administration needs to create a mindful curriculum at school. Professionals must commit to nurturing their social, emotional and physical wellbeing."

"Yes, I agree, and I totally understand why you say that. Current research and studies prove that this is the best way to maximize children's learning."

"Good. I'm glad you agree and understand that," Mrs. Magda said, feeling relieved that she didn't have to debate with her. Mrs. Magda firmly believed that any professional in the field of education had the responsibility to regularly update themselves with the latest research and information about it. So many findings had already indicated that the conventional and traditional way of schooling actually had a negative impact on all children, and that the advent of technology would one day make it obsolete. "To achieve this, Mrs. White, we need to make changes to create a more bicultural environment at school," Mrs. Magda continued. "I propose that the school should offer Arabic Calligraphy as a core class to all students. Bilingual education will benefit the cognitive abilities of all children. Also, the class will enhance their physical, creative and spiritual development."

"Well, this is an American school, Magda. Students come here to learn English. They can take up a foreign language if they like, but students have to adapt to what we teach them. If they don't like it, they will have to find another school. And there are plenty of schools in this country that offer Arab history and Arabic language classes," Mrs. White responded.

"I'm sorry, but let me remind you that your school is not located in America, but in Cairo, Egypt. Your school needs to be culturally appropriate. You know this is what current evidence-based research recommends. You know this is what inspectors are looking for now. You hired me to help you become more 'culturally appropriate', and that cannot be achieved without real changes," Mrs. Magda said firmly. She couldn't believe the nerve of Mrs. White. How could she not understand? How could she not see that the school was not bicultural, but rather the complete opposite?

"I understand what you are trying to say. But these are our values. Our edge lies in maintaining an American and International curriculum only."

"No. You do not practice what you preach. In fact, you contradict what you preach. You have an issue at this school. The Egyptian children are not assimilating well. This has created many problems in the past, and it will continue to do so if you do not address this now. Your teachers seem to think the problem is with the Egyptians, and that this has been the case since the school opened its doors in 1949. What they do not realise is that the problem is with the school and its environment, and *not* the students," Mrs. Magda said, trying to figure out how anyone could fail to see that. To think that the issue was with every single Egyptian who had attended the school throughout the decades was delusional, and the assumptions teachers had about them were simply deranged.

"Oh, really! And how is that so?"

"Can't you see for yourself how Egyptians at this school have nothing to do with Egypt and Egyptians? They can't even speak their own language! They only care about Americanizing themselves in order to fit in. Don't you see it in the way they slur their words, sway when they walk and relax in their baggy clothes?"

"Well, I do see that the Egyptians at this school are not like the ones I meet outside of it. But that has nothing to do with the school. It's more of a trend that is affecting the whole world. More people are becoming Americanized, and the American culture has become a strong force influencing many. The more people know of it, the more they want to be a part of it. And that's why the students in school are more Americanized than others."

"Oh, please. You know that's not true. Then how come the American students themselves are not as Americanized as the Egyptian ones?" Mrs. Magda argued.

"Because they *are* American. They don't need to prove anything."

"Exactly my point! The Egyptian students feel the need to *prove something*. And you know what that something is, right?"

"What?"

"They want to be cool. They want to be *so* cool."

"What does that have to do with being American?"

"They believe that by being American, they will be cool."

"Is this a joke?"

"Do you see me laughing?"

"No. But seriously, is it that bad?"

"'Bad' is putting it nicely. A profound crisis of identity is what is really going on with these students. Cognitive dissonance is what will happen to them after they graduate."

"Then what do you suggest?" Mrs. White asked.

"I suggest taking the necessary steps needed to create a bicultural environment. And there is no better way to do this than to introduce Arabic as a core requirement. My idea is to provide this opportunity through Arabic Calligraphy. It will offer a holistic discovery of the art, and will include its historical and spiritual aspects. And the amazing thing about this is that it is a low-cost solution," Mrs. Magda said, confident that her idea was the perfect answer to the problem.

"I'm sorry, Mrs. Magda, but this is going to be impossible to introduce as a core requirement. Students can learn about Arab Calligraphy in art or Egypt Culture Class. We offer these classes once a week. I can make this request to all teachers in both departments," Mrs. White said, rolling her eyes.

"I'm sorry, but I will not accept this as a solution. It will not work. My role here is to help make this school bicultural. So the school must represent both cultures equally. That's why Arabic Calligraphy will have to be a core class," Mrs. Magda responded. She was adamant that she would stand her ground. She could not *believe* how stubborn Mrs. White was being. How could she not understand that the creation of a bicultural environment required both cultures to be of equal importance and weight? Balance was key in this school, where the American culture was obviously tipping the scale.

"I don't know what to say, Magda..." Mrs. White said as Mr. Marron and Mr. Schwartz walked in.

"Hello. Sorry we're late, but we both had a few things to finish up before joining y'all," Mr. Schwartz said as he sat down.

"No worries, Brad. I already explained this to Mrs. Magda before we started the meeting," Mrs. White said.

"Ok. So can you brief us about what you've already discussed?" Mr. Schwartz requested.

"Sure," Mrs. White said. "Mrs. Magda believes we need to create a bicultural environment at school. She suggests we do this by offering Arabic Calligraphy as a core class. She says that this will be positive for the holistic development of all students, and that it will decrease the behavioral issues with the Egyptian students."

"I'm sorry, Mrs. Magda, but I think it would be a big mistake if we decided to change our curriculum. We cannot make it appropriate to Egyptian culture. We have standards that we need to maintain," Mr. Marron said.

"The standards that you need to maintain require that you dispel your assumptions, and be up-to-date with the latest evidenced-based research on education. Studies have indicated that everything you are doing is wrong. The science proves it. That's why the International Knowledge Authority are making it mandatory that schools become culturally appropriate," Mrs. Magda said, thinking that she would write all of this in the teachers' survey during inspection time. Did they think that this was a joke, or what? Mrs. Magda had earned her Master's Degree in Education with a specialization in anti-bias education. This was her passion. And she could not stay silent about the biased education in school anymore.

"Yes, and it was on that basis we hired you. That is how much change we are willing to make for this year, at least. Sorry we cannot do more," Mr. Schwartz said as he crossed his hands and stared up at the ceiling.

Mrs. Magda realized that Mr. Schwartz was a cold and disconnected human being. He could not even look her in the eye when he spoke to her. It worried her that the principal of Elementary was so insincere. She wondered how this affected the professionals, staff and young children at his school.

Mr. Marron seemed to be rigid in his behavior as well. It was obvious that he suffered from a superiority complex. His aura exuded arrogance. But unlike Mr. Schwartz, he was not aloof. Rather, he was aggressive. It concerned Mrs. Magda that he was not understanding and cooperative.

After taking a moment to think, Mrs. Magda said, "I'm sorry, but this does not work for me. I hope we can cooperate and come to a better solution. You have to address the *major* issue with Egyptian students at your school."

"Well, as of right now, I won't be able to provide more support. Maybe what I can do is have further meetings with the CEO of the school, and then we can talk about it later," Mrs. White said.

"Sure. I would appreciate that," Mrs. Magda said.

"Ok. I'll get back to you about this."

"Great! Ok, thank you for your time today. I'd better get going now so I won't be late for my next class," Mrs. Magda said, glancing at the clock hanging on the wall of Mrs. White's office.

Mrs. Magda was in a hurry to get to her class and out of Mrs. White's office. She had never felt so weak, defeated and small in her life. She didn't know why she'd let herself get intimidated by them. She was so shaken, and started to doubt her own abilities.

As Mrs. Magda walked to the high school building, she felt her stomach flip. She had never felt so humiliated before. She didn't understand why they seemed so uninterested in her proposal. If anything, she felt that her ideas and research were not welcomed and something they would probably mock later. Her arms weakened at the thought of that. She didn't know where she was going to find the strength to teach her next class. At that moment, she decided it might be best to take a few days off. She wanted to have time to recover from the stress and pressure that she had been under. She would email her students to let them know about her short break, and encourage them to brainstorm positive solutions for the issue at the library.

Meanwhile, back at Mrs. White's office, the three principals decided to ignore Mrs. Magda's proposal. They predicted that she would forget about it in a couple of weeks. They spent the rest of their time discussing the upcoming barbecue event that Mr. Schwartz was hosting it at his house the following weekend; everyone was looking forward to it.

When Mr. Schwartz and Mr. Marron left, Mrs. White asked Hala to throw Mrs. Magda's proposal in the trash.

Little did Mrs. Magda know that she would not hear from the principal or the CEO. After she returned to school from her short break, she realised that her wait to meet the CEO was in vain. Whenever she asked Hala or Mrs. White for any updates, the answer was always that the CEO was busy or traveling.

In the meantime, Mrs. Magda focused her attention on her students and classes. In fact, her students' creative response to the library issue took her mind off things for a little while. When they discussed it upon her return, it was a very intense class, with emotions running high. Mrs. Magda was surprised when Ossama told her that he did not know what to make of it. He played Ben Harper's "People Lead" to the whole class so they could better understand how he felt. He even wrote some of the lyrics on a huge sheet of construction paper, as they spoke the words he could not say. And now, beside the entrance of Mrs. Magda's classroom, hung these words of truth:

> *So as long as someone else controls your history*
> *the truth shall just remain a mystery*
> *for you can lead a horse to the water*
> *and not make him drink*
> *you can put a man through school*
> *and not make him think.*

Ossama believed that this was the first time in his life that he had learned how to actually think for himself. Snapping out of the delusion that he'd been living all these years was no easy process. But it was fortunate that Mrs. Magda was there for him, as were Maha, Laila and Mahmoud. This made unlearning everything that they had learned somewhat more manageable. After going through the stages of denial, anger and finally acceptance, the group decided that they must create awareness about this issue. So they created a club, called the "Christopher Columbus Did NOT Discover America Club". The club promoted anti-bias education, and their goal was to show how many people around the world were miseducated. The plan was to redress misinformed information. For example, in many schools, teachers taught students that the primary colors were green, blue and red, when in fact cyan, magenta and yellow were the true primary colors. The same went for believing that Pablo Picasso was the father of Cubism, when in fact it was Georges Braque.

Maha challenged Mrs. Magda most frequently, for it did not satisfy her to just spread awareness. She wanted to know more about the non-Western perspective, specifically the Arab one. She wanted to see the Arab world eye-to-eye. In an attempt to encourage this, Mrs. Magda recommended that she do some research outside of school. Her objective was to learn about a prominent figure in Egypt's modern history.

After days of researching and going to different old libraries, Maha became intrigued by a man called Nabil Ali. He was considered to be the prodigy of the Arab tech world, and had created the most advanced software and programs in speech technologies and linguistic database search engines. As Vice President of Research and Development at Sakhr Software, he was able to create fast and accurate Arabic and English linguistic translating engines. Maha hoped more books would be written about this man simply because there were not enough. She believed that he should go down in Egypt and the Arab world's history as the man who brought the Arabic language into the digital age. This genius of a man became a true inspiration for Maha.

Mrs. Magda was impressed to see her classroom becoming a place filled with active and engaged learners. It crossed her mind to point out to her students the drastic change in their learning behavior since the first day of class, but she decided to keep that to herself. She believed there was no use in bringing up that part of the past now, because their progress was so obvious to everyone. And it was nice, in such moments, to leave things unsaid.

In spite of this success, Mrs. Magda could not bear the weight of her disappointment in the administration. It had a negative impact on her motivation, and little by little, she lost the desire and hope of creating change at school. At that point, the thought of real change was nothing more than a farfetched dream. Mrs. Magda hit rock bottom. She lost her appetite. She rarely slept. And she was always irritable. The only thing she could do was pray to God for a miracle.

But even the reality of that seemed faint, because the situation at school took a turn for the worse during the time of the October 6 national holiday. The Egyptian staff and students discovered that school was to resume on that day, despite the fact that the whole country was to take a day off. Of course, when word spread, all the Egyptians at school fumed. Students decided to unite with the Egyptian staff, security and janitors to protest against it.

A petition was circulated and signed, but the administration soon discarded it. They sent a letter to everyone explaining why they could not have a holiday on October 6. Their reason was that a certain number of school days were needed to complete a whole academic year, and having October 6 as a holiday would jeopardize that. It would impact on everybody, especially the graduating seniors.

Saddened by the rejection of their request, many Egyptians did not show up at school that day. Even though this event upset Mrs. Magda, the way all Egyptians had united impressed her. They had finally gathered the courage to face the administration, and that, for her, was the first step in a positive direction. The administration might have rejected Mrs. Magda's proposal and stalled making changes, but something about this incident made her feel that change was going to happen soon. Maybe they were going to learn the reality of what they mocked. The thought of that made Mrs. Magda realize that she needed to stand up and put up a fight for what she believed in to create the change needed. She just didn't know if she had the strength to do it, especially since the administration clenched its iron fist towards any kind of change. And it was that iron fist that made Mrs. Magda feel stuck and hopeless.

CHAPTER TWENTY-ONE

Maha was so keen to start her lunch break soon, but she still had half an hour left until then. She needed to occupy herself with something, because she had finished her research work for English class way before everyone else. She didn't understand why she was still forced to stay in the library in spite of having completed everything. She decided to sit at a table beside the side exit and read her book, but that plan came to an end when Marwan joined her.

"Hey… Am I interruptin' somethin'?" Marwan asked as he grabbed a chair and sat beside her.

"No, not really. I was just trying to find something to do until lunch break. I'm done with all my work," Maha said as she put her book down.

"Yeah, me too. It's really annoying that we can't leave the library until Mrs. Hamilton excuses us."

"It's so Pre-K of her. Don't you think?"

"Totally."

"I guess it is what it is," Maha laughed.

"So what's up with you?"

"Nothing much. You?"

"Nothing much either. I'm just super excited about the winter trip to Luxor and Aswan and the social event."

"*Really?* That's like months away, Marwan," Maha said, shocked to hear that from him. She wondered why it was so difficult for her to be easily excited about these things. *Why was it so hard to be jovial about socials?*

"I know. But you know me. I always like to have something fun to look forward to."

"Ugh, Marwan. I feel like I'm the anti-fun whenever I speak to you."

"Hahaha!"

"Laugh away, Marwan. Go ahead! Laugh away," Maha said, hardly able to believe that he was agreeing with her. *Was she really Mrs. Anti-Fun?*

"Oh please, don't get me wrong! You are who you are, Maha! And I love that about you."

Uh-oh, Maha thought to herself. She felt very uncomfortable when guys expressed what they loved about her, because she never knew how to respond. She didn't want to risk anything getting back to Fahmy and his crew.

"Hmm. Oh please, Marwan!"

"Please what?"

"Please stop."

"Stop what? I didn't get started yet!"

"What are you talking about? You wanted to start something?"

"Yeah."

"What?"

"You."

"*Me?*" Maha gasped, shocked that Marwan was speaking to her that way. *What had gotten into him?* Maha's heart skipped a beat and she started to panic. She didn't want Fahmy to know about any of this. Unless time could fast-forward itself, she needed to find a way out of this conversation.

"Yes you, Maha. I really like you. And I want to us to be together."

Be together? Was he crazy? Had he lost his mind? Did he not know that Fahmy could ruin his life for this?

"Marwan, stop joking and fooling around!"

"I'm not! I have never been more serious in my life. I want you."

What had gotten into this crazy boy? Maha started to palpitate. Her palms got sweaty. She fidgeted in her seat. The only thing she wanted in her life at that point was to get out of there.

"I'm sorry, Marwan. But you know we can't be together."

"No, I don't! What do you mean, no?"

"What do *you* mean by what do I mean no? A no is a no!"

"*What?* You are telling me *no?*"

"Yes. I'm telling you no!"

"I can't believe this. You are telling me no?" he repeated.

"I can't believe that you can't believe this," Maha said. This was getting ridiculous. How could he not see that she was actually doing him a favor? Fahmy would seriously ruin him for this. Maha could only hope that one day, Marwan would thank her for this and see that she was actually protecting him.

"Of course I can't! How can you tell me no?"

"It really has nothing to do with you, Marwan. It has everything to do with me. I'm really sorry. I hope you understand one day," Maha said, wishing he would stop.

"Sure. Yeah. Whatever, after I've been demolished," he muttered, looking dejected.

"Please don't... I'm so sorry. I really have to go," Maha said as she realized that it was time for lunch break. She grabbed all her stuff and ran out of the library towards the bathroom. She locked herself in the stall and cried. She didn't know why she was crying, exactly. Was it because she'd hurt his feelings? Or because she was scared Fahmy would find out? Perhaps it was the pressure Fahmy put on her? Or that she was going to miss out on doing something that everybody around her was doing? All cried out, she knew that whatever the reason, she had to collect herself and go on with her day as if nothing had happened.

But that was never going to be possible at a school where word of mouth travelled faster than the speed of light.

Maha walked out of the high school building and instantly felt a difference in the way everyone looked at her.

"Oh yeah... There she goes! Heartbreaker," Maha heard someone say.

"No, you mean a flirt who leads people on," she heard another say. Maha didn't want to give in to her paranoia and assume it was about her, so she was very curious to find out who they were talking about. Then a few minutes later, Leena, Sylvia and Mariam came running towards her.

"What happened, Maha? Is it true about you and Marwan?" Mariam asked breathlessly.

"*What?* Me and Marwan what?" Maha asked. She panicked. Her heart trembled with fear. Her hands shook with tremors like waves. All she could think about was Fahmy and her father. Suddenly, her chest started to feel tight.

"Yeah. Yasmine just told us about what happened. She's really worried about you. She's looking for you," Sylvia said.

"Yasmine? Looking for *me*?" Maha asked, wondering why Yasmine was telling everyone about her and Marwan without talking to her first. That wasn't the behavior of someone who was really "worried". It didn't make sense that she would spread a story she hadn't confirmed yet if she was truly worried about her. *Wasn't it ironic for Yasmine, her best friend of 10 years, to be the source, if not the reason, of gossip about her?*

"Yeah, apparently she is concerned about you," Leena confirmed.

"Obviously," Maha said sarcastically.

"So what happened?" Mariam pressed her.

"Nothing much. Marwan and I talked after we finished our work early last period and he told me that he really likes me and wants us to be together."

"Oh no! Is he insane?" Sylvia gasped.

"He's probably got amnesia! Did he forget about Fahmy or what?" Mariam said.

"My thoughts exactly! I was very straightforward with him and told him no. I didn't explain to him why, though," Maha said.

"I guess this explains why Yasmine is saying you are a heartbreaker!" Leena said.

"*What*? Yasmine said that?" Maha asked.

"Yeah, and that you led him on!" Leena said.

"*What*? I don't understand why she would do that," Maha exclaimed.

"We don't, either," Mariam said.

"But she voiced her concern to everyone. She thinks you're slipping. Especially after the Ahmed incident in Coco Jungle, according to her."

"Ahmed incident? She knows the truth! He pursued me and I was trying to get out of it!" Maha said.

"Well, not according to her! She's also very worried about your smoking," Sylvia reported.

"She's the one who convinced me to smoke in the first place!" Maha said, wishing that her denial defensive mechanism would kick in. *How could Yasmine do this to her? And why?* There must be an explanation for all this. Maha was determined to speak to her first before jumping to any conclusions. The thought of losing another childhood friend so early in the school year killed her. She knew something like this would damage her for life, and that it would be irreparable. Everything was going wrong in such a short time period. Maha wondered if this was what divine storms looked and felt like.

"I know… And isn't it ironic that she and the rest of the girls want to do an intervention with you?" Leena asked.

"Exactly! They are the ones who date, drink and smoke and do way more than you, and yet *they* want to have an intervention with *you*," Mariam said.

"And why? Because they think you're 'slipping' even though they have slipped already," Sylvia said.

"I have to go speak to Yasmine," Maha said.

"Don't. You know how she is with confrontation," Leena cautioned her.

"No. I have to talk to her," Maha insisted.

"Please don't. You have to be careful," Leena said.

"Yes, please!" Sylvia agreed.

"What, you want me to quiet about this?" Maha asked.

"Just for now," Mariam pleaded.

"Let the melodrama that Yasmine created pass," Leena said.

"To be honest, I don't know if I can," Maha said, knowing that she couldn't stand the thought of pretending to be ok with Yasmine after all this.

"Let's talk about this after school, Maha," Leena said.

"Fine," Maha said. "I have to go now. I want to talk to Fahmy."

She was very lucky to find Fahmy, Yusuf and Seif hanging out at the kiosk. Maha felt her nerves rattle with fear at the thought of what she had to do next. But strangely enough, Fahmy was so happy to see her. Maybe he hadn't heard yet of what had gone down between her and Marwan.

"Hey, cuz," Fahmy greeted her.

"Hey, guys," Maha said.

Hey, M," Yusuf and Seif said.

"You ok? You don't look ok," Fahmy asked.

"Umm, yeah... I wanted to talk to you about something, but I don't know if this is the right time," Maha said hesitantly.

"Sure it is! But anyway, I think I know what you want to talk about," Fahmy said.

"You *do*?" Maha gasped.

"Yes."

"What is it?"

"Marwan."

"Exactly."

"Well, the guys and I want you to know that we are very proud of you! We are so happy that you put him in his place. That jerk crossed the line with you."

"Oh! You *are*?" Maha was so relieved to hear that. She was glad that they all knew she'd had nothing to do with it.

"Yeah! Good for you! Don't worry about the talk that's going on! We'll take care of that."

"You bet!" Seif agreed.

"Yeah, you bet! I'll personally make sure that Yasmine never talks about you again!" Yusuf said.

"Really?" Maha said as the tears welled up in her eyes. She was shocked by all this betrayal.

"For real, Maha. I want you to know that I never really liked Yasmine in the first place! She just talks and is full of drama." Yusuf said.

"What are you going to do?" Maha asked.

"Leave that to me. Please," Yusuf insisted.

"Sure," Maha said. She was glad for this unconditional support at that moment in her life. She suddenly realized that what had happened did not mean anything to her anymore. It was a good idea not to confront Yasmine about what happened. She did not want to feed into her drama. In the meantime, she planned to let anybody who told her that she needed an intervention know that *they* were the ones who needed it. It was at moments like this that Maha yearned for people to follow their own advice first.

Yasmine did not go home with Maha that day. She was apparently invited out to dinner with her stepsisters. And for that, Maha's attitude was gratitude for the rest of the day.

But that changed as soon as Maha arrived home. She immediately knew that there was something wrong when she didn't find her family sitting at the dining table and eating. She walked over to her parents' bedroom and was shocked when she didn't find them inside. She then went to Ayah's room and found her in tears, with Maya trying to calm her down.

Maha's heart beat so fast. She could sense that this was not good.

"Ayah, what is wrong?" Maha asked.

"Nothing, Maha," Ayah said through her tears.

"How is it nothing?" Maha asked. "Tell me what's going on!"

"Nothing, really. It's all going to be ok."

"*What* is going to be ok?" Maha asked furiously.

"Nothing much. It's baba."

"What? What's wrong with him? Is he ok?" Maha gasped, suddenly gripped with worry about her dad.

"Yes, he will be fine," Ayah said.

"Tell me what happened!" Maha demanded, ticked off at the suspense that her sister was creating.

"He fell while he was walking on the street. When he went to the hospital to make sure that he was ok, the doctors discovered that he'd had a heart attack," Ayah explained.

"*What*? Baba had a heart attack?" Maha screamed in disbelief. "Where is he now?"

"He's at the hospital. He has to stay there tonight. The doctor left him all day without explaining his condition to him. We just got through to him now!"

"What kind of doctor does that?" Maha asked, furious. "That's so unprofessional and unethical. His license should be revoked for stressing out patients with a heart condition."

"Calm down, Maha," Maya said.

"No! What is this nonsense? What did mama do?"

"Nothing. She called baba's doctor in Paris."

"And?"

"And the plan is for him to travel there tomorrow so he can operate."

"What is he going to do?"

"An open-heart surgery."

"Oh God! I can't believe this!" Maha said shakily, trying to take a moment to collect herself. This could not have happened to her dad! Not her dad! She hadn't realized how much she loved her dad until this very moment. She couldn't care less about anything else in the world, be it a university degree from an Ivy League school or whatever. Because all she wanted to do was to see her dad happy, healthy and strong again! That was the only thing she wanted. Everything else meant nothing to her.

"I know," Ayah said.

"I have to go to him at the hospital," Maha said.

"Ok, try to go quickly, because visiting hours end in two hours. I'll go down in a bit."

Maha dropped her bag in her room and ran out of the house. She got into her car and zoomed to the hospital where her dad was. She was relieved to find him awake. She ran in as soon as she got to his room and hugged him. He hugged her back for what seemed like an eternity.

"I'm fine, dear," he assured her.

"I'm sure you are. You are very strong," she said.

"No, not anymore," he said.

"Don't ever say that. You are *so* strong. And I'm so proud of you," Maha said, wondering if he knew that he was the king of all hearts. It was strange for her to discover that he did not realize how beautiful of a heart he had. It was so beautiful that no attack or blockage could harm it or him.

"You are the man of all men," Maha heard her mom tell him.

"So true, baba!" Maha could not agree more and was so happy to see him smile.

At that point, the nurses came in to check his blood pressure and glucose level. Maha left the room to answer her vibrating phone. It was Mahmoud. He'd just wanted to chat a bit, but Maha explained to him what had happened to her dad. Mahmoud insisted that he pass by her at the hospital, and Maha was touched by his support. When she walked back into the room, she saw Ayah, Maya and another lady with them.

"Maha, this is my friend Lisa," Ayah said.

"Nice to meet you, Maha," Lisa said.

"Nice to meet you, too," Maha responded.

"Lisa insisted on passing by when she found out that I couldn't go to today's workshop," Ayah explained.

"That's very nice of you, Lisa," Maha said.

"Oh no, it's nothing at all. This is the least I can do," Lisa insisted.

After about 30 minutes of conversation, Maha looked up to see Mahmoud and Mrs. Magda walk into the room.

"Mahmoud! Mrs. Magda!" Maha exclaimed, surprised to see her teacher.

"Hi, dear. I hope you don't mind that I came up with Mahmoud. I bumped into him at the reception downstairs. I was here to pick up my husband's blood test results."

"Oh! What a coincidence! Of course I don't mind. I'm so happy to see you. Please let me introduce you to my family. This is Mrs. Magda, my new TOK teacher."

"Very nice to meet you! We've heard so much about you," her mom said.

Mahmoud sat beside Maha and the group fell into easy conversation. For a moment, Maha could not believe how this experience had turned out to be one great big family affair. It was typical in Egypt that everyone considered each other family, even if they were not related by blood. Just like birds that flock together, Arabs liked to stick and move together. It was how many individuals developed their own sense of entitlement. On that day, as Maha looked at everyone around her, she felt blessed to have many sisters and brothers. And she realized that it was these little things that made the 'family' way of life the only and best way to live in Egypt and the Arab world.

That week, Maha lived on the edge as her father traveled to Paris for treatment. After conducting the necessary tests at the American Hospital, the doctors discovered that Maha's dad did not have to undergo open-heart surgery. Instead, the surgeons decided to put three stents in the place of the blockages. Maha's dad was relieved that he did not have to have major surgery.

In the meantime, back in Cairo, things were a bit more stable for Maha. Even Yasmine was drama-free. She texted Maha and offered all her support. So it was only inevitable that Maha decided to drop the issue with Yasmine. Maha realized that, especially during life-changing moments, there were many things that were simply not worth it. Anger, hatred and negativity were three of them. So, in a show of support, Yasmine spent hours with Maha cruising the streets of Cairo that week. Cruising had become their new tradition that brought them close once again. It was strange how music and car rides solidified their lifelong friendship. Maha was grateful, for she did not know how she could've survived without Yasmine's support.

Maha was overjoyed when her father returned back home with her mother and sister after about two weeks. On the day they arrived, Maha ran to the door and opened it for them. She hugged them all so tight. That day, she felt how deep her love was for her family. Her face lit up when she saw her father smile. To her, he was the king of all hearts. His love for his family and life was what could make his heart pump blood through the tightest of blockages, even if it meant that it had to squeeze through one drop at a time. Nothing in this world could stop this man from loving.

"I'm so glad you're back," she told her family.

"Us, too," her dad said as he walked to the TV room and sat on the couch.

Maha's mom, Ayah and Maha followed. Mary walked in to ask if anybody wanted something to drink or eat.

"Yes please, Mary," Maha's mom said. "Please make us some Arabic coffee and bring us some of the fresh dates that I got from Saudi Arabia last month."

"Ok, Madam," Mary said.

About 15 minutes later, the smell of the cardamom in the Arabic coffee filled the air.

"How nice. I love this smell," Ayah said as she got up and took the tray with four small cups of Arabic coffee and a box of rich Arabian dates.

"Wow, it tastes so good," her father said as he sipped from his cup and took a bite from his date.

"This *feels* so good," Maha said, excited to be embracing the beauty of her Arabic roots and feeding her soul with it. "I have to admit, there is nothing better in the world than this: sitting here with family, enjoying our Arabic coffee and dates."

"True," Maha's dad said.

"All we need is some Om Kalthoum," Ayah added.

"Oh wait, let me get that," Maha said as she quickly went to her room and found her Om Kalthoum CD. She put it in the Sony CD player and played "A Thousand and One Nights."

"Yaaa Alf laila we laila," Maha's dad said.

"Yes, what a timeless classic," Maha's mom agreed.

"So true," Ayah said.

"Too bad they don't make music like this anymore," Maha said as she appreciated the rhythm of Arabian sounds. It occurred to her that it was fleeting but perfect moments like this that made her wish she had the power to put life on pause.

CHAPTER TWENTY-TWO

Thursday, October 28, 1999
Egypt

Time passed at a slow pace throughout the rest of October and November. The gloom of winter had crept in. And in this case, it stole the light from everyone. The change of season was the culprit of this doom, and nobody could do anything about it. Mrs. Magda noticed that even Maha, Mahmoud, Ossama and Laila did not have what it took to fight it. They were not immune to its gloomy effects.

Mrs. Magda was so right in her observation, because it was during this time that Maha became a chain-smoker. Smoking helped her to escape from having to deal with the changes she couldn't face. Her pack of Marlboros was her crutch that she leaned on to get through it all. Smoking gave her the few minutes she needed to put everything in her life on pause. She smoked before and after school, and during lunch break. She even quit Cross Country. Her body bore witness to this toxic habit, and she got severe chest pains whenever she ran. So instead of quitting smoking, she quit running.

Everything else stayed pretty much the same. Sultan, well, he never replied to her message, and they ignored each other at school. Ahmed continued to pursue Maha. He even pressured Yasmine to help him get close to her. He had trouble forgetting her and their night at Coco Jungle. But Maha made it clear to him that she could not commit. Besides the fact that Fahmy and Yusuf could find out, she did not want to live another lie with her parents. It was enough that they didn't know she smoked. And anyway, they would never accept it. The idea of Maha dating was against their family values.

As for her friends, they were upset that Maha had distanced herself. But she could not hide from the fact that hanging out with them made her sick. Like, *literally* sick. Nauseous was how she always felt after their group outings. One time, she got especially ill after spending three hours listening to the girls talk about Sylvia. They criticized and judged literally everything about her – the way she talked, walked, dressed and even ate. When Sylvia joined the group later, as if by magic, suddenly everyone was friendly and nice to her, even complimenting her about the stuff they had criticized earlier. Maha couldn't tell which group suffered more – so-called white liars, or actual brown-nosers?

Anyway, in the midst of all this chaos, two things brought inner peace to Maha. Well, besides the smoking. The first was her art. She was busy preparing for the end-of-year I.B. Art exhibition. The second was her good friend Seif. He was the best thing that could've happened to her at the time. He was so Egyptian, and absolutely fine with that. If there had been a competition for the person least affected by an identity crisis at school, Seif would've won it. He was so cool that he was so Egyptian.

As for Mahmoud, bad luck hit him hard as he injured his left knee during one of his soccer games. His doctor had ordered that he rest it for at least three months, and that was enough for him to give up on his dream of pursuing a soccer career. Try-outs in England were taking place at that time, but his dad was not the obstacle anymore – his knee was. And for now, it was the hands of fate and God's doing that brought him his destiny. It was difficult for him to accept at first, so he resisted. He pushed himself to recover fast. But when that did not happen, he surrendered. Inspired by Maha, he too believed that perhaps what he hated was good for him.

Things with Ossama and Laila were pretty much the same. With time, Ossama changed his opinion about having a music career. He agreed with his parents, and this eased the tension between them. The only thing changing in Laila's life was that she was getting closer to Sultan. In fact, they were becoming almost inseparable.

When the last week of November arrived, excitement filled the air. The winter trip to Luxor and Aswan was just a couple of weeks away, and everyone looked forward to the change.

Even Mrs. Magda. She was going through a tough time at school and at home. The former was because she hadn't had any response from the administration about her proposal. The latter was because Saneya had suffered a family crisis, so Mrs. Magda could not rely on her help with the house on a regular basis anymore. Managing both work and home in Cairo was beyond challenging, almost nerve-wracking. But despite this, Mrs. Magda supported Saneya and her family through their tough time. Apparently, Saneya's husband, a delivery driver at McDonalds, had gotten into a legal issue with the company and was going to get fired. His colleague had falsely accused him of ruining one of the delivery motorcycles. Of course, the branch manager had to set up an investigation to find out exactly what had happened. After a few weeks of interrogations, it became obvious to everyone that Saneya's husband was innocent. The truth, according to many witnesses, was that one of the street children had accidentally bumped into the motorcycle and it fell. In an attempt to protect the children from any harm, Saneya's husband offered to pay for the damages. But the branch manager refused, and assured him that their insurance would cover the costs.

In the meantime, Saneya and her husband had gotten to know Zainab, the sister of the boy who'd bumped into the motorcycle. She was quite a charismatic character. Saneya could not stop talking about her to Mrs. Magda. She was so intrigued by Saneya's stories that she decided to go and meet Zainab where she cleaned cars next to McDonalds. When they met, Zainab talked to her about her family's plan to get themselves out of poverty. When Mrs. Magda found out that the family had been saving to build their own kiosk and that they were EGP 3,000 short, she decided to give them the money as part of the almsgiving that she was supposed to make for the Holy Month of Ramadan. It was coming up very soon anyway, and she had already considered the different charities to which she wanted to donate. Zainab was flabbergasted by her generosity and, according to what Mrs. Magda heard later, so was her family. It made Mrs. Magda happy to know that she'd made a difference in one person's life, let alone a whole family's life.

That's why she was so ready to enjoy herself in Luxor and Aswan. She felt she was in dire need of a nice break. The plan for the trip was to visit Aswan first, followed by Luxor a few days later. In Luxor, there would be a black tie social event taking place after the Sound and Light Show at the Luxor Temple.

CHAPTER TWENTY-THREE

On the day that the winter trip was scheduled to leave, Maha woke up late. She'd slept in because she did not have to go to school until 2:00pm. She dragged herself out of bed and changed into her clothes. Then she tied her hair in a low bun and ate her cereal fast. She bid her parents farewell, and headed down to the car. Her driver took her to school to meet up with the rest of the group.

Luckily, the streets were empty and she got there in 20 minutes. But when she arrived, she suddenly realized that she'd forgotten her dress for the black tie event at home. Annoyed by her mindlessness, she did not know what to do. She could not call her mom, because then she would never hear the end of her 'you're-so-last-minute' lecture. So she told the driver to go back home and ask Mary to give him the folded black cover that was on the couch in her room, and then to meet her at the entrance of Terminal 1 in 40 minutes.

After the driver left, Maha turned around and walked towards the group. She was so relieved to see Mrs. Magda. She realized that for some odd reason, talking to Mrs. Magda made her happy.

"Good morning, Mrs. Magda," Maha greeted her.

"Good morning, Maha! How are you today?" Mrs. Magda asked her.

"I'm ok, just a bit annoyed with the fact that I forgot my dress for the black tie event at home," Maha told her.

"Oh no! I'm sorry to hear that! Did you find a way to get it?" Mrs. Magda asked.

"Yes, I asked my driver to go back home and get it. He will meet me at the airport," she said.

"Great. Well, let's get on the bus now."

When Maha turned around, she saw Sultan walking towards the group. He looked so fresh and clean, and smelled like cool waters. His still-wet, thick hair was brushed to the side. Maha noticed that there was something a bit different about him, and it had nothing to do with how he looked physically. Rather, it was the new attitude that he wore. It looked like a ruthless one.

And there and then, Sultan's new attitude became a reality when he held Laila's hand. *What was going on? How could her two best friends who don't talk to her anymore possibly be dating? How could Sultan do this to her?* Less confusion is what she had asked him for. She found no joy in this kind of confusion whatsoever. *Why did he do this to her? Did he really love Laila? Did Laila really love him? Did Laila not know that Sultan was* her *best friend?*

Maha did not understand why she felt the way she felt. She could not pretend anymore. She could not resist the truth any longer. She hated him! She hated everything about him and wanted nothing to do with him ever again! She hated how he had a hold on her! She hated nothing in the world more than him!

Just then, Maha saw Laila let go of his hand to pick up her bag. But of course, like any gentleman, he stopped Laila and picked the bag up instead. And at that moment, Maha saw what she should never have seen. She saw a new silver bracelet on Laila's wrist with her name written in English on it. Maha could *not believe* that piece of scum had told her about the bracelet. That bracelet thing was theirs. Hers and Sultan's. He'd wanted her to wear more jewelry, and she'd promised him that she would get a silver bracelet with her name on it just for him. Even though she'd never gotten it, she never thought he could ever do something like that! This was so twisted! *Ugh!*

"Hang in there! I know it's weird," Maha heard Leena say, interrupting her thoughts.

"You mean twisted! I *hate* him, Leena. I *can't staaaand* him!" Maha spat.

"I'm sure you do," Leena said. "Let it go, Maha."

"*Let it go?*" Maha exclaimed in disbelief. "I hate him! I *hate* him! How can I let it go?"

"I'm sure you do," Leena said again soothingly. "Just forget about it for now. Let's get on the bus, listen to some good music, or read a book or something."

"Fine," Maha said. "But first, I need to ask Mrs. Magda if I can exchange rooms in Luxor and Aswan. I will *not* be able to share a room with her after this."

"Maybe you can switch with Menna. She's rooming with me. That way, we can share a room, and they share theirs," Leena suggested.

"Great," Maha said. "Thanks, Leena."

"Anytime."

As soon as they got on the bus, Maha got her Discman out. She listened to Keith Sweat's "Twisted" as she read her book, *The Unbearable Lightness of Being*. And as she read Kundera's words, "Life's first rehearsal is life itself," she imagined how interesting life would be if there were second rehearsals. She would've certainly re-rehearsed going back with her driver to get her dress. That would've dramatically bettered her day.

By the time Maha arrived at the airport, her driver was there with her dress. She ran to him and took the dress, and hurried to catch up with the rest of the group. After they'd all checked in, Maha went up to Mrs. Magda to talk to her about her room situation with Laila.

"I'm sorry to do this now, Mrs. Magda, but I need to change my hotel room in Aswan and Luxor. I had arranged to stay with Laila, but for several reasons, I will not be able to do that now. Can I switch rooms with Menna, who is rooming with Leena?"

"Sure, don't worry about it. As soon as we check in at the hotel in Aswan, I'll make sure to document the changes," Mrs. Magda said. "All I'll need to do at the hotel is provide the passports with the correct room number."

"Great! Thank you, Mrs. Magda."

"You're most welcome, Maha."

Maha spent the rest of the trip as far away as possible from Sultan and Laila. She did everything she could to ensure that their paths did not cross. So she hung out with Leena, Mariam, Sylvia, Mahmoud, Yusuf, Seif and Fahmy. She appreciated their company.

When they arrived in Aswan, Laila discovered that Maha had switched rooms with Menna. It was obvious to everyone that this was the end of their friendship. And just like that, a decade-long friendship had vanished into a figment of vague memories. Even though Maha knew that forgiveness was necessary, being a fool was not, and Maha hated nothing more in the world than when people tried to play her for a fool.

Maha did her best to engage herself in the day's sightseeing. The Abu Simbel and Kom Ombo temples captured Egypt's wondrous ancient civilization. Maha did not enjoy visiting the Aswan High Dam as much as the Botanical Garden, which was home to many plants, flowers and trees from all over the world. It was a masterpiece of the intricate web of nature's beauty. Being there restored her faith in the power of life.

It was a relief for Maha that most of the places they visited were out in the open air. It helped her sneak out from time to time to have a quick smoke without anyone noticing. For the first time ever, she smoked a whole pack in one day. She was exhausted by the first day's excursions, and it was no wonder that by the time they got back to the hotel, Maha was the first to go to bed.

The next few days passed by slowly. Maha was fine as long as she did not have to see or deal with Sultan or Laila. When their third night in Aswan came to an end, they all prepared to leave for Luxor. They were expected to arrive there early the next day, and attend the black tie social event later that evening.

When the group arrived in Luxor, they discovered that there was no sightseeing scheduled for the day. They were free to spend the day as they pleased around the hotel. The only commitment they had was the Sound and Light Show at 6:00pm, and the black tie event afterwards.

Everyone was enthusiastic about the event, except for Maha. She couldn't be bothered to get ready early. She preferred to tan by the pool and listen to her music. Leena also didn't care much, so they hung out until 5:00pm. Leena and Maha seemed to be the outcasts of the group that day. Or maybe the truth was, it was more than just that day. Anyway, they preferred to listen to music, eat pizza and drink the sunshine than feed into social pressure.

At around 5:00pm, Maha and Leena headed to their room. On their way, they were shocked by the sight of everyone decked out in lavish dresses, blinged up with the kind of gold that was so brassy. Thick layers of make-up could not hide the face of desperation to get noticed.

Leena and Maha got to their room and got ready in no time. They were able to dry their hair, moisturize, get dressed and accessorize in just 20 minutes. Maha needed an extra five minutes because she wanted to style her hair in a low bun and put on her gold earrings. It was amazing that they joined the rest of the group in the lobby at the same time, even though everyone else had spent hours getting ready. Once they were there, they decided to go on the same bus as Yusuf and Fahmy to the Sound and Light Show.

When Maha got to the venue, she was in awe of the beauty of the Karnak temple. The Sound and Light Show was special because it recreated the magnificent life of Thebes. With the help of music and lights, the show told the story of the temple and the pharaohs who built it. Even though it was now understood that their command was misguided, it was interesting to learn about how they lived. The show was magnificent and breath-taking.

After the show ended, the group moved into a venue not far away from the temple, where the social event was to take place. It was nice, Maha thought – the food was great and the music was phenomenal. The DJ played a mix of hip hop and pop songs, and Maha loved most of it, especially when he played Blackstreet's "No Diggity" and The Notorious B.I.G's "Hypnotize" right after each other. Maha couldn't help but have a blast – nothing could uplift her quite like the sound of good music.

After the DJ turned up the heat with "Hypnotize", he slowed it down a bit with Mariah Carey's "When I Saw You". Maha wanted to avoid the awkwardness of standing alone while everyone else slow-danced with a partner, so she walked outside the venue to smoke a cigarette. As she walked out, she sang the words to the song out loud, trying to match Mariah's high voice: "*Soft heavenly eyes gazed into me. Transcending space and time. And I was rendered still. There were no words for me to find at all. As I stood there beside myself. I could see you and no one else.*"

As if through a quantum leap, Maha found the words of the song manifest into her reality. She caught sight of someone sitting alone in the dark, and she could not help but feel soft eyes gaze into her. Time and space stopped. She stood there by herself, and she could really see no one else but… Sultan. He was still as their eyes met. His stare lured her as he took her in. She fell prey to his gaze, for she could not resist him any longer. The silence between them was tantalizing and uncomfortable all at once. So she started to fidget, while he continued to stare.

"Hi…." Maha said, wanting to break the silence.

"Hey…" he said in a low voice.

"Ummm… I wanted to smoke a cigarette but I can't find my lighter…. I think… I, umm, better go back inside and find one," she stuttered, not understanding why she couldn't find words to speak.

"Sure," he said again in a low voice.

"Ok. Bye," Maha said as she turned around and walked away. That weird feeling was creeping into her gut again. Maha walked fast out of Sultan's sight. She opened up the door to enter the venue, and stood there searching for anyone she knew. She caught sight of Yusuf who, to her surprise, turned away after he made eye contact. Shaken by the sequence of events, Maha paused for a moment to try and absorb it all. Yusuf? She didn't understand why he would look away, let alone walk to the opposite end of the venue. *Why was he walking away from her now?* This was all too confusing for her.

She was rescued by the appearance of Leena. She found out from her that there were shuttle buses going back to the hotel, and that sounded like the perfect plan of action for Maha. She snuck out of one of the side doors, and was on the first bus back to the hotel. As she got on the bus, she realised that nothing in her life would ever be the same again. Like, *ever* again.

When Maha got to the hotel, she fetched her Discman from her room and then went to sit by the pool. Staying in the room would have been too claustrophobic for her. She was in dire need of fresh air. When she got there, she lay down on a sun bed and stared into the starry night. She must've dozed off at some point while listening to 112's "Cupid", because she was startled when she heard Ossama's voice.

"Early night or what?" he asked.

"Hmm… Ossama… you startled me," Maha said a little blearily as she sat up and rubbed her eyes.

"Oh, I didn't realize you were sleeping," he said.

"Me neither, if that makes you feel any better."

"Hahaha, I love your sarcasm," he chuckled. "So what are you doing here all by yourself? Why aren't you with the rest?"

"Umm… Well, because… I don't know… I guess I just wanted to be alone," she said as she shrugged her shoulders. The thought of Sultan made her run out of breath.

"Really…" he said.

"Yes, really."

"I know you're not like the rest of the girls," he observed.

"Oh yes, Ossama, please rub it in and remind me again how I'm so different from everyone else," she said irritably.

"Well, you are. I don't get why you deny it."

"I'm not. I'm just like them. Why is it so difficult for you to see?" she asked. What she really meant to ask was why he didn't see how hard she was trying to fit in. She remembered that it had never taken any 'effort' for her to get along with her friends until sometime last year. Maha believed that changed around the time when she saw the real world.

It was when she went with her mom to donate food to street children, homeless families and the underprivileged. It was an experience that had changed her life forever. One day after school, during Ramadan, Maha's mom had needed her help to donate the food. Maha had tried to talk her way out of going. She was exhausted from fasting and wanted to nap until the call to prayer to break her fast. But that was not an option with her mom that day. So she went with her mom and the driver in their old white Lada Niva. Maha rarely rode in that car unless she was in Agami, a popular summer destination next to Alexandria. Her father had wanted her to learn how to drive that car, because he believed that if she could master it, she could drive any other car in the world. Anyway, going in the Niva meant she was going to a real slum area because normally she would ride the Mercedes or Peugeot for any errand. Little did she know that this experience was going to change her forever.

When they arrived at the outskirts of Heliopolis, her mom saw some construction workers sitting at a roundabout. She asked the driver to stop the car. After he did and before he got out, he told her mom that he would lock the car and close all the windows. Maha did not understand what was going on. Her heart started to beat faster. She saw her driver call out for one of the construction workers, who ran to him quickly. When the driver gave him the box of food, Maha could not believe her eyes when a herd of no less than a hundred men ran towards the car. Hunger drove them to beat each other up and shake the car back and forth. Maha was stunned by the way the car swayed. She felt real fear for the first time in her life, the kind that makes courage look like a sarcastic joke. No return to her comfort zone would ever make her forget the distorted face of a hungry man pressed against her window. The men screamed for food.

Maha could not help but feel guilty for the privileges that God had given her that day. She wanted to leave. She wanted to run far away from it all. After an hour of sorting the food out, Maha, her mom and the driver had an awfully quiet ride home. It was on that day that Maha not only learned, but actually *saw* how the circumstance of one's birth determined the way they lived. How she was going to get over the guilt, she would never know. But that day had changed her, because deep down in her heart, she knew that she had to do something about it.

"You've changed, Maha, is what I mean to say. I don't mean it in a bad way," Ossama explained, snapping her out of her memories. His cell phone started ringing. "Hold on a sec…" He slipped the phone from his pocket and answered it. "Hello… Yeah, man… I'm at the hotel… At the pool…. Ok, ok. I'll wait for you here."

"What's up?" Maha asked as Ossama hung up.

"Nothing much. It was Yusuf. He's here and he's coming to join us."

"He's here? He's coming now?" Maha repeated as she started to panic. She wished that this day of suspense would come to an end.

"Yes, I am… I didn't know you were here," Yusuf said from behind Maha.

"Oh, hey…Yeah… Well, I just came here to chill…" Maha stumbled, surprised that he'd arrived so quickly. She started to get up, wanting to escape this awkward situation. "And I'd better get going now."

"No, no. It's ok," Yusuf said as he inched closer to her. He put his hand on her shoulder and then ran it down her back.

What was he doing? Maha could not believe this! Yusuf, Mr. Don't-Go-With-Guys-To-Bookstores preacher man, was actually *touching her back?* How insane was this all?

"No, no… I really have to go check on Leena, and I really need to finish reading my book for English class," she said in a rush.

"What book are you reading?" he asked.

"*The Unbearable Lightness of Being.*"

"Hmm, is it a good book?" he asked.

"Yes," she said, wondering why Yusuf was asking these questions. *What had gotten into him?*

"I'd like to read it one day," he said.

"Sure, I can lend it to you when I finish it."

"I'd love that."

"Yeah, sure."

"Good, well… I guess that will save me a trip to the bookstore," Yusuf said, staring at her intently.

"Huh? I don't know what are you talking about, Yusuf!" Maha said, shocked by him. "I really have to go… Bye, guys."

Maha turned around and ran out of their sight. All of a sudden, her whole world had gone blurry, making it difficult for her to find her way back. She realized the more she panicked, the greater the blur. So she stepped to the side of the promenade, knelt down, and took a deep breath. With her knees and head on the floor, she inhaled for four seconds, held it for seven, and exhaled for eight. She kept on repeating this calming exercise until she felt better. All the while, she prayed that God would help her see clearly.

The group returned to Cairo a few days later. Maha collapsed by the time she reached home. She had a terrible fever that reached 41 degrees Celsius. Her body ached so hard that it hurt her to sit, stand and even lie down. She was in agony. She was delirious and could not talk. The nausea kept her from drinking and eating. Her family worried about her, and called Yasmine and Leena to find out what had happened on the trip. But they didn't get much information. They then called their family doctor, who told them to give her an aspirin and vitamin C, and to apply a cold compress to her forehead. He explained to them that Maha's fever was going to fluctuate a bit, and her body needed time to fight the infection. So Maha's mom gave her the medicine and left her alone to sleep. And with that, Maha fell into the deep sleep.

When she woke up, she felt much better. The aches were not as intense and she could lie down on her bed without feeling any pain. But she still suffered from severe nausea. Her mom came in with some chicken soup.

"I got this for you. It will help you feel better," she said.

"Mommy... I can't think about food right now. I'm feeling so nauseous," Maha groaned.

"Nauseous? You said nauseous?" Maya asked as she and Ayah walked into the room.

"Yes. Why?"

"It's just that May Britt, my naturopath, enlightened me about physical illnesses. She explained to me that they are a result of negative mental thoughts and emotional issues, and that the only way to heal is to release these thought patterns and replace them with positive ones," Maya explained. "In fact, there is this woman called Louise L. Hay who healed her cancer this way. She now has an amazing book about the different illnesses and how to overcome them. Anyway, the negative mental thought pattern for nausea is fear, and rejecting an idea or an experience."

"Interesting, Maya. Did anything happen on your trip that scared or bothered you?" Ayah asked her.

"Kind of," Maha said. "I can't talk about it now, though. So what do I do, Maya?"

"You replace this negative thought pattern with a new one. You have to repeat this affirmation: I am safe. I trust the process of life to bring only good to me. And keep saying it until you feel better. I hope you can relate to this, Maha?"

"Yes, Maya," she said as she teared up and repeated the new thought patterns. "I am safe. I trust the process of life to bring only good to me."

"Here, dear. Have a spoonful of soup," her mom coaxed.

"Ok, mommy. I'll give it a try," she said as she sat up and accepted the spoon her mom offered.

Two seconds after she swallowed the soup, she felt her stomach flip. She became dizzy and ran out of breath.

"I feel like I'm going to throw up," she moaned.

"Come on! Hurry to the bathroom," her mom said.

Maha ran to the bathroom and as soon as she entered, she knelt down on the floor and put her head inside the toilet seat. And threw up. She started crying, because she could not stop. She threw up again. She couldn't believe the amount of phlegm that was in her chest. It must have accumulated from her smoking. It was disgusting to even look at it. She was suddenly so turned off from smoking that the thought of a cigarette made her throw up again.

"Good, Maha, dear. It's obvious you are cleaning out your system. Let it all out," her mom said soothingly.

Finally, when Maha stopped, her mom asked Ayah to get a change of clothes for Maha, so that she could have a shower and change. When Ayah rummaged through Maha's closet to get her clothes, she saw a pack of Marlboro Lights hidden under her jeans. It was obvious that Maha did not want anyone to see it. Shocked to discover this, Ayah resolved to speak to Maha about it right after her shower. In the meantime, she took Maha's clothes to her mom.

Maha felt revived after her shower.

"You look much better, Maha," Maya told her.

"Yes, I think throwing up everything made me feel a lot better," Maha said as she got back into bed.

"Yes, you will be fine now. Now, excuse me while I go prepare the rest of the food in the kitchen," Maha's mom said.

"Ok," they all said.

As soon as Maha's mom left, Ayah turned back to Maha and showed her the pack of cigarettes she'd found.

"Can you please explain to me this?" Ayah said, shaking the pack.

"No, I can't, Ayah. I have no reason or excuse to justify it. But let me tell you, I'm never touching them again! After today's experience, I can't stand to look at them. Please get that pack out of my sight," Maha pleaded.

"You'd better not! But *how* could you Maha? *Why* did you?" she asked.

"I don't know. I was under so much pressure. And one day, when I was out with the girls, they offered me one. And with time, it increased to a whole pack," Maha said miserably.

"I understand you are under a lot of pressure, Maha! But *still...* That is no excuse," she admonished.

"I know," Maha said. "I just lost so many things in my life in such a short time..."

"Interesting," Maya interrupted. "You know that that's how addictions start – when people are not able to cope after change, or the loss of someone or something. It's the search for lost human connection that makes people use things, if you know what I mean."

"Exactly, Maha! No number of cigarettes will ever bring back to you what you lost," Ayah said. "You have to face it and accept it."

"I know. I get that now. I promise I'll never do it again, even if I have to walk alone. I will never let anything or anyone bring me down again," Maha promised.

"Good! I'm glad to hear that," Maya said.

"Me, too! I guess we live, we learn," Ayah said.

"I guess so. I'd better sleep now, girls – I'm so tired," Maha said wearily.

"Ok. Hope you feel better soon," they both said.

CHAPTER TWENTY-FOUR

Mrs. Magda's home
Thursday, December 10, 1999, 4:40pm
Cairo, Egypt

Mrs. Magda was so happy to be back in Cairo. She'd missed Maher so much, and was excited about Ramadan preparations. Nothing made her happier in the world than giving and helping out those in need. She liked to prepare and distribute about 100 ready-made meals each day throughout the month of Ramadan.

She loved Ramadan so much because it was a sacred month. She enjoyed waking up before dawn prayer to have her suhor, the last meal before the next day's fasting. And she loved nothing more in the world than to perform her dawn prayers. It was so humbling to witness the mighty power of God. There was no other force in the world that could mobilize billions of people the way a call to prayer did. No power in the world was greater than that. Indeed, life was a miracle.

Mrs. Magda could not wait to dedicate her time and self to God during the holy month. She was glad that there was only one more week left of school before the two-week long Christmas break. Ramadan was to start after the first day of the break, and school would resume during the third week of Ramadan. The good news for Mrs. Magda was that after two weeks of the new term, there was going to be another break for the Eid celebrations.

The last week of school before the break passed quickly. Mrs. Magda was pleased with her students' assignment rewrite. When Maha, Mahmoud, Ossama and Laila saw their 'before' and 'after' grades for the assignment, they could not believe their progress. Mrs. Magda read their journals and was happy to see a significant improvement in her students' abilities to write and communicate their ideas well. Mrs. Magda's favorite was Mahmoud's entry about the verse, "But perhaps you hate a thing that is good for you, and perhaps you love a thing that is bad for you." He explained how these words from the Quran had the power to not only heal his past pain, but also inspire him to be optimistic about his future. He also mentioned that it was good for him because his relationship with his family was becoming solid again. He said that when he discovered that nothing at all, not even soccer, compared to the feeling of belonging to his family, he saw how sweet and loving his family really was. After all, what was the point of being a successful soccer player if you had no one to share that success with? He would never give up his family for anything in the world.

During the few days before the start of Ramadan, Mrs. Magda spent her time preparing for the iftar she wanted to her have at her house. She planned to invite her and Maher's extended family on the third day of Ramadan, and they were expecting 60 guests in total. As stressful as it was to arrange such an undertaking on her own, Mrs. Magda was so excited to do it. Not only did it make her forget about the issues in her life, it also gave her so much pleasure to cook and decorate the house. Mrs. Magda wanted to have a memorable feast that day.

She and Saneya spent endless hours deciding on the menu for the iftar. After a few days of brainstorming, Mrs. Magda finalized their choices. The plan was to offer a nice variety of healthy dishes that were an authentic fusion of European and Middle Eastern cuisines. They wanted to make two kinds of soups – lentil and creme de volaille – as well as four salads: fattoush, salade Russe, potato salad and tabouleh, in addition to hummus, baba ghanoush and tahina. She also wanted to offer a variety of choices for the main dish. The menu included chicken fatah with chick peas and yoghurt, sharkaseya, dolma, samboussak, saneyat kobeba, vol au vents, rice, torly and picatta. For dessert, she was going to offer the traditional basbousa, baklawa and konnafa. She felt that this would make for a perfect iftar for the whole family to enjoy together. She also wanted to offer the best dates from Saudi Arabia for her guests to break their fasts with at the call to prayer.

On the day of the feast, the guests arrived at sunset in time for the call to prayer, and broke their fast with the nutritious dates. Everyone then served themselves from the dining room. Mrs. Magda was on cloud nine, because everyone was commending her on how delicious and scrumptious the food was. Many of her guests returned for seconds, thirds and fourths, and Mrs. Magda believed that actions certainly spoke louder than words that day. The evening had an amazing, positive vibe because everyone was happy to reunite. After dessert, they all gathered around the TV in anticipation of the upcoming family shows. All were enjoying being the big family that they were.

Family in the Arab world was everything, and everything revolved around family. This sense of belonging was at the heart of everyday life for every family. Where they lived, what they ate and how they behaved was crucial to their identity. Arabs could not survive without the human connection of their families, neighbors and friends. Arabs who lived without this connection were like birds without wings.

It was fortunate that Mrs. Magda and Maher's families got along so well, even though, at first, both families were not too keen on their union because they were so different. Many doubted whether they would be able to get along. Maher's father had been an integral figure in King Farouk's old guard, and his line of work was aimed at protecting the monarchy. Mrs. Magda's family were the complete opposite: they were keen on preserving the Egyptian culture and identity, and Mrs. Magda's grandfather was an influential figure in this movement. It was a miracle that both families got along despite these differences. They all put their politics aside for Mrs. Magda and Maher, and all were grateful for that. Well, except for Mrs. Magda's great aunt who, from the first day she met Maher, had an issue with how he wore his socks. It was unbelievable how this concern troubled her throughout all these decades. Maher himself didn't understand why his sock-wearing ways offended her, let alone why she even took it personally in the first place. It was one of those things that Mrs. Magda liked to laugh about. She liked to take such family affairs lightly.

Following the successful iftar, Mrs. Magda spent the rest of Ramadan in solitude. She prayed and read the Quran, went to orphanages and helped those in need. She also went to some of her friends' and family's iftars. She could not have wished for a more peaceful time, especially after those last two difficult months at school. It was nice to get her mind off all the negativity there. In fact, she had sorely needed this time to strengthen her faith and trust in the process of her life.

Mrs. Magda's peaceful Ramadan routine came to an end on the first day of school. She could not believe how disrespectful the environment at school was during the holy month. Unlike all the other institutions in the country, school resumed like any normal day. People worked regular hours. Food was available for everyone. In fact, some non-fasting students teased the fasting ones with their food. It amazed her; the attitude was an insult to every single Muslim. But because she was reconsidering working at the school the next year anyway, Mrs. Magda was willing to let it pass.

That was until she received a letter from the school about the upcoming Eid holidays. The letter was an apology to all Muslims that the school would not be observing the Eid holiday that year, for the same reason they couldn't give the national holiday off in October. This letter fueled the flames of the fire. All staff, students, parents and even security and janitors received this letter. Mrs. Magda could not believe the nerve of the school. How could they make such a decision?

Mrs. Magda could not handle it anymore. She immediately went to Mrs. White's office. When she arrived, she asked Hala to arrange for her to speak to Mrs. White.

"Sorry, but Mrs. White is busy today," Hala said.

"Well, sorry, but that won't do it for me this time. Find some time for me to speak to her," Mrs. Magda demanded.

As she said it, she saw Mrs. White walk from behind her and into the office. It looked like she'd had a meeting somewhere outside the building and was just returning.

"Great timing!" Mrs. Magda said to Hala. "Leave it to me. I will speak to her now."

"Ok," Hala said, intimidated by Mrs. Magda.

"Mrs. White," Mrs. Magda called. "Just the person I was looking for."

"Well, great! What can I say, this is perfect timing!" Mrs. White said, gritting her teeth and resisting the urge to roll her eyes. "Please come into my office."

"Sorry, I won't be able to. This will be quick," Mrs. Magda answered.

"What's the problem now?" Mrs. White asked.

"I just got the letter informing us that the school will not be offering the Eid holiday this year."

"Yes, about that… Unfortunately, it didn't fit our schedule and we are sorry about that. But the dates are inconvenient for the school," Mrs. White said.

"*Inconvenient*? Watch your words before I report you to the inspector," Mrs. Magda spat.

"Report me? Why?" Mrs. White said, suddenly looking worried.

"Yes, report you! You are *far* from being a culturally appropriate school. You bear no consideration for our people, language, culture, religion and even holidays. Only a biased school would do the things you do. I don't understand this! If you don't appreciate our culture, then why are you here in the first place? What brings you to our country? Why don't you stay in your country where none of these issues will be an *inconvenience* to you?" Mrs. Magda exclaimed.

"Excuse me! Do not speak to me like that. You've crossed the line. What I meant was that the *dates* were inconvenient, not you or your culture. I promise that was not my intention," she said firmly, trying to intimidate Mrs. Magda.

"Well, that's not what you said. You must be held accountable for your words. You are the principal of this school, after all. As for crossing the line, you crossed my line a long time ago. I need to know how will you rectify this situation," she demanded.

"I'm sorry you feel that way. As for the holiday, I will see now what I can do," Mrs. White said evasively.

"'See what you can do' as in not respond to me, like you did with my proposal for calligraphy classes? Or what, exactly?" she said fiercely.

"No," Mrs. White mumbled, keeping her gaze on the floor as she was too embarrassed to even look Mrs. Magda in the eye.

"Good! Because it will not work this time," Mrs. Magda said. "Also, consider today my last day of work at this place."

"*What*? Come on, Magda! You are blowing this out of proportion. You are taking this personally. You are being too emotional."

"Well, what do you want me to do? Obey your orders and be quiet?" Mrs. Magda asked.

"Of course not! Please give me some time to see what I can do about resolving everything," Mrs. White said.

"Time? I believe that I have given you more than enough time. It's not good enough for me. I have no faith or trust in you or this institution. I have to go now," Mrs. Magda said. When she turned around to walk out of the waiting area, she saw how many people had gathered around. They'd seen and heard everything that had gone down between her and Mrs. White.

"I am sorry, Mrs. White! But I cannot tolerate this either," Hala suddenly chimed in. "I agree with Mrs. Magda. I'm not Muslim, but I want to support her and walk out with her."

"Hala, you just can't walk out and leave," Mrs. White cried. But it was too late. Many other people from the floor joined Mrs. Magda, too. Not all were Arab, let alone Muslim. In fact, they all represented different cultural backgrounds.

"There is a limit to everything. And enough is enough!" Mrs. Magda said.

"Yes! Enough! Enough! Enough!" the crowd, which had now swelled to about 50 people, chanted back.

Little did Mrs. Magda know that word of what had happened between her and Mrs. White had spread like wildfire. Even the faculty heard of it. Students, janitors and security rallied with each other to walk out of school without her even knowing.

When Mrs. Magda walked out of the administration building, she could not believe her eyes. Hundreds of people were waiting for her on the field. Mrs. Magda walked towards the group and met Sherif and Ahmed. She discovered that they were responsible for the gathering.

"We can't do this anymore, either," Ahmed told her.

"We can't turn a blind eye any longer," Sherif agreed.

"Exactly!" Mrs. Magda exclaimed.

"They can do whatever they want to do, but we don't have to put up with it! We are all going to walk out with you today," Ahmed said.

And just like that, Mrs. Magda realized that this was divine intervention. She saw how the power of God worked in a mysterious way. She was grateful for His guidance. She knew that He was never unjust. And if anything, when good was done, He doubled it in rewards.

"We cannot continue to work this way. Respect goes both ways. They have to be respectful to us and our culture," Mrs. Magda announced to the crowd.

"Yes! Enough is enough!" they all cheered.

Mrs. Magda then ran to her classroom to retrieve her belongings, and returned to the group to lead them out of the school.

All kinds of people stood together as a group: janitors, chefs, security, messengers, staff workers, faculty and even students. Mrs. Magda was so happy to see Mrs. Stone and Mr. McMan there as well.

"We are commited to the healthy development of all students," Mrs. Stone said.

"That's why we are here. We want to help Egyptian students. We want them to maximize their learning potential, just like the rest," Mr. McMan agreed.

"I'm so happy to hear that! Thank you," Mrs. Magda said gratefully. She couldn't believe that they were beginning to change their outlook and see reality for what it really was.

Mrs. Magda was surprised when she saw massive crowds of people walking from different side streets towards the main road, Horreya Street, or Freedom Street as many liked to call it in English. She almost fainted when she saw Zainab join the crowd holding Haga So'ad's hand. They followed Khalifa and another boy. Mrs. Magda wondered what brought them there. And why was Zainab holding Haga So'ad's hand?

As soon as Zainab saw Mrs. Magda, she pulled her mom's arm and ran towards Mrs. Magda. Khalifa and the other boy ran after them.

"Oh my God, it's you!" Zainab shrieked.

"Yes, it is. What are you doing here?" Mrs. Magda asked.

"You, who? What is going on here? How do you know Madam Magda, Zainab?" Haga So'ad asked.

"She's the nice lady who gave me the money for the kiosk, mama," Zainab told her.

"You? No! I can't believe this! What a small world!" she said. "You saved my and my family's lives!"

"I can't believe this either! What a coincidence. I'm happy it all worked out," Mrs. Magda said, amazed at how things seemed to always come right in the end.

"Oh, my! I'm so happy we answered Ahmed's cousin's call and came," Haga So'ad said.

"Ahmed who?" Mrs. Magda asked.

"He's the janitor who works here. He's calling everyone to come and protest. I don't get it, how can educated people not give you the Eid holiday off?"

"I can't believe this! He did that… and you came? We don't get it either. That's why we are protesting."

"Yeah, my cousin owes Ahmed a favor, that's why he agreed to it at first. But now that I know you are the one who helped us, I want you to know that we will never leave your side. We'll get more people to come if we have to."

"I really don't know what to say," Mrs. Magda's voice shook as she tried to swallow her tears. She couldn't believe how things took their own course and worked out so beautifully. Her heart beat with gratitude.

"Don't say anything. I know more people are coming from other schools. This issue has gone viral."

"Oh, wow! God is great!" were the only words that Mrs. Magda could find to say.

The group felt empowered as more people joined. Their numbers were growing rapidly, and now thousands seemed to block off Horreya Street. They knew that the school could not survive any longer. It was obvious to many now that they were creating a lockdown. It was surreal how the sequence of events fell like pieces of a puzzle into place. That day, the school witnessed the beginning of a change that would revolutionize it forever.

In the meantime, the administration called for an emergency conference call. They needed to address the crisis.

"What are we going to do now?" Mr. Marron asked.

"Well, I can't do anything, because even the security are part of the crowd. I have to go and talk to Mrs. Magda at the main entrance. We can resolve this issue with her diplomatically," Mr. Schwartz said. "We are going to have to compromise and give them the Eid holiday. We will have to find a way to make up for the days missed later in June."

"All agreed?" Mrs. White asked.

"Yes," they chimed.

"Then let's hurry to meet them at the front gate," Mrs. White said as she heard her other phone line ring. "Wait, I have another call… Let me get that. I'll put you all on speaker."

"Ok, sure," they both said.

"Hi," Mrs. White said as she answered the incoming call.

"Hi, Rebecca. It's Robert Flynn from the British International School."

"Hi, Robert."

"I just wanted to check with you if what I heard is true. Do you really have a protest going on outside your school? Is the school on lockdown?"

"Yes, Robert. I'm going to go and handle the situation now."

"Ok, great! Please do give the people their holiday. None of this is worth it. I don't want the internal environment at my school disrupted. Many Egyptians are starting to get ideas from what is going on at your school."

"Oh, no. I'll deal with it and update you later," she said as she heard her third line ring. "Hello?"

"*Oui, bonjour.* It's Edith from the Lycée."

"Oh… Please don't tell me that you're calling to ask about the protest, too?"

"Yes, I am. Please, you have to fix this soon. Give them the holidays. There is no need for problems."

"Yes, I know. I'm about to do that now, but everyone is calling me," she said as the fourth line rang. "Oh, no. Please all of you hold until I answer this call. I have you all on speaker." She connected with the fourth call and answered wearily, "Hello?"

"Hello, Rebecca. It's Malte from the Deutsche school."

"Hi. So I guess you've heard about the protest and lockdown as well."

"Yes."

"Ok, well… You are on speaker with the middle and elementary school principals from my school, and the principals of the British school and the Lycée. I want you all to know that I will go down now to resolve the issue. This will all be over soon. I'll update you all when it is."

"Ok…" they all said and Mrs. White hung up. She took a deep breath and walked out of her deserted office building.

Mrs. White hurried to the front gate and saw that Mr. Schwartz and Mr. Marron had arrived before her. Mrs. White could not believe the number of people standing at the front gate. She searched for Mrs. Magda, but could not see her anywhere. She stood on one of the benches and asked for everybody's attention. But nobody listened to her. She was as good as invisible.

That was until she found Mrs. Magda and got her attention.

"Mrs. Magda, please! I need to talk to you! I'm sorry for all this, and the administration wants to fix it. We want to resolve this issue here and now," Mrs. White screamed.

Mrs. Magda heard Mrs. White and walked over to her. "Well, we have a list of demands that are non-negotiable for us. If you don't agree to them, then there is no point in continuing to talk any further. Ok?"

"Sure! Tell me your demands," Mrs. White said hopefully.

"We want you to create appropriate prayer rooms for everyone in the school. You will adjust your calendar to accommodate our national and religious holidays. You need to be more mindful of the working hours of all Muslim employees during the holy month of Ramadan. You will increase the wages of underpaid staff. All salaries must meet the minimum wage requirement. You will offer Arabic Calligraphy classes, as well as Arabic and Islamic classes according to the requirements of the Ministry of Education in Egypt. Only Muslims will take Islamic classes, but all children will learn Arabic. Foreigners will take Arabic as a Foreign Language class. You will respect us and our culture. You will dispel the assumptions you have about Egyptian and Arab students. You will promote anti-bias education. Teachers must take a course in anti-bias education. You must provide non-Western perspective books in your library and classes. Your curriculum must ensure the holistic and healthy development of all children, including their social, emotional, cognitive and physical development. You will provide healthy and nutritious food from now on," Mrs. Magda listed their demands.

"Fine, Mrs. Magda. We will do it all! We'll work on making and applying all these changes," Mrs. White promised.

"Great! Then you are going to have to sign off on all these demands. Maha, please can you give Mrs. White the paper with the list of our demands?" Mrs. Magda asked, turning to Maha.

"Yes, sure," Maha said, brandishing the printed list.

"Here you go. Please sign this in agreement that you will commit to making these changes, and that they will be in effect as of April 24, 2000. Also, in the event that you do not follow through, we will demand the resignation of your whole administration," Mrs. Magda demanded.

"Ok! I will do that now!" Mrs. White took the paper and pen from Mrs. Magda and signed it.

Nobody could believe that Mrs. White had signed the document. They were ecstatic that they had succeeded in achieving their goals! The sounds of joy filled the air as everyone celebrated.

As the crowd began to disperse, Mrs. Magda called Mrs. Salwa to fill her in on everything that had happened. Mrs. Salwa was so pleased with the news. She congratulated Mrs. Magda for being an inspiration to everyone. She requested that Mrs. Magda send copies of the signed papers to her. She wanted to file them at the organization's headquarters so that they could hold Mrs. White accountable for her progress. Mrs. Magda agreed to the idea and promised to mail her the papers later.

After Mrs. Magda finished her conversation with Mrs. Salwa, she was so eager to go home and tell Maher the amazing news. She could not stop praying and thanking God for what had happened. When she arrived home, she saw Saneya and told her the good news. She then went to her room and prayed. After she finished reciting her verses, she knelt in a child's pose on the floor and rested her forehead on the ground. As she repeated the words, "Glory to the Lord my Exalted" three times, the truth suddenly became clear to her: We *were* all one. Interconnected. And because that was so, one was us all. She understood the value of this truth, and that's why she knew that it was important not to hide it.

After Mrs. Magda finished her prayers, she saw Maher and told him the wonderful news. He was so happy for her and proud of her. He called for an amazing evening of celebrations.

CHAPTER TWENTY-FIVE

American School in Cairo
Sunday, January 3, 2000, 2:42pm
Cairo, Egypt

Unlike many other families, Maha's family was very happy with what had happened at school that day. They believed that this was the very first step in the right direction. They couldn't be more content that their daughter was going to have the opportunity to get a high quality education at an international school, and learn Arabic and Islamic as per the recommendation of the Ministry of Education. This was a phenomenon in the field of education in Egypt. They were glad that ACS was going to be the very first school to break such grounds.

It was sad, however, that it was only Maha's family that felt that way. That became clear when Maha's mom picked up her home phone when it rang right after Maha told her the story.

"Hello," Maha's mom said.

"Hi. I'm Faiza. I know you don't know me, but we are a bunch of moms on conference call and we wanted your opinion on the disaster that happened today."

"Disaster?"

"Yes. We are all very upset. We can't believe that our children will be educated like the Egyptians."

"*Like the Egyptians*? Um, please correct me if I'm wrong, but aren't you all Egyptians?" Maha's mom asked pointedly, wishing that old washed-up passé mentality would disappear forever. It was the kind of mentality that made many Egyptians believe the more English, French or German a person spoke, the more aristocratic and intellectual they were. Those who didn't would be considered *balady,* or the opposite of aristocratic.

"Yes, we are. What I meant is that we are not like the *other* Egyptians."

"Oh, please. I'm sorry, but I don't get it. Seriously, how can you speak like that?"

"Because it is the truth. Now, seriously, are you happy with what happened today?"

"Yes! I'm glad that Maha will learn her language and religion at school."

"*What*?" Maha's mom heard a bunch of moms gasp at her words.

"This is unacceptable," Faiza said. "The standard of education will be worse because the curriculum will not be as International and American as can be."

"Excuse me, you've got it all wrong. Read the research. These changes will make our children more intelligent and balanced."

"Really?" one mom asked. "I didn't know that. I'll look into that."

"Whatever the research says, I am telling you that this is *degueulasse,*" Faiza said. "Wait, hold on, we are adding two more people on the line. Nagwa and Samar, welcome."

"Hi," Nagwa said.

"Hello," Samar said.

"What do you think about the disaster that happened today?" Faiza asked.

"I think it's disgusting! I think that new veiled teacher is the cause of all this! What's her name?" Samar asked.

"Magda," Nagwa replied.

"We have to get rid of her," Samar said. "I have to talk to the principal and tell her to let her go. She's trouble."

"Don't say that about her. You don't even know her," Nagwa argued.

"Yes," Maha's mom agreed. "You don't."

"Please, let's give Mrs. Magda a chance. She's making positive changes, and she is a very good woman. This might be good for our kids," Nagwa continued.

"I totally agree. Everything that she is doing is evidence-based. She is not violating any law, value or rule," Maha's mom added.

"I don't care about the research. I care that my children are not educated like the Egyptians. I'm paying too much tuition money for all this," Faiza said.

"I agree," Samar said. "So please, ladies, count me out when you speak like that. I'll make sure the administration know this when I speak to them. I have nothing to do with you two."

"What? Why all this drama?" Nagwa asked.

"Do as you please. I'm sorry, I have to hang up now. I'm really busy," Maha's mom said. She didn't have time for this kind of talk. Maha's mom had the strength to walk away from negativity. And Maha recently seemed to inherit that quality from her.

"What was that all about, mommy?" Maha asked.

"Nothing important at all, dear," she said.

"Ok, then I'll go inside now and take my shower in a bit."

"Ok, dear. Relax and take it easy now," her mother smiled at her.

"Will do, mom," Maha said as she walked to her room.

Relaxing seemed to be an unlikely possibility, though, when she logged on to her MSN and email. She found an email from some anonymous person with attachments of Laila's MSN chat history. Apparently, someone had hacked into her email and chat and shared her entire history. This was, like, the biggest fiasco to hit ACS ever!

Maha found an instant message from Leena.

Yo. Did you get Laila's chat history and emails? Did you read them?

I just saw it right now. What's goin on? Maha responded.

Nobody knows much. But everybody is guessing it's Sultan or someone he knows.

What!?! Sultan!?! Y wud he do that? Aren't they dating?

No not nemore. Apparently, they broke up after Luxor. He broke up with her!

What!?! Y? Maha typed as her heart palpitated. She remembered the last time she saw him and her heart melted. It sank down deep.

Nobody knows. But neway, please be careful when u read that crap. U will be shocked! She talks bout every1. Even me and Selim!

What! No way! What did she say? Maha asked.

Say!?! More like what she did!

What did she do?

After she found out that Selim & I broke up, she talked 2 Thalia & told her 2 go for him cuz he was into her, Leena responded.

What!!!???!!! NOOO WWAAYY! She is so conniving & manipulative!!

I know. Whats sick is that she texted me right after Thalia telling me how sorry she wuz 2 hear about the break up.

Wuuuuuttt!!! Nooooo!!! Double-faced, conniving and manipulative!!

Yeah I know! Yo, this girl is ruined! She's such a has-been.

Ugh! Yeah!! I don't even wanna imagine what she wrote bout me. I don't think I wanna read it. Even though I'm curious, Maha admitted.

You don't have 2 read it. I can summarize, Leena offered.

Shoot plz.

You & Sultan – ur fallout is all her doing! She told Sultan that u talked about him behind his back. She also told him that Fahmy would ruin him if he contd talking 2 u. Apparently, Fahmy and Yusuf bullied him sometime last Monday. They warned him to keep his distance from you, Leena wrote.

Maha gasped out loud as she read Leena's message. *WUT!!! FAHMY?? YUSUF?? WHY WUD THEY DO THAT TO SULTAN???*

Oh come on Maha, u know how Fahmy is all so protective over u! So that's no surprise! The surprise is Yusuf! What's up with that?

I dunno. I'm in shock.

Anyway, U & the girlz – she told Yasmine and all the girls that you were slipping ever since u hung out with Ahmed and started smoking. They said that they were worried u were changing. Also, apparently Marwan had talked 2 Yasmine and told her that he was in2 u and that he wanted 2 ask u out.

What What What!!! Maha gasped again as she replied. *Why would she ever do that? What did I ever do to her? And why wouldn't Yasmine tell me about Marwan & tell Laila? I seriously don't get this.*

Yo, look, it's obvious it has nuthing to do with u. She did this to every single person in school. That's just the way she is.

Yeah, I guess. Well I ain't goin to read ne of that crap. I'm trashing it all! I'm so taking the high road on this one.

Good 4 u girl!! Be proud! Leena wrote.

I am :) Especially after what happened 2day!

Yeah I'm on a high!! It was epic. I feel great things are going to happen.

Me 2.

C u tomorrow.

Yeah. Peace out.

And indeed, by April 24, 2000, the school was a changed one. There were four prayer rooms available to all staff and students, and not just Muslims. The curriculum had been enhanced and was more holistic. Staff received an increase in their salaries. The library had a few new non-Western perspective books. Teachers registered to take online courses on anti-bias education. Also, the first Arabic Calligraphy, Arabic language and Islamic classes started that day. Fortunately, the families of students who objected to these changes could not do anything about it. They were living in a time where their mentality was clearly outdated.

The students were curious to discover what their new classes had to offer. Maha was especially eager to have her first calligraphy class. When she walked in, she met her new teacher, Mr. Zenhom. He briefed the class about the task ahead. He told them that he wanted them first to trace the different letters on separate sheets. After that, he asked them to pick a sheet from the stack of papers on his desk. On these sheets were two- and three-letter words that he wanted them to trace. He asked all students to work at their own pace and enjoy the experience.

Maha got her Discman out and listened to Ben Harper's "Fight For Your Mind". She quietly sang the words to herself as she worked:

> *If you're gonna step step on in*
> *if you're gonna finish you got to begin*
> *don't you fear what you don't know*
> *just let that be your room to grow*
> *you got to fight for your mind*
> *you got to fight for your mind*
> *while you got the time*
> *you got to fight for your mind.*

She immersed herself in her calligraphy while she thought about the lyrics. She enjoyed learning how to master the reed pen and ink to form the twists and turns of each letter. Once she felt confident with the pen, she traced the letters. She got up and went to Mr. Zenhom's desk and pulled a sheet from the stack of papers. She was eager to start writing two- or three-letter words.

It didn't matter to her that she didn't immediately master the art of writing in Arabic. She just wanted to write. When she turned the small paper around, she found the letters (h) and (b), standing for 'hob' or 'love' in Arabic. Underneath was a little English explanation of the root word: *Hob (love) comes from root h b (hab or seed)*. She thought that it was so significant how two letters and one syllable in the Arabic language revealed the meaning of the many definitions of love. If love's root was a seed, then its form was its shape and its content was its growth.

As Maha traced the word, she reflected back on all the events of the school year so far. Even though nothing had really gone back to how it used to be, she realized that she *was* happy. It was the first time she'd noticed that she felt that way. It was a liberating feeling to know that *she'd done it*. She'd survived everything because she had the love to get her through, be it from herself or her family. And it was at that moment that she realized her purpose in life: to show how love was such a powerful force on earth. It could make or break someone. She could not hide this truth anymore. She could not imagine a life for anyone without it, not even for her worst enemy. For the first time, in the most heartfelt way, she mindfully prayed for herself, her family, her friends and even her haters to live a life full of love.

Acknowledgments

I would like to express my gratitude to Brendan McNulty, for the amazing support; Jenna Barlow, for the brilliant editing and proofreading; and Peter Barlow, for the superb cover design. I would like to thank my wonderful mentor, May Britt Searty, and excellent yoga instructor, Sofia-Maria Searty, for the valuable learning that helped in the making of this book.

I owe special thanks to my family, friends and those who saw me through this book. Among them: Mehrez Wasfy, Magda Gawish, May Wasfy, Mayssa Wasfy, Nader Aboushadi, Mohammed Wasfy, Seif Khalifa, Leena Khalifa, Virginie Lyko, Farid Aboushadi, Pakinaz Doss, Reem Saleh, Sandy Samaan, Dina Abou El Nasr, Shaimaa Hammad, Heba Sherif, Yasmine Bassiouny, Nancy Gaballa and Aliaa Ossama.

Made in the USA
Charleston, SC
08 June 2016